If the Gods Are Good

If the Gods Are Good
The Sacrifice of HMS Jervis Bay

Gerald L Duskin and Ralph Segman

Crécy Publishing Limited

If the Gods Are Good
The Sacrifice of HMS Jervis Bay

First edition published in 2005

A CIP record for this book is available from the British Library

ISBN 0 859791 07 6

Printed in England by Biddles

Crécy Publishing Limited
1a Ringway Trading Estate, Shadowmoss Road, Manchester M22 5LH
www.crecy.co.uk

CONTENTS

Preface 7

Acknowledgements 9

Introduction A Climate of Desperation 11

1 The *Scheer* Breaks Out 35

2 A Family Reborn and Death of a Sister...................40

3 In Command 50

4 The Conscripted 'Cruiser' 59

5 The Captain..71

6 In All Respects Ready 82

7 The Fifth of November 90

8 Out of Nowhere 95

9   Ranging In 104

10 Rain of Steel 115

11 The Lower Depths 129

12 Someone Else is Getting Away 133

13 Every Ship for Herself......................................139

14 Into the Icy Sea 152

15 We Go Back...163

16 Search and Getaway 177

17 The *San Demetrio* Saga 185

18 End of the String..200

Epilogue..210

Appendix 1 HMS Jervis Bay Officers and Crew 225
    5th November 1940

Notes...232

Bibliography...240

Index 247

About the Authors 255

Preface

JUST as fate, in several guises, created the flow of the battle in our story, it brought Gerald L Duskin and me together to create this book.

Jerry read about the naval engagement the day it was reported in Philadelphia newspapers. The morning of 6 November 1940 was chilly and blustery at his self-owned corner news-stand, where the fourteen-year-old—who had been stricken by polio as an infant—hawked the *Inquirer,* the *Bulletin*, the *Record*, and the *Daily Racing Form*. The front pages of the dailies carried reports of the uneven confrontation of the German pocket battleship *Admiral Scheer* and the British convoy escort HMS *Jervis Bay*. Germany falsely claimed the entire convoy was sunk. The bigger news with banner headlines that day was the re-election of President Roosevelt—another polio victim—to his third term. The juxtaposition of the two stories imprinted the naval action in young Jerry's psyche.

A few months later at Leary's Bookstore Jerry found a volume of poetry by Gene Fowler entitled 'The *Jervis Bay* Goes Down.' Thus started years of collecting a book here and an article there about the births of the two ships, the historical times that preceded the battle, the battle itself, and the deaths of the ships. The 1975 American edition of a book first published in 1956 by the German captain of the pocket battleship kindled Jerry's latent desire to develop a book of his own on the event. When his marriage broke up in 1978, the first thing he removed from the family house was his treasured *Jervis Bay/Admiral Scheer* material.

Jerry made seven trips to England between 1984 and 1999, where he interviewed some of the few remaining *Jervis Bay* survivors, family members, and naval historians. He conducted research in the Public Record Office, the Imperial War Museum, the library of the National Maritime Museum, and the Churchill Archives at Cambridge University, poring over books, declassified papers, reports, articles, audio tapes, and photographs. Visits to the US National Archives (containing a complete corpus of German war materials), the Library of Congress, the Nimitz Library at the US Naval Institute, the library at the Washington Navy Yard, and the Canadian Ministry of Defence added to a collection that filled an entire room's bookshelves and file cabinets.

After retiring as an economist from the US Department of Commerce, Jerry moved into the field of technology transfer (commercialisation of the results of scientific research), and he represented the National Organisation on Disability in a consortium of associations that lobbied for and gained passage of the Americans with Disabilities Act of 1990. That, curiously, is what brought him into contact with me.

For most of my working life I wrote about science and technology for newspapers and magazines. My biggest story (for the US Information Agency), published around the world, was one I ghosted for Alan Shepard, who had just completed the first American manned space flight. After about twenty-five years in the field, I moved into technology transfer. In helping set up a new type of small sawmill in Philadelphia's Fairmount Park to process dead trees into firewood for bundling and sales by mentally disabled youths, I made Jerry's acquaintance.

In 1995, after I retired, my wife Mattie told me about a cousin who had become paraplegic in a motorcycle-racing accident. I began seeking information that could be useful to the disabled, despondent young man. The only knowledgeable person I knew, though distantly at the time, was Jerry. At the end of our telephone conversation (in which he was unstintingly helpful), we discovered that each of us had a book as his next project. He invited me to look over the material he had been collecting for more than twenty years. It was a truckload, but it contained the ingredients of such a good story that I agreed to collaborate in producing a manuscript.

Living about 250 miles apart (Jerry in Washington and I in Pittsburgh), we moved along in fits and starts. It took three years to organise the material, comb through it, reorganise the selected pieces, hunt down missing elements, and work up an outline. The initial writing, several consultations and critiques, two major rewrites, and almost non-stop editing took several more years. With the manuscript finally acceptable to us both, we approached many agents and publishers with many a nibble. Finally we placed it with the Naval Institute Press.

A few weeks before the contract for publication in the USA was received, Jerry Duskin suddenly died. It was a shock to all of us who knew him and loved him. It was especially tragic since the acceptance of the manuscript would have been the highlight of his life.

Ralph Segman

Acknowledgements

THE toughest challenge in writing this book was that so few of the *Jervis Bay* survivors were alive to give us their experiences and their feelings during the battle. Much of the action and most of the quotes came from *The Jervis Bay* by George Pollock and *Pocket Battleship* by Theodor Krancke and H J Brennecke, published in 1958 and 1956, respectively. We are fortunate and thankful that crew members Everett Morrow and, especially, Sam Patience were able to give us a personal sense of their near hopeless ordeal. Convoy officers and crewmen H C Fellingham, Hedley Jones, and R F McBrearty fleshed out our understanding of the merchant seamen's role in the harrowing encounter. Barbara Fegen and Gillian Cooper, both nieces of the *Jervis Bay* captain, and nephew Nicholas Fogarty Fegen provided considerable family background. Additional German information came from Max Bugge and journalist Cornelia Gerhard. All told, this book was constructed from about 190 sources, including declassified documents, naval and political histories, interviews with naval historians, news reports, magazine stories, and books by members of the convoy and other well-versed authors.

We also thank all the other generous and knowledgeable people who helped us gather information, critiqued various stages of the manuscript, and encouraged us over the years it took to put the story in print: Jerry Bortman, Michael Chappell, Larry Glaser, the late Mark Lewis, Joseph Marriott, Klaus May, Patricia Park, Andrew Patience, Sid Pollack, Ed Sharon, John Waller, and many others. And, especially, for her unflagging support, gracious patience, and sharp editorial eye, my late wife Mattie Segman.

Introduction

A Climate of Desperation

As the German pocket battleship *Admiral Scheer* approached HMS *Jervis Bay* and her convoy HX 84 on 5 November 1940, World War II was already in its fifteenth month. For Great Britain it was a time of desperation. Most of Western Europe had been overrun by the Nazis, and the remnants of the British Expeditionary Force had been evacuated off the continent. The Soviet Union, Germany's treaty friend and enemy-to-be, had joined the Wehrmacht in ravaging Poland, and shortly afterward invaded Finland and took over Lithuania, Latvia, and Estonia. Adolf Hitler's Italian counterpart, Benito Mussolini, had sent major forces across the borders of weaker nations in North and East Africa and Southern Europe. Japan had already seized China's Manchurian province and had begun occupying major port areas on the East China and South China Seas.

The Political War

Hitler's early strategy had been to grab targeted areas one at a time, while assuring Britain and France that Germany was merely reclaiming its natural borders. For four years, as he rebuilt the German army, navy, and forbidden air force in the face of flaccid League of Nations criticism, he also succeeded in a clever variety of bloodless take-overs. His promise of a reinvigorated Germany induced the people of the coal-rich Saarland to vote for reunification with the 'fatherland' in 1935. The next year German troops marched into the demilitarised Rhineland, again with minor protests by some of the league's members.

Hitler opened 1937 by declaring the Treaty of Versailles null and void. This stirred up little more than newspaper reports. The next year, still in step with his politically adroit plan, he sent his army across the southeastern border into Austria, the nation of his birth, and proclaimed to cheering crowds that it was now a province of the Third Reich. Western silence continued. Then, later in 1938, his confidence at new heights and scornful of a British and French mutual-protection pact with Czechoslovakia, the Nazi leader demanded sovereignty over that country's Sudetenland region. British Prime Minister Neville Chamberlain and French Premier Edouard Daladier sought to appease Hitler by agreeing that their eastern partner should hand over the territory. The betrayed Czechs had no choice but to give in to the pressure from both sides. Chamberlain, pleased with his own capitulation, was moved to deliver his infamous 'peace in our time' speech. Five months later, undeterred by widespread disapproval, Germany occupied Czechoslovakia's regions of Bohemia and Moravia without firing a shot.

The Nazi leader's campaign of 'peaceful' take-overs was so successful that in early 1939 he blithely seized the Free City of Memel, which had been separated from Lithuania by the League of Nations. On the heels of this move, he signed an oil-supply deal with the Romanians, who agreed to leave security to the German army, yet another form of occupation.

With the Third Reich expanding like a river in flood, other despots grabbed onto the Führer's tail. The insurgent Generalissimo Francisco Franco, just before he took over the reins in Spain on 1 April, signed a convenient treaty of friendship with Germany. In May, plotting to conquer Bolshevism and the West, Mussolini and his new crony Hitler formed a 'Pact of Steel.'

Hitler felt emboldened at that point to make a play for Polish territory, including the Free City of Danzig, adjacent to Poland's port of Gdynia. Despite British and French attempts to get them to compromise, the Poles refused to give in. German threats of force and political strong-arming only provoked them into preparing a military defence. Then Great Britain unexpectedly enacted a conscription to beef up its armed forces, a move shrugged off by Germany as a bellicose bluff.

The Führer next brought a strange new cohort into the fold, Soviet leader Josef Stalin. Already in a pact with Japan, Italy, and Spain against the international spread of communism, Germany played both sides of the field to strengthen its position. Stalin had equally venal reasons for joining in the Machiavellian game. With this German-Soviet agreement, by late August, all dictators in Europe—fascist and communist—and Japan were teamed up in an anti-West, anti-democracy concord.

By this time, the Nazi chief was deeply annoyed that his nearest neighbour to the east would not allow another in his string of easy occupations.[1]

The Land War

The stubborn, independent Poles forced Hitler into his second major miscalculation. (For the Führer's first error, see the section 'The Sea War,' below.) On 1 September 1939, Germany opened World War II with a full-scale invasion. Using Poland as a guinea pig, the Wehrmacht introduced the world to *blitzkrieg* (lightning war)—the fusion of massive air power, armour, motorised infantry, and internal subversion. The Poles resisted fiercely and occasionally outfought the invaders. But they had no realistic chance to beat off the monster. Then, on 17 September, Soviet forces crossed the eastern border. Squeezed between the two huge war machines, Poland surrendered in early October. By virtue of a prenegotiated partition, Germany took over the western half of the country and the USSR the east.

Though for a time the rapid conquest gave much of the world the fearful impression that Nazism was the wave of the future, it was the beginning of the end for the 'Thousand-Year Reich.'

Hitler had no intention of going to war against Britain until the mid-1940s. By then, he would have subjugated the rest of Europe, including his friend Stalin's country as far east as Moscow. He counted on the timorous Western democracies sticking to the sidelines. But two days after the invasion, Britain and France finally recognised the futility and peril of appeasement and declared war on Germany. This unexpected Western spunk mucked up Hitler's timetable.

During the Polish campaign, Germany had left a few divisions on the French border. It was a great opening for the reunited Allies, but as Hitler had expected, their forces were not yet capable of applying military pressure. Their trousers were hitched up, but, as Winston Churchill later commented on the prior British and French neglect of their armed forces, 'This battle had been lost some years before.'

It was the beginning of a stretch when 'action' in Western Europe was little more than military build-up, skirmishes, diplomatic manoeuvring, and propaganda. Western newspapers disdainfully labelled it 'The Phoney War'; to Germans it was *Sitzkrieg*. American journalist William L Shirer felt that the Allies had bungled their only chance to gain an early advantage: 'The French government had insisted from the start that the [Royal] Air Force should not bomb targets in Germany for fear of reprisal on French factories, though an all-out bombing of the Ruhr, the industrial heart of the Reich, might well have been disastrous to the Germans. It was the one great worry of the German generals in September, as many of them later admitted.' The day after Britain declared war, the Royal Air Force (RAF)—whose commanders reasoned that the sea was not German soil—bombed naval vessels near Wilhelmshaven. One of their targets was the *Admiral Scheer*, which fate kept intact for her later encounter with HMS *Jervis Bay* when Flight Lieutenant K C Doran hit her with two 500-pound duds. This raid was one of the few aggressive forays that interrupted the Allies' idiosyncratic conduct of the first eight and a half months of the air war. Until Hitler launched his attack on the West, few British and no French sorties were flown over Germany except to drop propaganda leaflets.[2]

A German military aircraft, lost in the clouds, was forced down near Mechelen-sur-Meuse in Belgium on 10 January 1940. Major Helmut Reinberger scrambled out of the plane with a briefcase and put a match to its contents. Belgian soldiers retrieved the papers, stamped out the flames, and took Reinberger prisoner. He later grabbed the papers and threw them into a lighted stove. Again the Belgians saved them with little charring. What they had captured was a copy of German plans to invade Belgium and Holland on 17 January. They passed copies to Holland, France (also a target), and Britain. It was then that the Allies realised that what their journalists and some politicians mockingly referred to as a phony war was a time of Wehrmacht planning and marshalling for a *blitzkrieg* on the West.

Informed of his bad luck, Hitler postponed the invasion. That stroke of fate with its resultant four-month delay in the attack was a major factor in saving Britain and possibly the whole Western world from subjugation by the Nazis. It allowed the island nation that much more leeway to rebuild its armed forces, especially the RAF.

The German general staff immediately began making drastic changes in the invasion plans. Though distracted by the early April start of the Norway/Denmark campaign, they completed the back-up blueprint by the end of the month. Hitler set the new date for 5 May. Then the usually confident supreme commander got jittery. He set the kick-off back a day, due in part to an uncertain weather forecast and also because his Foreign Office was strangely concerned about violating the neutrality of the countries they were about to invade. Paranoia about information leaks and treachery—triggered by a rumour that a Belgian envoy was going to the Vatican—compelled the Führer to postpone the invasion to 7 May, then 8 May. General Alfred Jodl, concerned by his leader's panicky behaviour, noted in his diary: 'May 8. Alarming news from Holland. Cancelling of furloughs, evacuations, roadblocks, and other mobilisation methods...Führer does not want to wait any longer. [Air Reich Marshal Hermann] Göring wants postponement until the 10th, at least...Führer is very agitated; then he consents to postponement until May 10, which he says is against his intuition.'

On the night of 9 May, as the Wehrmacht poised again to strike into the Low Countries and France, the Führer suddenly regained his brass. He crowed to his general staff: 'Gentlemen, you are about to witness the most famous victory in history.' He was in high spirits and rewarded his chief meteorologist with a gold watch for an encouraging weather forecast. At dawn, the German forces crossed borders from northern Belgium to Holland and Luxembourg. Like other Hitlerian victims, the Belgians and Dutch had counted on neutral behaviour saving them from German clutches (despite their having found plans for the aborted 17 January invasion). They had refused British and French requests to strengthen fortifications on their soil. The Allies reacted quickly to the invasion, racing heavy forces from northwestern France to a natural defence line along the Dyle River running through eastern Belgium and Holland...headlong into a trap devised by General Erich von Manstein.

France had built the 'Maginot Line,' a string of sophisticated strongholds along its German border from Switzerland to Ardennes, the southeastern corner of Belgium. The French believed the mountainous, forested Ardennes was impassable to heavy armour, so they set up light defences along its border. After the Allied rush to the Dyle line, the most powerful German force, Manstein's Army Group A, which had been concealed until then, launched a drive into the 'impenetrable' corner. His armour quickly filtered through the forests and negotiated the hills. The panzers spilled out through the weak defences onto the French lowlands and reached the English Channel on 19 May. The Allied armies were cut off on three sides by the Germans and backed up against the English Channel.

Luxembourg fell on the day of the attack, the Netherlands surrendered after five days, and Belgium lasted less than three weeks. It took just thirty-six days for Hitler's troops to enter Paris. Germany occupied the northern part of France, including its Atlantic and Channel coasts. Under the armistice agreement, the collaborative Vichy government was allowed to administer the occupied area under German authority and the southern half of the country relatively freely.

Hitler's one error in this otherwise brilliant campaign was that he let many of the enemy's elite troops slip through his fingers. The British quickly realised their only resort was to evacuate as many of their trapped men as possible from the Dunkirk area. The result was one of history's most stupendous military escapes.[3]

On 28 May, not quite three weeks after he replaced Chamberlain as Prime Minister (the same day as the invasion of the Low Countries), Winston Churchill gathered his War Cabinet together. The group considered a proposal by the opportunistic Mussolini that Italy, in exchange for some territorial concessions, would act as an intermediary for war-ending negotiations. Churchill, who did not favour negotiations, told the other four members: '[Hitler's] terms would put us completely at his mercy. We should get no worse terms if we went on fighting, even if we were beaten.' Two members, the still politically powerful Chamberlain and his ally Lord Halifax, argued against this assessment and pushed for negotiations. Clement Attlee and Arthur Greenwood said bargaining with Hitler would be a terrible blow to British morale. Continued defeatism of the two senior members discouraged the new Prime Minister.

As soon as the meeting adjourned, twenty-five ministers who were not members of the War Council streamed into the room for a briefing by Churchill (in what Sir Martin Gilbert portrays as 'one of the most extraordinary scenes of the war'). He had not seen most of them since their appointments. Minister of Economic Warfare Hugh Dalton noted in his diary:

> He was quite magnificent. The man, and the only man we have, for this hour. He gave a full, frank, and completely calm account of events in France. Now it was necessary to fight our way through to the Channel ports and get away all we could…We should certainly be able to get 50,000 away. If we could get 100,000 away, that would be a wonderful performance…
>
> 'And I am convinced,' [Churchill] concluded, 'that every man of you would rise up and tear me down from my place if I were for one moment to contemplate parley or surrender. If this long island story of ours is to end at last, let it end only when each of us lies choking on his own blood on the ground.'
>
> There were loud cries of approval all around the table.

An hour later, the War Cabinet resumed its discussion of Mussolini's proposal. Buoyed by the ardent support of his other ministers, a now fiery Churchill 'pounded the table' and got unanimous agreement to reject negotiations.[4]

The Dunkirk evacuation began three days before the War Cabinet's decision to fight to the death. Three factors helped the Allies. First, the terrain enabled them to set up an effective perimeter around the embarkation sites, and the French and Belgian armies fought effective rearguard actions. Second, Hitler stalled the advance of Manstein's Army Group A for three days in order to conserve his panzers for the coming attack on the French armies defending Paris. He did not want to expend them on the Dunkirk remnants, which Luftwaffe chief Göring assured him would be destroyed by his bombers and fighters. The third factor was the Royal and French Navies, the many seagoing civilians, and the Royal Air Force, all of which pitched in with their ships, boats, and planes to bring off the evacuation.

About nine hundred British and French ships and small craft engaged in the exodus between 25 May and 3 June. More than 80 merchantmen and warships, many small boats, and 177 RAF planes were destroyed in the effort.

Despite the horrendous losses, the rescue went astonishingly beyond British expectations. More than 338,000 men—112,000 of them French—were ferried across the Channel. In the two weeks after Dunkirk, and before France surrendered, another 144,000 British soldiers, 18,000 French, 24,000 Poles, 5,000 Czechs, and a few Belgians escaped from other Channel ports. And about 24,000 British troops were evacuated from Norway. Though it was hard to foresee at the time, the deliverance of more than 555,000 bedraggled Allied fighting men was the outcome of another error that hastened Hitler's defeat.

Believing a German invasion attempt was imminent, Churchill on 4 June delivered a speech to the House of Commons that contained one of his most stirring, uplifting perorations: 'We shall fight on the seas and oceans, we shall fight with growing confidence and growing strength in the air, we shall defend our island, whatever the cost may be. We shall fight on the beaches, we shall fight on the landing grounds, we shall fight in the fields and in the streets, we shall fight in the hills; we shall never surrender.'[5]

On 10 June, when it seemed obvious that Germany was on its way to defeating the Allies, Mussolini, 'with a jackal's sense of occasion,' as historian Paul Kennedy put it, declared war on Britain and France. He sent nearly 500,000 poorly equipped, incompetently led, half-hearted troops into the French Alps and the Riviera. About 100,000 French soldiers, though demoralised by the imminence of surrender, retained enough esprit to hold them to a standstill.

It was an occasion for the wolves, too. As Germany was completing its occupation of most of Western Europe, its Soviet 'friendship treaty' partner took over the governments of Lithuania, Latvia, and Estonia. A few weeks later, Stalin annexed those countries into his system of soviet socialist republics as a buffer against an expected flip-flop in Hitler's profession of friendship. Before the end of June, the Soviets, helped by political pressure from the reluctant but still deceptive Hitler, incorporated a portion of Romania.

About the same time, Germany occupied the Channel Islands, the only British territory the Germans would set foot on during the war. Most of the 90,000 residents of the main islands—Jersey, Guernsey, and Alderney—remained there throughout the war. Hitler committed a full division with major armaments to the occupation, where they would stay isolated and unutilised until they surrendered peaceably at the war's end.[6]

The abrupt collapse of France surprised everyone—the French, the British, the rest of the world, and even Germany. Ironically, the Napoleonic success of Hitler's battle plan disrupted his schedule and left him unprepared to take advantage of the sudden opportunity.

Britain was extremely vulnerable, possibly more than ever before in history. Most of its army's heavy equipment lay abandoned on the continent. Just after the evacuations, it reportedly was left with about twenty tanks. Though the country was about to ratchet up arms production, its current output was inadequate. The Royal Navy was open to air attack. And, despite the rescue of more than a half-million soldiers, Churchill said only a few brigades of well-armed, well-trained troops were prepared to meet invaders by the beginning of July. His military chiefs told him their only hope was to keep the convoy routes open and to maintain air superiority against invasion. They all agreed that survival hinged on the morale, resolve, and endurance of the British people. The only person capable of lifting the nation to such sustained heights of spirit and grit was the silver-and-steel-tongued Churchill. Fate had put the right man in place when he was needed.

The prime minister's first priorities in July 1940 were to expand and speed up aircraft and other arms production, to fortify the island against seaborne and airborne invasion, and to render the formidable French fleet useless to Hitler.[7]

Hitler, not privy to Churchill's sources of information, believed Britain had thirty-five well-equipped divisions (about 500,000 men) to throw against the German army. He was not ready to cross the Channel against a defence that strong without the Luftwaffe first softening it up. In response to his directive, the Wehrmacht High Command (OKW) issued an order that began: 'the Führer has decided that an invasion of England may be decided upon under given conditions of which the most important is considered the gaining of air superiority.'[8]

The purpose of the instruction was to start preliminary thinking about invasion requirements and to pick the earliest possible landing date. Two weeks later, Hitler surprised the OKW with an urgent follow-up: 'Since England, in spite of her militarily hopeless situation, shows no signs of coming to terms, I have decided to prepare a landing operation [Sea Lion] against England...The preparations...must be completed by mid-August.'[9]

On 19 July, ten days after starting intermittent air attacks on

British defences, especially the RAF and its infrastructure, Hitler addressed the Reichstag and offered Britain an option of peace or 'unending suffering and misery.'[10] He added, with an uncharacteristic touch of ragged humour, that Churchill was ready to skip out to Canada and get his hands on the gold he had sent there. (He did not reveal his plan that, after the expected surrender of Britain, 'the able-bodied male population between the ages of seventeen and forty-five...will be interned and dispatched to the Continent.')[11]

The prime minister told his cabinet, 'I do not propose to say anything in reply to Herr Hitler's speech, not being on speaking terms with him.'[12]

The task of making a curt response was given, with sublime Churchillian irony, to Lord Halifax, one of the senior cabinet members Hitler counted on to bring about a peaceful capitulation. Declared Halifax, perhaps a little grimly: 'We shall not stop fighting till freedom for ourselves and others is secure.'[13]

In early August, the Führer issued Directive 17, which set the invasion day between 19 and 26 September. This was the last best opportunity of the year for Sea Lion. The next favourable confluence of high tides and good weather would not occur until spring. Because the Germans had been delayed by three major errors—lack of a Channel-crossing strategy and preparations, a gross overestimate of the remaining strength of the British army, and a late start of the Luftwaffe's bombing campaign—the Wehrmacht was left with this one-week span to mount the landing operation. The order for Sea Lion Day was to be given after Göring's bombers and fighters had pummelled the RAF for two weeks. All preparations had to be completed by 15 September.

A few days after ordering the planning for a cross-Channel landing, the impatient Hitler told the startled OKW to prepare a blueprint for an invasion of the Soviet Union. While he wallowed in the delicious prospect of drubbing the irritating British, he was not about to be caught napping again in the wake of a quick conquest. His generals preferred to concentrate on Sea Lion, but they lacked the courage to seriously object to the Führer's timing. This decision marked the beginning of the scatter and dilution of Hitler's military power. By 5 August, four days after he ordered the attack on Britain, the OKW laid out a preliminary plan for a spring 1941 offensive against the USSR.

Also during this period, Hitler's ally Mussolini determined that his forces in Africa (stationed in Abyssinia [Ethiopia], which had been occupied by Italy since 1936) were overwhelming enough, and he sent them into Sudan, Kenya, and British Somaliland, where his troops outnumbered the Tommies, 342,000 to 40,000.[14]

All during the summer of 1940, Britain prepared feverishly against an invasion that was expected at any moment. Despite the then continuous German air attacks, their war plants increased production of tanks, guns, aeroplanes, warships, and other heavy equipment. By the beginning of autumn, the army at home had gone from post-Dunkirk defencelessness to a well-trained core of three armoured divisions and seventeen others (more than 300,000 men) ready to face an assault on their shores. About two-thirds of Britain's 1.5 million Home Guard volunteers (all over forty years of age) had graduated from broomsticks to rifles.[15]

The British also began developing some desperate anti-invasion schemes. Churchill wanted to do something dramatic: 'Just as Drake singed the King of Spain's beard, I want to singe Hitler's moustache.' The Prime Minister approved an incendiary defence called operation Lucid. Captain Augustus Agar (Captain E S F Fegen's superior immediately before he was assigned to the *Jervis Bay*) directed the project. He brought in Morgan Giles as a special-assignment staff officer. Giles later told an interviewer at the Imperial War Museum:

> Agar said Churchill had been taking advice from the Petroleum Warfare Department who had been doing experiments with a mixture of Admiralty oil and diesel and petrol in the Thames with barges. This mixture ignited and boiled the [water] beneath it which bubbled up and made it run around like quick silver...
>
> He said, 'I've been told to mount an operation to get four or five old Admiralty tankers, fill them with this mixture, and go across the Channel and attack Calais and Boulogne where the Germans are mustering huge numbers of Rhine barges for the invasion.'
>
> The tankers had volunteer crews, about a dozen in each ship. The idea was that they would sail them across, take off all but three of each crew, steer the ships in, and crash through the booms. Each remaining crew would lower a little speedboat to water level, scramble down, and have some chance of escaping. A couple of minutes later scuttling charges would explode and the ships would begin to settle down.
>
> Then ignition charges would operate and this extraordinary mixture would start running around the harbour and burn up the barges and the troops in them.

In an experiment off the rocky shore just east of Portsmouth, an oil mixture was delivered into the water and ignited. 'A wall of flame of such intensity raged up from the sea surface,' the head of the Petroleum Warfare Department said, 'that it was impossible to remain on the edge of the [30-foot] cliff and the sea itself began to boil.'[16]

Two weeks after Mussolini's forces swept into Egypt, the three fascist powers—Germany, Italy, and Japan—completed a round of aggressive diplomacy and lined themselves up against the rest of the world. On 27 September they signed the Axis Pact, agreeing that each would declare war on any other country that made war against any of the three, except in Germany's or Japan's relations with the Soviet Union. They hoped the pact would deter the United States from allying with the British and from disputing Japanese ambitions in Asia.

At a follow-up meeting in early October, Hitler warned the Italian leader against any new adventures and offered to help him in Africa. Mussolini declined. A week later, without alerting his Axis partner, Hitler sent the first contingents of a 'military mission' into Romania, ostensibly to rebuild the Romanian army. His concealed purpose was to help newly appointed Prime Minister Ion Antonescu put down a rebellion in order to provide Germany with a stable base for the coming attack on the USSR.

Mussolini, vexed at Hitler's attitude and at not being informed in advance about the Germans' Romanian incursion, declared: 'Hitler always faces me with a *fait accompli*. This time I am going to pay him back in his own coin.'

Accordingly, the self-styled Caesar, against advice from his general staff, pushed the war button without giving Germany a heads-up and sent his army into Greece on 28 October. Hitler reacted in a fury, not only because of Mussolini's precipitate action but also because he was sure Britain's Mediterranean forces would come to the Greeks' aid and thus be within bombing range of the Polesti oil fields in Romania. As it turned out, the Italian army again was insufficiently equipped and poorly led, and was not prepared for the cold weather or for the strong, spirited Greek resistance. Forced to aid his Axis partner, Hitler experienced another setback. Again he was distracted from the more compelling strategic objectives of conquering Great Britain and the Soviet Union as far east as Moscow.

A few days before the bungled Greek affair, another would-be ally drove Hitler to near-incoherence. On 23 October the Führer arrived in his armoured private train at the Franco-Spanish border town Hendaye to confer with Generalissimo Franco and convince him to fulfil his promises to join the Nazi crusade.

Franco, indeed, had told Hitler many times that when Spain was prepared; it would enter the war on the German side. These assurances were made when Germany was almost certain to roll over Britain. The first objective was to be Gibraltar. But, if Spain was to be involved, according to Franco, Germany must first supply it with 700,000 tons of grain for its people, food and equipment for its army, and aircraft and artillery. He also demanded that Germany support Spain's territorial claims in Morocco. In return, Spain would attack Gibraltar with its own troops, and not, as Hitler wanted, with military help from Germany. Franco actually had been edging away from a deal with Hitler. Two weeks earlier, President Roosevelt had offered Spain wheat if it would stay neutral. Britain had not collapsed. And it was receiving increasing support from the 'neutral' United States. To the Generalissimo, now, the war's outcome was no longer certain. The railroad car meeting went on for nine hours, with Franco incessantly repeating his demands. Hitler, in exasperation, finally jumped up and ended it. He later told Mussolini, 'Rather than go through it again, I would prefer to have three or four teeth taken out.'[17]

The Air War

The sustained massive bombing that touched off the celebrated Battle of Britain started on what the Germans called 'Eagle Day,' 13 August 1940, when Reich Marshal Göring transmitted an order to the Luftwaffe: 'You will wipe the British air force from the sky. Heil Hitler.' (The British say the battle began with the 10 July bombings of Channel shipping and docks in Wales.) He gave his fliers four days to cripple the RAF over southeastern England and four weeks to totally destroy it. As a curtain raiser, the previous day his planes damaged five airfields and put a major radar station out of action.

The Eagle Day attacks mounted about five hundred bomber and one thousand fighter sorties. The RAF managed to raise seven hundred fighter flights against them and downed forty-five German aircraft while losing thirteen. Two days later the Luftwaffe sent some eighteen hundred aircraft across the Channel, and the British met them with one thousand Spitfires and Hurricanes, the largest number of sorties on any day in the Battle of Britain. The score again favoured the RAF, seventy-five German planes destroyed against thirty-four of their own.

Göring did not know the British had strengthened their air defences by linking thirty-two radar stations into a network. All incoming data were relayed to a single processing centre, giving Fighter Command very early and accurate information on approaching German formations. The data were quickly analysed, and packets of instructions were fed out to sector communicators, each of which was associated with a fighter group. The sector stations continually radioed updated and timely guidance to their planes. With this ingenious system, the British were able to use their outnumbered aircraft very efficiently. On 17 August the RAF shot down seventy-one German planes at a cost of twenty-seven.

In view of the large size of the Luftwaffe, however, the Germans' losses were not as punishing to them as were the RAF losses to the British.

Without the network, RAF fighters would be reduced to a confusion of butterflies, exposing the Royal Navy to devastating air attacks and the island nation to a virtually irresistible Wehrmacht invasion. But Göring, a World War I fighter ace and successor to Manfred von Richthofen (the Red Baron) as commander of the legendary Flying Circus, was, like his Führer, egotistical, intolerant, and disdainful of the value of science and technology. 'Gadgets' like radar meant little to him. His aircraft commanders, knowing he wanted to hear only about victories, exaggerated British aircraft losses. Playing into Göring's narrow preconceptions, his intelligence chief, who had quickly puzzled out the co-ordinated British radar communications system, reported instead what he thought his arrogant chief wanted to hear: that each RAF squadron was controlled by a single radar station and therefore could easily be feinted away from primary bomber formations.

The Reich Marshal thought he had the RAF beaten. But he did not realise that the Germans' ability to hamstring the British communications stations was their decisive advantage. His most egregious error was not caring to understand the nuances of the air-defence network. This character flaw of their commander blinded the Luftwaffe to Fighter Command's considerable flexibility and mobility.

Göring started the great air battle with strategic attacks on anything related to the RAF. So, by sheer association rather than by tactical design, his bombers began sorely damaging key radar and sector stations. The British quickly replaced them with mobile transmitters, which were not very useful—except that their rapid deployment led the Germans to believe the radar/communications sites were returned to full operation. Three days into the campaign, Göring removed them from the target list, declaring: 'It is doubtful whether there is any point in continuing the attacks on radar stations, since not one of those attacked has...been put out of action.'

During a bad-weather lull in air operations from 19 August to 23 August, the Reich Marshal again reversed himself and decided to intensify his campaign to eradicate the RAF by retargeting supporting infrastructure as well as fighter planes and airfields. Then he cleverly changed the Luftwaffe's tactics, sending in small groups of bombers with large numbers of fighter escorts on daytime raids to engage and destroy the British defenders. After dark, profiting from the RAF's lack of night-fighter capability, German bombers made unescorted attacks to stretch the defences and allow the Britons no respite. The night raids, using Germany's secret new radio-beam navigation/bombing system (which somehow got through Göring's anti-technology filter), were startlingly effective.

For two weeks, the Luftwaffe flew an average of a thousand sorties a day against the full range of RAF-related targets. Göring was coming close to his goal, though he was not aware of the paramount factor in his success: six of the seven key sector-communications stations in the southeast were badly damaged, and Britain's Fighter Command network was almost shut down. The smaller RAF now was suffering as many aircraft losses as the Germans, a level of attrition that by the end of August had tilted the British air defence into a potentially disastrous nosedive.[18]

About two months earlier, an intelligence coup promised to help the British relieve some of the strain brought on by the German night bombings. At the suggestion of his science advisor Frederick Lindemann, Churchill invited R V Jones, the twenty-eight-year-old deputy director of Intelligence Research at the Air Ministry, to a cabinet meeting on 21 June. Jones revealed evidence supporting his belief that the Germans were using a radio-beam system to aid bombers on their night missions. His report at first was met with a mixture of incredulity, derision, and awe. He said his people had deciphered an intercepted German message containing the word *knickebein* (dogleg) in reference to an air raid near Retford. (He did not reveal that the decoding was done with a German Enigma machine obtained from a Polish source before the war started.) Two days later, a Luftwaffe prisoner of war, who had antiwar sentiments, revealed that *knickebein* was a code name for a two-beam navigation/bombing system. Jones said the beams were transmitted from widely separated sites in Europe and intersected over the targets. A flight of bombers winged along one beam to the target, and as they crossed the second beam, their bomb-releasing mechanisms automatically triggered.

Churchill asked Jones to confirm the existence of such beams and, if necessary, see to it that countermeasures were developed. By the beginning of September, the British had devised an electronic scheme (code-named ASPIRIN) that jammed the German transmissions and reduced their night-bombing efficiency.[19]

Just before the jamming started, another intervention of fate, together with Nazi vindictiveness and myopia, led to the rapid recovery of the RAF and ruined Hitler's last opportunity to put Fighter Command out of business. It started on 24 August; the first night of Göring's intensified campaign to obliterate the RAF. During an attack on the industrial outskirts of London, several planes, unable to find their targets, jettisoned their bombs and inadvertently killed people in the financial district. This went against strict orders not to bomb civilian areas, lest RAF bombers retaliate on German cities. The Nazis had promised the German people they would never see an enemy warplane. The next night, the unimaginable happened: eighty-one RAF bombers released their loads over Berlin. A larger force bombed the German capital two nights later. 'The Berliners are stunned,' wrote journalist William L Shirer. The Führer was shocked and humiliated. He reacted hysterically. The British would pay for this barbarism. He ordered the Luftwaffe to switch tactics to massive night bombings of London. He would exact revenge by razing the capital city and shattering the resolve of the infuriating British. Success, he thought, might even make invasion unnecessary.

The new bombing campaign was launched on 7 September. Göring saturated London with nearly 1,300 planes, surprising everyone, including the RAF, whose night-time defence was weak. In the first two raids more than 840 people were killed and 2,300 wounded. The attack was the beginning of what Britons came to call 'the blitz' (which was to continue almost unabated for eight months). The civilian casualties were anguishing and the damage vast.

But so, too, was the damage to Hitler's strategy of conquest. Instead of pressing for the few more days or weeks needed to finish off the RAF, and probably moving on to a momentous victory, he took his vengeful eye off the prime target. The switch in German attacks from RAF sites to the city of London gave Fighter Command a quickly seized opportunity to patch up the radar/communications network. In less than a week, the RAF regained its effectiveness. Soon it would begin making the Luftwaffe pay heavily for the Führer's personal foible.

By 14 September the Germans were near victory. On 15 September—the day Fighter Command returned to full operational status—the Luftwaffe shifted to exclusively daylight bombing with a huge attack on London, confident that the RAF was no longer viable. But this time their formations did not sail through British butterflies. The Spitfires and Hurricanes again were quickly guided to positions where they pounced on the attackers. They downed sixty German planes while losing twenty-six. On that day, British fighters shook the morale of the exhausted German bomber crews, who had been assured by Göring that the RAF was on the verge of collapse.

It was, said Churchill, the crux of the Battle of Britain—one of the decisive battles of World War II. Germany would not be able to dominate the Channel for the twenty-four hours needed to mount a successful invasion. Indeed, since early September, British bombers had destroyed or damaged 21 troop transports, 214 barges, and 5 tugs in French ports—about 10 percent of the invasion fleet. Two days later, Hitler postponed operation Sea Lion indefinitely. Although the British people were not aware of the invasion deferment, and despite the continued massive bombing and casualties, their high morale endured and toughened. Within the next several months, the frustrated Luftwaffe bomber force took such heavy losses that it never regained its overwhelming superiority.[20]

The War at Sea

The Battle of the Atlantic started at the outbreak of the war with the dispatch of eighteen U-boats and the pocket battleships *Deutschland* and *Admiral Graf Spee* into areas of expected heavy British maritime traffic. The United Kingdom, suffering the consequences of its earlier neglect of the Royal Navy, countered with a system of inadequate patrols and lightly escorted or often unprotected convoys.

The German navy began scoring some successes, sinking about 350,000 tons of Allied shipping in the first two months of the war. In mid-September 1939, U-29 torpedoed the British aircraft carrier *Courageou*s, which went down with 518 members of her company. The *Graf Spee*, operating in the South Atlantic off Brazil, sank its first merchant ship at the end of the month. Extremely concerned about the new surface raiders, Britain and France sent eight hunting groups— three battleships, three aircraft carriers, and fifteen cruisers—into the Atlantic, Pacific, and Indian Oceans in search of the elusive *panzerschiff*. This reaction gave the Germans just what they wanted: large numbers of Allied warships tied up on wild-goose chases.

However, disregard for his navy was the first major blunder in Hitler's drive for conquest. (We have already seen his second error; in 'The Land War' section, above.) In March 1938 the Führer had approved Admiral Erich Raeder's seven-year 'Z Plan' to construct a fleet—including 56,000-ton battleships, aircraft carriers, and 249 U-boats—and assigned it top priority over other armament programs. The new armada was to be capable by 1945 of taking on the Royal Navy and choking off Britain's sea routes. Unfortunately for Nazi Germany, Hitler's impatience to grab eastern lands and his intolerance for disagreement (in this case, Raeder's) resulted in resources being taken from the navy and given to the army and air force for the invasion of Poland. Britain's unexpected entry into the war and the rapid expansion of its fleet made the island virtually impregnable to the Wehrmacht, except for the brief post-Dunkirk period and the first months of the air battle.[21]

On 14 October 1939 the Germans gained some revenge for the scuttling of their High Seas Fleet at Scapa Flow at the end of World War I (see chapter 2). Just after a moonless midnight, U-47's captain, Lieutenant Commander Gunther Prien, one of the future stars of the German submarine fleet, surfaced outside the British naval base and was shocked to see the area brightly lighted. An unexpected aurora borealis was illuminating the entire anchorage. Reckoning that he still held the advantage of surprise, he decided not to abort his mission. The incoming tide carried the surfaced U-boat astonishingly fast toward the channel separating the islands of Lamb Holm and Mainland. Prien picked his way between two sunken blockships guarding the anchorage. His gut tightened as the submarine's bottom scraped rocks and her starboard bow brushed along a blockship cable. It was a close call, but he passed into the waters covering the remains of his country's sunken fleet.

Skirting the northern shore, he spotted the 27,500-ton *Royal Oak*. Luck was with him as the aurora faded and the night turned black. He fired three torpedoes from about 3,000 yards. One exploded far forward and caused little damage. While the battleship's captain sent men toward the bow to assess what he thought was an internal malfunction, Prien swung U-47 around, aimed the stern tubes, and launched three more weapons. In three minutes all torpedoes detonated, one of them setting off a giant explosion as it hit a magazine filled with cordite. The *Royal Oak* sank in thirteen minutes, and 833 men died. Spotted by occupants of a car, the U-boat raced back along the shore and escaped between the blockships on a tide that had begun to ebb.

Hitler was jubilant: a naval victory, a great propaganda coup. An Admiralty board of inquiry could not figure out how the U-boat had entered Scapa, but concluded she could not have used the channel she had in fact slipped through.[22]

Allied shipping losses to U-boats, surface raiders, aircraft, torpedo boats, and mines averaged about 175,000 tons a month until the end of 1939 and rose to a 220,000-ton level in the first two months of the next year. The rate dropped off to 155,000 tons for two months when U-boats were called in for Germany's invasion of Norway. It rose in May to 288,000 tons, partly due to British naval losses off Norway, and more than doubled in June as a result of the Dunkirk evacuations.[23]

One of the war's key, but little known, events occurred on 10 May (coincidentally, the day Germany invaded the West and Churchill was named Prime Minister). The Germans had given some thought (not a priority in Hitler's landlocked mind) to occupying Iceland, but the British got there first. Major General H L Davies later wrote:

> Only one thing was needed to complete the Nazi aim [after taking Norway and Denmark] of effectively blocking our north-west approaches. This was the occupation of Iceland. With Iceland in their grasp [as Admiral Raeder understood] Germany could develop aerodromes, seaplane and submarine bases, and naval anchorages athwart our convoy routes...Is it too much to say that, at this moment in time...the ultimate outcome of [World War II] hung in the balance?[24]

Churchill agonised over the possibility that a German take-over of the French fleet, the fourth largest and one of the most modern in the world, would confront Britain with 'mortal dangers.' He empathised with his defeated ally, but he was hard-nosed and uncompromising about the survival of his country with honour. Top officials of the Vichy government and officers of the French navy had insisted they would not allow their warships to fall into German hands. However, Churchill did not trust Pierre Laval and his puppet administration.

During the confusion of the collapse of the Allied defences, troop evacuations, and armistice negotiations, French minister of marine Admiral François Darlan had ordered the French Atlantic fleet to evacuate their home bases. Some two hundred, mostly small naval craft and two old battleships had arrived in British ports by early July. When Darlan heard about this, he instructed them to sail to Mediterranean bases in France or North Africa. The Admiralty seized the vessels with minor resistance, confirming Churchill's belief that Germans could easily take over French capital ships.

The modern strength of the French fleet was now in North Africa, many of the vessels recently arrived from the home ports on the Atlantic coast. In Algeria, at the adjacent bases of Oran and Mers-el-Kebir, lay the cream of the navy: the two new battleships *Dunkerque* and *Strasbourg*, the two modernised battleships *Bretagne* and *Provence*, and thirty-five smaller ships. This cluster, which could become a powerful extension of Hitler's navy, was Churchill's prime target in what he called operation Catapult.

On 3 July, Vice Admiral Sir James Sommerville stationed his own formidable fleet off Mers-el-Kebir. He reluctantly relayed an Admiralty message to the French commander, Vice Admiral Marcel-Bruno Gensoul. It presented four alternatives: the French ships could join the British fleet, or reduce their crews and sail to British ports, or sail to the French West Indies for disarmament, or, in lieu of any of the first three alternatives, they could face destruction within six hours. The fourth choice sorely grieved Sommerville; it infuriated Gensoul.

'This was a hateful decision,' Churchill later wrote in *Their Finest Hour*. 'The French had been only yesterday our dear Allies… On the other hand, the life of the State and the salvation of our cause were at stake. It was a Greek tragedy.'

Gensoul rejected the British alternatives. British Intelligence intercepted a message from Darlan to Gensoul that read: '…(Orders have been given) to all French naval forces in the Mediterranean to join you immediately in fighting order….Call in submarines and air force if necessary.' Partly in light of this message, the Admiralty would not compromise. In a delaying mode, Gensoul held his ground. A few more fruitless back-and-forths, and a heartsick Sommerville ordered his ships to open fire. The *Dunkerque* was put out of action, the *Bretagne* sunk, the *Provence* beached to keep her from sinking, and a destroyer heavily damaged. No hits were registered on British ships. More than 1,200 French sailors were killed.

Another, smaller French fleet anchored in Alexandria was presented with similar demands by Admiral Sir Andrew Cunningham. The French commander, Cunningham's friend Vice Admiral René Godfroy, decided to mount a quixotic charge through the British blockade. Cunningham appealed over his head to the good sense and honour of the French ships' companies. Confronted by his men's overwhelming preference to disarm, defuel, and reduce crews by two-thirds, Godfroy yielded.

Churchill might not have turned on his former ally if he had known that Darlan had destroyed France's major Atlantic harbour installations and the ships still in them before the Germans moved in. Darlan had never told him what he had done. (And, despite their anger over the British attacks on their ships, the French again were true to their word when, in the face of a November 1942 German attempt to seize their fleet at Toulon, they scuttled seventy-seven of their most technologically advanced warships.)[25]

The Royal Navy had developed an asdic device, which they believed was so effective in detecting and combating submerged U-boats that construction of anti-submarine convoy escorts was neglected. The Germans quickly discovered that asdic could not spot a surfaced U-boat. And the first British naval radars, carried by few ships at that time, were not capable of detecting a small conning tower poking above the water. In effect, British convoys were stone blind to U-boats at night.

The disadvantage for U-boats was that a tight clutch of convoy ships was as hard to find as any of the independent merchantmen scattered over the ocean. They were aided by German intelligence, which had discovered the broad swath of North Atlantic shipping lanes and kept them informed of the times of departures from Halifax and other Canadian assembly ports. Despite the concentration of spies in the embarking areas, intelligence could not ferret out the precise routes of individual convoys or their escort makeup.

Nevertheless, when routine warfare against merchantmen was renewed after the Norway campaign in early summer, the average monthly toll reached 420,000 tons. It was the beginning of what German submariners called 'the happy time.' The losses became so severe that the British were forced to re-route their convoys, causing organisational snafus and port congestion.

But these successes were not enough for the commander of the U-boat force, Admiral Karl Doenitz, who believed the war could be won by choking off British supply routes. Doenitz could well have been a hero, had the Führer and Grand Admiral Raeder paid attention to his plea for a war-opening three hundred U-boats. He later wrote in his memoirs: 'That out there in the Atlantic a handful of U-boats was being called upon to fight a battle that would decide the [outcome] of the war was something that the continentally minded German Government and High Command...were both, unfortunately, quite incapable of grasping.'

To increase the sinkings to a strangulation level, during the late summer, Doenitz developed the 'wolf pack' tactic. Its purpose was to locate convoys more efficiently and devastate them. A group— say, a half-dozen U-boats—would line up perpendicularly across a suspected convoy route. Separated from each other by about twenty miles, they would constitute a 'drift net' about a hundred miles long. Once contact was made with a convoy, positions would be transmitted to U-boat Command in Germany, which then would direct the other boats to the target (a system that, curiously, resembled RAF Fighter Command's network). Methods of attack would be left up to the U-boat commanders. Their approach normally would be at night—when they were least visible to asdic, radar, and the naked eye—and one or two of them would infiltrate the convoy and attack from within.

At the beginning of September, Doenitz's U-boat strength was fifty-seven, of which only twenty-seven were available for patrols. The new approach was so adroit that the small fleet, with some six or seven boats out pack-hunting at any given time, was able to sink an extravagant number of merchantmen—an average of eight enemy vessels per U-boat per patrol at peak success.

The first notable wolf-pack attack came on 20 September against the forty-one-ship convoy HX 72. Its escort HMS *Jervis Bay*, commanded by Captain Edward Stephen Fogarty Fegen, had been ordered back to Halifax a few hours before. The convoy was spotted by Prien, who had one torpedo left after earlier actions. He reported the location to U-boat Command and continued shadowing and transmitting bearings. The other five U-boats in the pack were directed to the convoy. The attack started the following night, after a Royal Navy vessel met the convoy to accompany it to port. U-99 fired the first torpedoes and sank three ships before the new British escort reacted. U-100 slipped inside the convoy array and, while the escort frantically hunted her for four hours, torpedoed seven ships. All told, HX 72 lost twelve vessels.[26]

Back on 15 May, as the *blitzkrieg* tore into Belgium, Holland, and France, Churchill cabled US President Franklin Delano Roosevelt requesting 'the loan of forty or fifty of your older destroyers.' He was referring to the 120 or so four-funnelled World War I vessels that had been 'mothballed' and lashed together at several naval stations since the end of that war. Churchill felt that these rust buckets could be cleaned up, repaired, greased and oiled, and refitted with British asdic equipment, radar, and anti-aircraft guns. The Battle of the Atlantic was heating up, and the old four-stackers could be useful in patrolling and protecting convoys in the interim until new corvettes, destroyers, and cruisers began sliding down British ways in great numbers.

But Roosevelt was in a domestic bind. He was discouraged by a deep-seated American isolationism. And he was breaking an American tradition, first articulated in George Washington's refusal to run for a third term. Coming to the end of his own second term in an extremely malevolent international climate, with the Americas as a future target of the totalitarian powers, Roosevelt and his supporters were convinced that the continuity of his leadership was crucial. He did not want to jeopardise his re-election by engaging in a prolonged battle with the powerful isolationists in Congress, who probably would filibuster over the issue of destroyers for Britain. His ambivalence was heightened by the uncertainty of Britain's survival.

The president's inclinations, however, were beginning to gain influential support. One great boost came from General John J Pershing, the revered former commander of the World War I American Expeditionary Force in France, who told the American people in a radio address on 4 August that 'all the things we hold most dear are threatened.' He said the British needed the destroyers right now, and the next few weeks would be critical. If these vessels could be used to reinforce the Royal Navy, he said, they could 'save us from the danger and hardship of another war.'

On the same night, Colonel Charles A Lindbergh, aviator hero and spokesman for the isolationists, told forty thousand roaring supporters in Chicago that the United States should cooperate with the Nazis if Germany won the war. The speech, coming on the heels of the Pershing appeal, caused an uproar. Senator Claude Pepper of Florida said the American people would have to decide whether to follow the advice of General Pershing or that of 'the chief of the fifth column in this country, Colonel Lindbergh,' who had been decorated by Luftwaffe chief Göring.

The day before the two speeches, Churchill's cabinet had approved US Navy Secretary Frank Knox's idea for swapping a ninety-nine-year lease on Atlantic bases for the destroyers. The British proposal was considered at a meeting of Roosevelt's cabinet, at which it was decided to find a way to bypass Congress and consummate the deal, fast.

It was not to be simple. Roosevelt wanted Churchill to pledge publicly that if Britain fell, it first would transfer its fleet to Canada to continue fighting. Churchill felt that raising the spectre of defeat would severely damage British morale, which he had striven so hard to elevate. He also thought that Britons might resent the deal as one-sided: trading their island havens for floating rust. The Prime Minister wanted his people to view the swap as generous and dedicated to a common cause. The president wanted the American people and Congress to see it as a hard-nosed business arrangement.

An ingeniously simple solution to the impasse was devised by State Department legal adviser Green H Hackworth: first, in exchange for fifty destroyers, Britain would lease to the United States six bases in the Bahamas, Jamaica, Antigua, St. Lucia, Trinidad, and British Guyana, satisfying the American need for an unsentimental Yankee trade; second, two other, more strategically useful bases in Newfoundland and Bermuda would be outright ninety-nine-year gifts, entirely separate from the destroyers, allowing Britain to be perceived as grateful and generous to a nation that had been helping it since the Nazi onslaught started. The deal was signed on 2 September 1940.

Churchill was elated, not so much for the old destroyers as for the realisation that the United States had sidled closer, irrevocably close, to the status of ally.[27]

The German submariners' 'happy time' peaked in October with three major convoy actions, including the single most devastating U-boat attack of the war. That battle involved a slow (about seven knots) thirty-four-ship convoy, SC 7, out of Sydney, Nova Scotia, and a wolf pack of eight U-boats. On the night of 16 October, U-48, under Lieutenant Commander Heinrich Bleichrodt, made contact but lost it when he was depth-charged by the escorts, a particularly strong group of three destroyers and several smaller ships. They were several hundred miles off Ireland. Doenitz, at submarine command, ordered the pack to line up across the presumed route of the convoy, and contact was regained the afternoon of 19 October.

At 10 pm, seven U-boats began the attack at the perimeter of the convoy formation. Lieutenant Commander Otto Kretschmer took his U-99 unseen between two destroyers and became part of the convoy. For him it was a feeding frenzy; in three hours he destroyed nine ships. The total score for the pack that night was twenty-one of the loaded merchant vessels. The slaughter was called 'the night of the long knives' (the same metaphor used for Hitler's paranoid murders in 1934 of more than a thousand early supporters).

The following night, convoys HX 79 and HX 79A lost twelve vessels.

The September and October average of shipping sunk by the Germans was more than 440,000 tons, three-quarters of which was put under by U-boats. In October, Doenitz's fleet achieved an all-time monthly record of 60,000 tons per submarine at sea. The sustained loss of merchant vessels starting in July was approaching the 600,000-ton level that the U-boat admiral reckoned would starve Britain into suing for peace. It was done with fewer than 20 percent of the underseas raiders he had requested.

On 5 November Churchill told the House of Commons, 'More serious than the air-raiding has been the recent recrudescence of U-boat sinkings in the Atlantic approaches to our island.'[28]

The Stage is Set

As the only survivor among the targeted Western European nations, Britain had for the moment held back the Nazi onslaught. Though defeated on the continent, the island nation had used the English Channel and the Royal Air Force masterfully as its first lines of defence in holding off a German invasion. Not knowing Hitler had called off Operation Sea Lion, the British people expected it could come at any time. The devastating blitz continued. And the phenomenal success of the new U-boat campaign of the last four months brought them face to face with the possibility of fatal food and material shortages. The men who sailed the cargo ships not only felt the threat along every mile of the seaways but worried almost constantly over the lot of their families and friends back home.

At that time the military power of the Axis partners and their Soviet comrade of the moment, the Nazi political and racial doctrines, and the Führer himself altogether seemed invincible.

Still, Britons were encouraged by the increasing US involvement in the war effort and by the re-election of the more-than-sympathetic Roosevelt to an unprecedented third term. In spite of their precarious situation, their morale was sky-high, for they knew they could depend on each other to fight together, to the death if necessary.

With this sense of the wartime climate on 5 November 1940 now in place, the curtain rises on the classic one-sided battle between the German pocket battleship *Admiral Scheer*—feared by the British even more than U-boat wolf packs—and the vulnerable, lightly armed, former cargo liner *Jervis Bay,* lone protector of the thirty-seven ships of convoy HX 84.

1 The *Scheer* Breaks Out

THE *Admiral Scheer* sailed smoothly above the Arctic Circle, far north of the Royal Navy blockade. The day was 30 October 1940. Her crew hardly noticed the pocket battleship's rise and fall on the long, gentle swells. As she passed between the northeastern tip of Iceland and Jan Mayen (a Norwegian island—the site of a German meteorological station—recently occupied by free Danish forces with British help), Captain Theodor Krancke changed course, aiming her sleek new clipper bow southwest toward the Denmark Strait. It was to be the most dangerous part of his projected breakout into the North Atlantic. The narrow passage lay between Iceland and Greenland, where British sea reconnaissance was intensive.

The raider was about to run into good, yet painful, fortune. Her 'frog in the jar,' the ship's meteorologist had forecast a weather change for the worse. To the Germans, worse was better. A storm could interfere with enemy patrol visibility and tilt the advantage to the *Scheer*.

Cloud cover developed during the afternoon. The wind picked up from the northwest and began pelting the ship with sleet and snow. As the sea rose, her pitch and yaw increased. Many new sailors in the 1,300-man company felt the ponderous rhythms mainly in their guts. The storm continued building, far beyond the frog's expectation, and near nightfall it had evolved into a heavy gale. In spite of the breakers pounding her bows, the *Scheer* managed to generate up to twenty knots toward the strait's entrance.

Krancke cleared the upper decks, except for the anti-aircraft gun crews. Bo'sun Hellgert[0] sent a man out with a safety line around his waist to cover some exposed ammunition. When he realised the job could not be done with one pair of hands, he shouted over the shriek and crash of the storm that he was going out to help.

Hellgert waited for a lull and then bolted over to the gun's ammo cache…just as a huge wave cascaded over the starboard side.

Another gun crew heard moans after the water washed off the deck. Two of them, secured by ropes, crept forward and found the man the Bo'sun had sent out lying unconscious against a side of the superstructure. They lifted him upright between them and draped his arms over their shoulders. Then, battling the wind, snow pellets, waves, and spreading ice patches on the deck, they found the nearest hatch and somehow got him down to the sickbay. Both his thighs were broken. He was lashed to a secured cot. On coming to, he stammered out what he remembered to First Officer Ernst Gruber:

'...boatswain came out to help me...[took] off his coat...to be able to move quicker. We'd just got a case loose...enormous wave broke over us. I was flung against something...and I felt a terrible pain in my legs and that's all I know.'[1]

A report that Hellgert and another crewman were missing and presumed overboard quickly reached the bridge. At a risk of swamping, the captain immediately brought the *Scheer* about. He ran a searchlight pattern, but its reach was limited by the precipitation and the spume streaking across the violently tossing surface. After an empty half-hour, Krancke grimly accepted his own judgement that no man could live more than a few minutes in the frigid water whipped up by that terrible Arctic gale. He gave up the rescue diversion and resumed his southwestward course.

These were the crew's first losses of the war, and the men fell into a mass melancholy—a prayer here and there, a few words about their lost mates. Then they got back to bringing their ship and themselves through the storm.[2]

By early morning, the wind had intensified to hurricane force. Gritty air carrying spray and globs of foam shrieked at nearly 100 miles an hour through the superstructure and around the masts and lines, and peppered everything in its path. Its direction shifted to northeasterly and waves began pounding the *Scheer's* stern. Normally, for the safest ride, the captain would turn her bows into the sea and backtrack her course until the storm played out. But Krancke was anxious to attack a British convoy that German intelligence had signalled him would be in an unpatrolled zone in the North Atlantic halfway between Canada and Ireland. He was willing to endure the punishment of the worsening storm because he wanted to keep that appointment. The following sea, though it threatened loss of control and even capsizing, actually added a few knots to the ship's pace.

Dawn was about to make the ocean visible when the *Scheer* lurched into the Denmark Strait and turned a few more degrees to the south.

The captain was sure British patrol planes were grounded ((he didn't know British naval aircraft had not yet started sweeping the strait). If the Royal Navy had ships in the area, they could not be expected to spot and identify the pocket battleship through the snow, spray, and heavy seas. In spite of this security, on 31 October the *Scheer's* men were a shaken crew.

The strait was the worst place to be in a polar hurricane. Only 180 miles wide at its narrowest, it had become a kind of wave speedway. Great rollers 60 to 70 feet high, driven by the predominant northeasterly flow, swept through the passage from the ship's stern while other giants, kicked up by winds from other directions, criss-crossed them and set up chaotic patterns. Wave-modeller Hendrik Tolman estimates that a storm of such energy must have raised one in a hundred crests to 90 feet, with an occasional monster towering 110 feet. Men who could see out bridge windows and portholes were terrified by these sudden sheer mounds that reared over the wild seas higher than the ship's fighting mast and bore down on them like a thundering herd of elephants.

Because of the *Scheer's* 616-foot length and her loaded displacement of more than 16,000 tons, she rocked and heaved in what seemed to be slow motion while the foamy chop danced crazily all about her. At times she ploughed down the front of a great wave, jammed her bows into the trough, and then was lifted stern first, back up the same wave. As the crest rolled under the ship, it acted as a fulcrum suspending her forward and aft sections above the water like a seesaw. Many ships would have broken in half across the beam, but the *Scheer's* structure was strong enough to withstand such stress. More than once she came close to capsizing when unexpected breakers slammed into her sides and superstructure as she was fending off the repeated pounding and lifting at her stern.

Crewmen struggled to keep to their stations and do their jobs. The few who ventured into the face of the wind kept their mouths shut tight, or they felt 'as though they were being blown up like a bellows.'[3] Unsecured equipment and loosened fittings bounced off bulkheads. Krancke was slammed into a corner of the bridge along with the helmsman. Exposed ventilators lost their covers, and seawater flushed into food-storage compartments, ruining beans and converting flour into sacks of paste.

Men who were not needed to keep the vessel moving through the storm took to their bunks. They found themselves feet high, then head high with the plunge and lift of the ship. When she heeled—as much as 37 degrees—they grasped handrails or any solid bulkhead fitting to keep from being flung out of their berths. The sickbay filled with injured sailors who managed to stagger up and down the heaving companionways to get there…or who somehow were bundled there by concerned shipmates.

When Lieutenant Kurt Breithaupt finished his watch tour and an acrobatic lunch, he reeled back to his cabin for some rest before his next tour. It looked as if the Gestapo had been through the room. His things—chairs, books, alarm clock, desk and dresser drawers and their contents—were scattered all over. They continued sliding and tumbling around the floor. Like a vaudeville comic, he tried hopelessly to gather them and put them back where they belonged. Quickly giving up, he teetered to his bunk. But rest was impossible. Breithaupt had to fight to stay in place. The noise was like hammers and frying pans banging on his skull. Because he couldn't read a book or do anything else, he settled for staring at his laundry articles, hung over a radiator to dry, and marvelled as they alternately stood out like windblown pennants and then slapped against the bulkhead.

The radar operator, grasping his chair with cramped fingers, spotted a ship 6,000–7,000 yards to port. The captain suspected she was a British armed merchant cruiser patrolling the strait. He knew most Royal Navy ships did not yet carry search radar, so he shifted his ship's bearing a few degrees to the west and kept the pocket battleship beyond naked-eye visibility.

At midnight, Meteorological Officer Defant, who had forecast the storm, appeared on the bridge. His face radiated preternatural joviality. Hanging on like the rest of them, he raised his voice above the cyclonic din.

'Well, gentlemen, are you satisfied with me?'

'Too much of a good thing,' the navigation officer mumbled, informing Defant of the loss of the two men. 'You must have pulled the plug too hard.'[4]

As the *Scheer* emerged from the Denmark Strait on 1 November, the storm began tailing off. It had put the crew through a terrible ordeal, but it also had concealed their breakout. First Officer Gruber allowed them time to calm down. Then he called some of the officers onto the bridge and told them to pull themselves together and start cleaning up.

The men first assessed the extensive, mostly minor damage. The worst of it was two wrecked motor boats hanging from their davits, one of them a total loss. Washroom basins were torn away from the plumbing. The outside ventilator covers were lost. Luckily, the ship's Arado scout plane, secured on its rails about forty feet above the waterline, had survived almost unharmed.

Repairs got under way. When it was safe to negotiate the outside decks, the cleanup crew dumped shattered china overboard. They pumped water out of the cabins and the lower levels. They straightened out the messes in various work areas and then put their jumbled personal effects back in order.

Doctors and medical aides, as soon as they were steady enough on their feet, began setting bones; treating bruises, gashes, sprains, and concussions; and taking care of other injuries, including the captain's hand, which had been crushed against the bridge wall.

Before the end of the day, the men brought shipboard conditions to near normal, and the *Scheer* sailed on to her 5 November rendezvous with convoy HX 84 and its escort HMS *Jervis Bay*.[5]

2 A Family Reborn and Death of a Sister

T HE sun, always welcome on the Orkney Islands, added some brightness and colour to the British Scapa Flow naval base. It was 21 June 1919. The seventy-four interned German warships rode high on the quiet waters of the anchorage off the northeastern tip of Scotland. As a fleet, they were probably the finest naval vessels in the world. But they were manned by rebellious skeleton crews, some close to mutiny. Shattered by their country's defeat in World War I and by chaos at home, they had been stuck for six months in this damnable enemy harbour waiting for politicians in some French place called Versailles to decide what was to become of Germany, of its navy, and of themselves. Few of the men had any inkling of the intense event they were about to be part of.

That morning, about four hundred excited schoolchildren clambered aboard the Admiralty tender *Flying Kestrel* at Stromness for an outing among the seemingly quiescent ranks of enemy warships. The youngsters buzzed and shouted and giggled and pointed at the few sailors they could see on the lofty German decks. Some crewmen thumbed their noses at the noisy little intruders. A few made obscene gestures. Most of them ignored the children and continued complaining to each other, playing mouth organs, and pacing the boards, and snoozing.

Around noon, the *Flying Kestrel* put about for her return to Stromness on Mainland Island. No one aboard could tell at that moment that the greatest act of self-destruction in naval history was under way.

A few minutes later they heard a brass bell clang and saw the crew of the *Friedrich der Grosse* scramble over the side into lifeboats. They gaped and screamed as the huge battleship heeled over and sank. The tender revved up to full speed and sped the children homeward through what became a horrifying scene of giant ships listing deeply, bows or sterns rising toward the sky, sinking. Abandon-ship bells reverberated all around them as boatloads of German sailors headed shoreward. The sight and sounds of the dying ships terrified the children.

James Taylor, a fifteen-year-old boy on the excursion, wrote in *Teacher's World*: '...out of the vents rushed steam and oil and air with a dreadful roaring hiss, and vast clouds of white vapour rolled up from the sides of the ships. Sullen rumblings and crashing of chains increase the uproar as the great hulls slant giddily over and slide with horrible sucking and gurgling noises under the water.'[1]

By mid-afternoon, fifty-two ships were under the still-roiling, littered surface of the Flow. The Royal Navy managed to beach the other twenty-two.

After signing the 11 November 1918 armistice, the disorganised German government surrendered two hundred U-boats (fourteen others were scuttled). The Allies shared the submarines and converted most of them into scrap. The fate of the surface vessels of the German High Seas Fleet was a different story. British, French, Italian, and American admirals of the Naval Council could agree only that the entire fleet would be disarmed and temporarily confined to German harbours under Allied supervision, and that the seventy-four most modern warships would later be transferred to the Allies.

Final disposition of the ten battleships, six battle cruisers, eight cruisers, and fifty destroyers became a bone of contention among the naval leaders. The French demanded a quarter of the ships as a fruit of victory. The Italians also wanted a share of the naval spoils. In the process of reducing the size of its fleet while maintaining global maritime supremacy, Britain opposed the strengthening of the French and Italian navies. The Americans, who twenty-five years later built the world's most powerful navy, were satisfied to let the others thrash it out for themselves.

The squabble was ended by the Supreme War Council (the highest civilian level), which ordered the ships interned outside Germany until the peace conference at Versailles determined their fate. That pleased the admirals, who had suspected the Germans would scuttle the ships if the peace treaty demanded a handover of the High Seas Fleet. The Naval Council decided the vessels should be moored temporarily in the security of Scapa Flow, about eighty square miles of water surrounded by islands on all sides but the south, under surveillance of the Royal Navy. Considering their anticipation of a mass scuttling, this preference of a deep-water harbour for the internment showed incredible lack of foresight. In a shallow-enough anchorage, a ship with her seacocks opened would bottom out before totally submerging.

By 27 November, seventy of the German ships, guns disabled and radio equipment silenced, had settled in the Orkney waters. The remaining four anchored there by the following January.[2]

About 20,000 men had sailed the warships to Britain. Their morale was in a sorry state. Several of the battleships and battle cruisers fell under control of revolutionary agitators, who managed to intimidate, dominate, and even terrorise their officers. In a hand-written message dispatched to Berlin, fleet commander Rear Admiral Ludvig von Reuter reported, 'All restraints of obedience and discipline were completely dissolved.' He branded his flagship *Friedrich der Grosse* 'a madhouse.'[3]

Since the possibility of scuttling the fleet had been on his mind, Reuter was exasperated by the breakdown in the shipboard efficiency he needed to co-ordinate seventy-four simultaneous sinkings before the Royal Navy could seize the ships. The brigs were too small to accommodate all the near-mutineers. So he worked out a scheme to subtly reduce the ships' crews. He gradually sent them home, especially the worst of the troublemakers, until he was down to 1,700 men—enough, he hoped, to quickly and quietly pull off a scuttle. And he transferred his flag to a less disorderly ship, the cruiser *Emden*. His British overseers paid little attention.

During the internment, the admiral was not kept current on progress at the peace table. The British allowed him to receive the *Times* of London but made sure it was always four days late. Radio communications were blacked out. Little effort was made by Berlin to update the admiral; his superiors regarded him as no more than a set of strings to be pulled when they were ready.

Reuter was a square-faced man with a small grey moustache. A deep crease cut straight down from each corner of his tight, slightly bowed mouth, delineating his chin. When he spoke, his jaw seemed to slide up and down like Pinocchio's. But, though he was dejected, in an almost hopeless fix, he was nobody's puppet.

The admiral had his own agenda. Being ignored by his leaders and held in a time warp by the British was not enough to erase his inner strength and his passion for doing what he thought was right. He would make a decision based on three possibilities:

  1) if Germany rejected the peace terms, he would scuttle the
  ships before they could be seized;
  2) if German negotiators got the fleet on the table as a
  bargaining chip, he would preserve the ships;
  3) if Germany accepted the peace terms, he would surrender
  the fleet.

He secretly developed a scuttling procedure with his seventy-four captains.

Four days after the Allies agreed on the peace terms and passed them to the Germans, Reuter read about them in the 10 May 1919 edition of the *Times*. The overall demands were harsh: losses of land, people, and natural resources, and huge reparation payments. Naval limitations were grim, as he had expected. The interned ships and fifty-two more would be surrendered to the Allies. The German navy would be restricted to a small number of old ships. The admiral was devastated.

On 16 June, the impatient Allies set a deadline of 21 June for Germany to accept the conditions of their forty-day-old proposal or face a resumption of the war. The news got to the *Emden* on 20 June. Some officers on a German dispatch boat reported the Reichstag's opposition to the treaty.

Stranded without official information or instructions from Germany, Reuter felt that the time had come for him to make a decision. He based his call on the former Kaiser's order that no German ship be allowed to be taken by an enemy. In effect, a scuttle policy had already been articulated.

He did not know that on 20 June a flurry of political activity had wiped out opposition to the treaty and the Reichstag had agreed to accept the terms. The deadline had been moved to the evening of 23 June, and the Royal Navy's scheduled seizure had been set back to that morning. Had timely news reached the admiral, he would have opted to hand over his ships to the Allies.

Instead, early in the morning of 21 June, when Reuter heard that Vice Admiral Sir Sydney Freemantle had sent a large part of his Scapa Flow fleet out to sea on a training exercise, he virtually glowed in the brilliance of fortune's smile upon him. It was the only good thing that had happened during the long months of the internment.

Just after 10:00 am that morning, the German commander raised 'D G' code flags, alerting all ships to be ready for instructions. A half-hour later he told the yeoman to send the prearranged scuttle command: 'Paragraph eleven. Confirm.'[4] The signal was passed from ship to ship by semaphore or Morse lamp. Only then did most of the sailors learn that their vessels were about to go to the bottom. It took about an hour for the message to reach the seventy-fourth ship. The admiral did some anxious deep breathing, praying the British had not caught on to all the signalling, until the first confirmation came back. An hour and a half after 'Paragraph eleven' was signalled, the crews opened the valves, and the first gouts of seawater entered the hulls of the High Seas Fleet.

By 5:00 pm, fifty-two of the most advanced warships in existence had gone to the bottom. A livid Admiral Freemantle raced his squadron back to the harbour and took into tow and beached the remaining twenty-two. The *Flying Kestrel*, after debarking her shaken young passengers at Stromness, returned to the turmoil and managed to pull the settling battleship *Baden* to shore.

The response to the scuttling had a comic element. As described by Dan van der Vat in his book *The Grand Scuttle*: 'The British were publicly indignant and privately relieved; the Germans officially regretful while protesting their innocence, but privately proud. The French were furious and vengeful, while the Americans shrugged their shoulders.'[5]

The Versailles Treaty limited the German navy to six old battleships, six light cruisers, twelve destroyers, and twelve torpedo boats. It allowed twenty-year-old vessels to be replaced, but at a drastic reduction in proportions. That meant the substitute for a 25,000-ton battleship could displace no more than 10,000 tons, the size of an 8-inch-gunned heavy cruiser. Construction of U-boats and aircraft was *verboten*. German naval leaders were beside themselves with rage. In one stroke Germany had morphed into a third-class sea power.

At least they had their Admiral Reuter, a hero who had 'outwitted' the British at Scapa Flow. It was especially important to the Germans that he had restored honour to what they regarded as their undefeated navy, and that many of the recently rebellious, slovenly sailors were again proud of their leaders and ready to take orders.

Following the signing of the peace treaty on 28 June, German admirals—together with naval architects and politicians—began spinning visions of a powerful new navy. Their crucial advantage was that the war's destruction had been mainly on enemy soil, while their own industrial infrastructure had been left intact. Nevertheless, it was going to take ingenuity, audacity, and guile to activate their shipyards under snooping Allied noses.

Reuter further stirred German hunger for recapturing past glories in his 1921 book *Scapa Flow*: The Account of the Greatest Scuttling of All Time with his call to action: 'The men of the interned force know that the sinking of the fleet represented only a part of their task. The greater one, the rebuilding of the fleet, still lies before them.'[6]

Under the moderate Weimar Republic, despite the post-war chaos, societal aimlessness, and horrendous inflation (130 billion marks to the dollar), the navy's commander in chief, Admiral Paul Benecke, laid the keel for the first replacement light cruiser in 1921 and launched her in 1925. The *Emden* (named for Reuter's scuttled flagship) displaced 5,600 tons and carried eight 5.9-inch guns. She was the last German naval vessel to stick to the Versailles restraints.

Benecke and his successor in 1924, Admiral Hans Zenker, were intent on maintaining and improving U-boat design capabilities, notwithstanding the ban on German submarines. They established a clandestine bureau in the Netherlands, funded by sham companies, to design and construct U-boats and run sea trials. By 1928 prototypes lay on secret slipways in Spain and Finland.

Two years after Zenker took command, the Germans floated their first replacement 'torpedo boat,' which at 924 tons was four and a half times heavier than allowed by the treaty and more powerfully armed than the prescribed destroyers. This was a test of the mettle of the League of Nations and its major members. Their response was silence.

During Zenker's command of the navy, the time came to replace their antiquated battleships. German naval leaders and designers deliberated, innovated, and thrashed out the characteristics of a revolutionary cruiser/battle-cruiser hybrid that would be effective against any navy and, at the same time, pass the scrutiny of Allied observers. After four years of debate, political scheming, and technological development, Zenker approved plans for the *Deutschland*, the first of three *panzerschiffe* (armoured ships). She was commissioned in 1933. Her sister ships, the *Admiral Scheer* and the *Admiral Graf Spee*, entered service in 1934 and 1936.

Each carried six 11-inch guns and topped out at twenty-seven knots. With the exception of three old but fast British battle cruisers, no other nation's warships could compete with that combination of firepower and speed. The *Deutschland* class's purpose was to destroy faster but weaker ships and run from more heavily armed but slower ships. They were going to be formidable raiders against the British merchant fleet. The shocked Allies marvelled at their advanced technology and dubbed them 'pocket battleships.' The *New York Tribune's* John Elliott wrote: 'They are a remarkable example of German ingenuity. Without violating the terms of the Treaty of Versailles, Germany in her pocket battleship has created nervousness in every Admiralty in the world.'[7]

Elliott was fooled. An honest 10,000-ton cruiser under the massive burden of six 11-inch guns would be reduced to scrap from the blasts and recoils of their salvoes. What escaped his and other observers' notice was that the Germans had packed the ships with far more steel than they let on—3,600 tons of it in the *Scheer*. That was what gave her the structural integrity to support heavy turrets and barbettes and to resist the muscular kickbacks of her big guns. More than two inches of armour along her belt, backed by empty space, and three inches of steel in her bulkheads and vital parts protected her from torpedoes and the shells of all but the largest capital ships.

Convinced he could get away with such fiction, Adolf Hitler, about to be named chancellor of Germany, privately bragged, 'If I say a ship is 10,000 tons, then it is 10,000 tons no matter how big it actually is.'[8]

The League of Nations and the Allies, some of whom suspected the violation, again backed off in the face of German contempt.

The *Scheer's* big guns, not subject to treaty limitations, generated great muzzle velocity (2,957 feet per second), a flat trajectory (8 percent elevation for a nine-mile shot), and potent impact. At 21.5 miles, they outranged all but the most modern, large-calibre cannons. They were set in triple turrets, one forward and one aft. The ship's medium armament, eight 5.9-inchers, placed amidships port and starboard, could put shells on a target more than fifteen miles out. She also carried six 3.4-inch and eight 1.5-inch anti-aircraft guns, ten machine guns, and eight torpedo tubes. With her superb fire-control system—five stereoscopic range finders, seven bearing directors, and one of the first naval radars—the pocket battleship projected awesome firepower.

Much German inventiveness went into weight-saving schemes. They used the advanced technology of electric arc welding to eliminate the bulk of hundreds of thousands of rivets. That reduced the weight of the *Scheer's* hull by 15 percent. Aluminium went into many struts and girders. In opting for two three-gun turrets instead of the traditional three double turrets, the designers took major chunks out of the total amount of steel incorporated in the big-gun systems and in the ammunition trunks and magazines.

The pocket battleships were the first capital vessels powered by lightweight, quick-starting diesel engines. The *Scheer* was propelled by eight linked engines developing about 54,000 horsepower. Space normally filled by boilers was used for extra fuel, storage, and accommodations, giving her longer time at sea—19,000 miles at nineteen knots—than any other capital ship.

The *Scheer* approaching a German port with her crew in dress whites.*(Imperial War Museum)*

Her two-seater Arado 196 monoplane with twin pontoons perched on a set of rails abaft the funnel. It was launched by a compressed-air catapuLieutenant The men called it 'the parrot' in affectionate recognition of its drooped nose. Its large Perspex dome, although set over the wing, provided wide angles of vision forward and aft for the pilot and observer/gunner, respectively. The Arado could cover a triangular pattern to a range of more than one hundred miles. On its return, the ship generally executed a sharp turn into the wind to create a 'duck pond,' a temporary smooth landing area for the pontoons. A derrick lifted the plane and replaced it on the catapult rails.[9]

For two years after her commissioning at Wilhelmshaven, the *Scheer* sailed through a series of shakedown trials and work-up training cruises in the Baltic Sea, the Atlantic, the Irish Sea, and the English Channel. Several problems emerged. The engines vibrated excessively between twenty-one and twenty-three knots. Stabiliser equipment was even noisier than the diesels. At a list of 12 degrees, the flow of lubricating oil to some propulsion units was cut off. Spray from the bows interfered with bridge visibility in heavy seas and high winds.

When the Spanish Civil War broke out in July 1936, Germany and Italy (siding with the Nationalist rebel forces under the fascist Generalissimo Francisco Franco) and the Soviet Union (supporting the socialist-leaning Republican government) all sent warships to Spanish waters for experience under operational conditions away from home ports and to test their new weaponry in near-battle situations. Other nations' ships cruised around the Spanish coasts or entered ports to protect their interests and their own citizens in the country. Hitler dispatched the *Admiral Scheer*, the *Deutschland*, some light cruisers, and smaller boats to Spain. On 29 May 1937 the Germans started getting more than they had bargained for.

That day the *Deutschland* and two torpedo boats were moored at Palma. Eight Republican aircraft bombed the harbour, scoring some near misses on the Nationalist cruiser *Baleares*. The cautious Germans left Palma and dropped anchor in Ibiza. Five days later, a Republican force of two cruisers and eight destroyers hove-to offshore and appeared ready to open fire. While all eyes were focused on the Spanish warships, a pair of three-engine aircraft descended out of the sun and hit the pocket battleship with two bombs and a near miss. Thirty-one men were killed and seventy-five wounded. The *Deutschland* was ordered home, and the *Scheer* was immediately recalled from sea duty to replace her stricken sister ship.

The fury in Germany was palpable. Hitler ordered the *Scheer* to bombard the coastal town of Almería. Under Captain Otto Ciliax's command, she sailed to the harbour and pounded shipping installations, barracks, other defensive facilities, a shore battery, and civilian areas. Fired in anger for the first time, her guns poured 239 rounds into the Spanish community. Estimates of civilian casualties from the bombardment vary from nineteen to hundreds killed, with up to eight thousand people losing their homes.

The *Scheer* ended her Spanish patrols in mid-1938. Into the late summer of 1939, she engaged in a series of exercises and training cruises. At the beginning of World War II (1 September), she was at the Schillig Roads anchorage off Wilhelmshaven.[10]

In an early evening mist four days later, the *Scheer's* deck watch was relaxed. On an upper level mast platform, the anti-aircraft officer and a Luftwaffe officer studied aeroplane recognition charts. Suddenly, some blips on the screen of the naval base's new radar indicated a flight of aircraft about one hundred miles to the west. As happened in the sightings at Pearl Harbour two years later, inexperienced technicians assumed they were friendly planes. After a while, the loudspeaker blared: 'Three aircraft at six o'clock. Course, straight towards *Scheer*.'

They were identified as German Heinkel He 111s. Then the Luftwaffe officer shouted, 'They're not ours. They're...Bristol Blenheims.'

Royal Air Force Squadron 110, led by Flight Lieutenant K C Doran, flew under a 500-foot cloud ceiling, spotted a large merchant ship straight ahead, and beyond her the *Admiral Scheer*. The British pilots saw laundry hanging over the warship's stern and crewmen idling on the deck. Even before the ship's air-raid alarms started jangling, Doran took his Blenheim just above mast height and unloaded two 500-pound bombs. Both clanged off the deck, ricocheted off superstructure, and chunked into the water. They failed to explode because their fuses needed eleven seconds to arm—not possible at the bomber's low altitude. A second Blenheim got a near miss, also a dud.

The Arado reconnaissance plane, its catapult, and a small gun were slightly damaged by the bombs. The ship's anti-aircraft gunners downed two planes, one of them a Blenheim and the other a friendly Junkers Ju 52 whose pilot failed to give recognition signals.

Saved by pure good luck, the *Scheer* underwent quick repairs. Captain Theodor Krancke took command at the end of September.[11]

Misfortune, which harassed the *Scheer's* sister ships, was about to hit the pocket-battleship fleet. In November, fearing the *Deutschland*, because of her name, might be sunk and played into a propaganda disaster by the British, Hitler changed her name to *Lützow*. The Führer's lack of confidence in his navy could be taken as an ill omen.

But not for the *Lützow*; it was the youngest sister that suffered.

The *Admiral Graf Spee*, which had the name *Admiral Scheer* painted on her bows in a pointless attempt to confuse the enemy, had claimed only 50,000 tons of enemy merchant vessels in the first three months of her commerce-raiding cruise in the South Atlantic and Indian Oceans. In early December, with an eye for better pickings, Captain Hans Langsdorff put her on a course to the estuary of the Rio de la Plata off Uruguay, a region of dense shipping.

Commodore H H Harwood, commander of one of the Royal Navy's eight task forces hunting for the *Graf Spee*, anticipated Langsdorff's move. He stationed his ships—the heavy cruiser *Exeter* (8-inch guns) and the 6-inch-gunned light cruisers *Ajax* and *Achilles*—in an intercept pattern at the mouth of the river. The three cruisers were no match individually for the raider, but together they stood a chance.

On 13 December, the raider's lookout sighted masts. Feeling blessed, her captain made ready to attack the supposed gaggle of British merchantmen. He realised too late that he was heading straight into an ambush.

The *Graf Spee's* 11-inch artillery concentrated on the *Exeter* and tore her to shreds. But, for reasons never revealed, her medium guns at first scored zero hits on the light cruisers. The *Ajax* and the *Achilles* (the latter a New Zealand ship) freely nipped at her heels. The captain then allowed the wounded Exeter to slip away and turned his main armament on the two yipping tormentors. He severely damaged the *Ajax* and dropped a few shells on the withdrawing *Achilles*. Though the pocket battleship was protected by armour, she did not get away free; according to one of several estimates, she took above-deck damage, mostly superficial, from two eight-inch and eighteen six-inch hits. In a decision that led to the *Graf Spee's* end, the overly cautious Langsdorff retreated to Montevideo harbour for repairs. Uruguayan authorities gave him three days to patch up and leave their territorial waters.

As the Germans worked on their ship, the Admiralty concocted British Broadcasting Company stories about a powerful Royal Navy force approaching La Plata. Berlin fell for the misinformation and signalled Langsdorff to scuttle his ship. On 17 December he followed orders with six torpedo warheads and treated hundreds of thousands of spectators on the waterfront to a tremendous sound and light show. While it was not the *Lützow* (formerly the *Deutschland*) that was forced to commit suicide, Hitler nevertheless suffered a major propaganda and naval defeat. Captain Langsdorff shot himself three days later.[12]

3 In Command

THEODOR Krancke joined the German navy as a cadet at age nineteen. He was born 30 March 1893 and brought up in landlocked Magdeburg. Though his family maritime tradition went no further than the bathtub in their small house, he took to the sea like a young polar bear. His training included tours on the cruiser *Victoria Louise* and at the naval school at Murwik. This sequence was typical of his future: sea duty, land duty, sea duty, land duty...In World War I he began showing his leadership potential as an ensign and then lieutenant, junior grade with the IX Torpedo Boat Flotilla. After a series of staff positions ashore, in 1921 he was given command of a minesweeper, then a torpedo boat. That experience earned him a promotion to lieutenant and a three-year teaching assignment at the Torpedo and Intelligence School. His next tour of sea duty began in 1927 as torpedo officer aboard the old *battleship Schleswig-Holstein.*

Captain Theodor Krancke, commanding officer of the pocket battleship *Admiral Scheer*. (*Bordkameradschaft* Admiral Scheer*)*

During the 1930s Krancke's career moved inexorably ahead like a tidal bore. He was put through a year's executive training, raised to lieutenant commander, and given command of the 4th Torpedo Flotilla Group. By then a promising leader in the burgeoning German navy, he bounced through a series of increasingly responsible shoreside assignments: staff officer at Torpedo Boat Flotilla Command to the Defence Ministry (where he was promoted to commander and soon after captain), then supervisor of the German Naval Academy. Two months after World War II began, the now highly respected senior officer was given command of the *Admiral Scheer*, one of the prides of the new *Reichsmarine,* and was charged with securing the North Sea area. The ship cruised there quietly for a few months.[1]

As early as October 1939, the navy's commander in chief, Grand Admiral Erich Raeder, had begun trying to convince Hitler to seize air and naval bases in neutral Norway, partly for the protection of cold-weather shipments of Swedish iron ore down the Norwegian coast. During the warm months, when the Gulf of Bothnia was ice-free, shiploads of the vital mineral were transported across the German-dominated Baltic Sea. Germany depended on Sweden for about three-quarters of its high-grade ore.

Winston Churchill, then First Lord of the Admiralty, had felt that Hitler could be defeated if German industry were deprived of Swedish iron. He had proposed laying mines in Norwegian territorial waters, but Prime Minister Neville Chamberlain chose to honour Norway's neutrality and scotched the plan. When the Soviet Union attacked Finland, however, the British and French began organising a force to land on the northern coast of Norway and cross northern Sweden, ostensibly to aid the Finns. Once in Sweden, their actual mission would be to take control of the ore deposits. Hearing of this plan via Germany's efficient intelligence network, Raeder raised the level of his pitch to Hitler. 'It is important to occupy Norway,' he urged.[2]

Unaware that the Soviets and the Finns had begun negotiating through Swedish intermediaries, the Allies, still using the pretext of helping Finland, decided that on about 20 March their troops would land at Narvik, the Norwegian ore shipment terminal, and several other northern coastal towns, then move on to the ore fields. They expected Norway and Sweden to cooperate. Their plan was slapdash, and their presumptions about Scandinavian intentions were unwarranted.

German groundwork for the invasions of Norway and Denmark began in earnest in late January 1940. Just after he had docked the *Admiral Scheer* at Wilhelmshaven for a major refit early in February, Captain Krancke was called away to serve temporarily as one of the three chiefs of a new special planning staff. He reported directly to Hitler and General Jodl, chief of the Wehrmacht (Germany's armed forces) operations staff. Wehrmacht Commander in Chief General Wilhelm Keitel, Jodl's father-in-law, outlined their mission: 'Your task is to prepare an operation for the occupation of Norway [and Denmark]...We are in possession of information...indicating that the British...intend to occupy the ports of the western coast of Norway in co-operation with the French...Given our situation of naval inferiority, [such an Allied success]...would be a major setback for us.'

Krancke later said, 'Inasmuch as both Hitler and Jodl allowed us to work in peace, I was under the impression that they were not firmly resolved to execute the operation.'[3]

In mid-February Churchill made a decision that, while unrelated to the Norway landings, resulted in a leg up for the Germans. On his instructions, the destroyer *Cossack* stopped the German tanker *Altmark* (returning from her final supply rendezvous with the late *Graf Spee*), and with her boarding party wielding revolvers and cutlasses in nineteenth-century Royal Navy tradition, repatriated 303 captured British merchant seamen. The encounter took place in a fjord, angering the Norwegians (though they did not object to the Germans transporting prisoners of war in their waters). It enraged Hitler. He ordered his staff to accelerate the planning.

Except for some data on the Norwegian army, intelligence was meagre, and this impeded Krancke's group. They had to use travel guides, tourist brochures, and hydrographic charts. To the captain's credit, they quickly drew up naval recommendations that were the backbone of the entire operation. They proposed simultaneous landings at all main Norwegian ports, with warships and aircraft delivering the first wave of troops.

Both sides kept altering plans and changing dates. Churchill resurrected his scheme to mine Norway's coastal waters. Unaware of Hitler's plan to invade, he set back the occupation of the northern Norwegian ports to 8 April. The Germans kicked off their operation on 7 April. As virtually the whole German fleet was involved, the Royal Navy sensed something unusual was underway. But, while laying a pattern of mines along the coast, they sent their main force out to sea against what disorganised intelligence and preconceived notions had told them was a German raid on shipping. This promised to be a clash of major warships, a mouth-watering prospect to many high-level officials of the old naval school.

The Admiralty then thought the Germans might be on their way to Norway. It informed the fleet, but only after a significant delay of four hours. Churchill added to the jumble by ordering the occupation troops to disembark from the ships of the First Cruiser Squadron that were about to carry them to Norway. Instead, he sent the ships out against the phantom German raiders. The Tommies, languishing at British docksides, would have been in Narvik before the Germans landed on 9 April.

By contrast, meticulous planning and near faultless execution, speeded up in response to the boarding of the *Altmark*, led to successful invasions by the Germans. They took over Denmark in twelve hours. The landings at Oslo, Kristiansand, Stavanger, Bergen, Trondheim, and Narvik went like clockwork against minor opposition by the ill-prepared Norwegians.

The Norwegian campaign ultimately was costly to both navies. Britain lost an aircraft carrier, two cruisers, seven destroyers, a sloop, and four submarines. Germany, considering the smaller size of its fleet, suffered proportionally much greater casualties from which it never fully recovered. Three *Reichsmarine* cruisers, ten destroyers, and six U-boats were sunk. Three old battleships and several smaller craft were damaged.[4]

The *Admiral Scheer* before she was refitted with a raked bow and a light tubular fire-control mast. *(Imperial War Museum)*

While almost the entire navy engaged in the Norway operation, the *Scheer* was high and dry in Wilhelmshaven, having her innards and her topside reworked to make her a fitter warship. Engine vibrations, which had stressed the crew and interfered with the fire-control system, were damped by rebuilding the underpinnings of the diesels. She was given raked bows to reduce the water taken on in heavy seas, a problem that might have affected her ability to weather the killer storm she later encountered in the Denmark Strait. Her pagoda-like fighting mast was replaced by a lighter, tubular structure. The radar in the new mast was coupled to the forward range-finder. By the end of June, the *Scheer's* refit was completed, and with the take-over of Norway and Denmark accomplished, Krancke was relieved of his temporary post and resumed command of his pocket battleship.

After the five-month lay-up, the crew needed retraining and the ship had to be put through a series of sea trials. Krancke took the *Scheer* on some runs in the Baltic, then back to Wilhelmshaven for minor repairs and adjustments. He next led her through working-up exercises with the *Nordmark*, her designated mid-ocean supply ship. By 23 October, nearly fourteen months after the war started, the pocket battleship was provisioned for her first raiding cruise, and she made ready to sail from the Baltic base at Gotenhafen.

Before the tugs nudged her away from the quay, two captains, old friends of Krancke, came aboard for a farewell. One of them laced his send-off with an uncalled-for dose of pessimism: 'You haven't got a fifty-fifty chance. More like ten-to-one against. The British have had time to improve their defences and after the *Graf Spee* business they'll be on their toes.'[5]

This forecast preyed on Krancke's mind. After a while, Admiral Raeder's philosophical/practical assessment of naval warfare slipped into his consciousness and helped him shrug off the anxiety: 'Success and failure are only a hairline apart. A wrong decision or one a minute late, the wrong interpretation of a message, a bad change in the weather, an unfortunate hit—any of these can change

Grand Admiral Erich Raeder reviewing the *Admiral Scheer* crew. (*Bordkameradschaft* Admiral Scheer*)*

victory into defeat in a twinkling. In the same way, an apparently hopeless battle may turn into a victory through errors of the enemy.'[6]

The diesels began turning the *Scheer's* twin screws, and she slipped past the harbour mole. Krancke then stopped the engines and mustered the crew at the stern. As the ship lay dead in the quiet water, he revealed their mission: to devastate a Halifax convoy, disrupt British shipping and naval operations, and then head south and stir up more trouble for the British.

He stressed the courage, fighting tradition, and much greater strength of the Royal Navy. 'If we have to fight,' he said, 'then let each man on board this ship do his duty in the spirit of the great sailor whose name she bears.'[7]

What the captain knew in his heart and did not tell his men was that German naval leaders also considered the Royal Navy's tactics orthodox and conservative. In fact, Raeder's intent in the early part of the war was to do the unusual and surprising, and cause the British to go off in all directions. They believed that the Admiralty would adjust to new situations hesitantly.

Restarting the diesels, Krancke set a westward course, then swung the ship north toward the Great Belt, between the Danish islands of Fyn and Sjaelland, on her way to the Kattegat and the North Sea.

The *Admiral Scheer* crew relaxing with the tail of the Arado scout seaplane just visible above the turret. *(Bordkameradschaft* Admiral Scheer*)*

It was night time in the belt. The chain of a buoy marking a wreck that had not been entered on navigation charts fouled one of the *Scheer's* propellers. The ship hove to again, and her engines stopped. A suited diver dropped off the stern into the cold autumn water. By noon the next day he had freed the undamaged screw, and the ship resumed her cruise. Nine hours later, as she passed through the Kattegat between Denmark and Sweden, her wireless room received a message from Naval Command Group North that British submarines were on patrol in the Skaggerak around the northern tip of Denmark. They were instructed to turn back to Kiel and enter the North Sea via the Kiel Canal just below the base of the Danish peninsula.

These two early interruptions strummed the alarm nerves of the crew. Were they an omen? After months of hanging around Wilhelmshaven, running work-ups, and making adjustments here and there while the war was raging, it was easy for the frustrated men, some of them superstitious, to imagine more trouble ahead. The mission schedule was already retarded. Would bad luck keep piling up? Was their operation foredoomed?

The captain sensed the jitters spreading through his crew. He reassured them that internal butterflies were normal at the start of a major cruise. He ordered the anchor dropped for a night of calming down. They set sail for Kiel in the morning.

On 27 October, the *Scheer* passed through the canal into the mouth of the Elbe River. The day was sunny, the visibility excellent—especially for any patrolling British submarines and aircraft. She was given a destroyer and fighter plane escort, but no enemy appeared. At twilight the escorts dropped off, and the pocket battleship continued due north. Before dawn the next day, she took cover in an isolated fjord near the Norwegian port of Stavanger. That night—four days later than planned—Krancke moved north, evading five patrol planes from RAF Squadron 269, then west toward his next objective, the Denmark Strait.[8]

After completing the arduous, unobserved passage through the strait, as described in Chapter 1, Krancke set a course for the British convoy route and rang the engine room for full speed.

Given a few days of light duty to recover from the terrible battering by the storm, the men settled down and discussed their rough experience and the captain's qualities of leadership. What mattered most was that fate had dropped them into the worst storm they would ever experience and that Krancke had brought them through it. That he had risked everything searching for the lost crewmen warmed their hearts. The more they talked, the more their admiration for him rose, and the greater their trust. They were glad to be serving under him.

Krancke was fairly tall, an inch or two over six feet, with a lean physique. He held himself easily erect. His long face tapered somewhat, but his chin was strong. He wore his straight brown hair parted on the right side. Premature bags hung under his hooded blue eyes—a characteristic developed by many commanders responsible for the lives of other men. Crow's feet spanned from the corners of his eyes, probably a consequence of years of squinting out to sea. His thin mouth sometimes twisted down on the right side, depending on his state of mind.

If there is a look of a commander, Krancke had it. He projected a spare authority and an aura of experience and intelligent judgement. His modulated baritone, in a striking, peculiar way, seemed directed down his gaunt nose straight at those he talked to. At the same time, there was compassion and a kind of playfulness in his eyes. He often loosened up his officers with a funny story or some banter. When relaxing or formulating plans, he always lit up a black cigar.

Krancke's destination was a North Atlantic area bounded at 52–54 degrees north and 32–35 degrees west. The high command believed Halifax-to-Britain convoys generally sailed through that approximately 120-by-120-mile square. They expected convoys HX 83 and HX 84 to be there between the fourth and sixth of November. German Naval Intelligence had sent him that estimate. The information on which it was based was easy to come by. Nearly everyone in Halifax knew when the ships were gathering to leave port: the taxi drivers who drove the ship captains from their vessels to naval headquarters and back, the clerks in the harbour shops, families who put up the sailors in comfortable quarters between trips. And whoever worked for the Germans certainly knew. The only task for intelligence was to intercept radioed convoy cyphers, estimate the times of convoy passages within the target area, and signal them to the *Scheer*.

No one except the convoy captains and the port's naval control-of-shipping officers knew the exact routes and the composition of their escorts. It was no secret to the Germans, however, that convoy protection at this early stage of the war was makeshift and usually minimal, sometimes absent. Under way, the convoy ships maintained their positions in the array and observed radio silence, though some receivers leaked detectable oscillations. Krancke's task was to find them and destroy them. He needed the Arado seaplane's reconnoitring sweeps to have more than a lottery chance.

Although the storm had let up two days before, the sea on

3 November was still heavy. Seaplane operations would be hazardous, and the parrot was confined to its rails. The *Scheer* combed the target square with no sightings. Krancke was concerned that he would miss the convoys. He consulted his electronics and decoding officers, but they reported no trace of convoy radio oscillations. Routine activities continued aboard the anxious raider.

Just after a discussion started about publishing a ship's newsletter, the alarm bells rang. The crew pounded the decks and companionways to their action stations. A lookout pointed to the tops of two masts. The captain quickly joined him on the foretop observation platform. She was a single ship bearing west, probably in ballast, not worth going after and revealing the *Scheer's* breakout and position. Krancke reminded the disappointed crew that their first objective was to find and destroy a convoy.

The North Atlantic swells continued into the next day. They sighted another westward-bound vessel and let it go. Again the crew groused. They wanted action.[9]

The morning of 5 November dawned with a broken overcast advancing toward clear skies to the south, and a calmer though still slightly rising and falling sea.

'Well, Pietsche,' Krancke said to the Arado pilot. 'What do you think of the weather today? Good enough to risk coming down in the sea?'

Pietsche grinned. 'If you care to make me a duck pond, sir, I think it'll be all right.'

'Good. Get moving, then.'

Lieutenant S Pietsche and his observer Gallinat hustled into their seats and pulled the transparent dome over their heads. The pilot started the engine as the torpedo officer ran a pressure check on the catapult's air tanks. Pietsche quickly raised the engine to an intensely high pitch, then settled it back to a steady roar. The spinning propeller flashed in the morning light. A thunderous clap…and compressed air blew the straining seaplane down the greased rails. It dipped slightly, then gained altitude.

A teddy bear dropped off the catapult onto the deck. 'Bad sign,' said the sailor who retrieved Pietsche's charm.

'Don't worry your head,' one of the mechanics said. 'He's got mascots by the dozen. All his girl friends give them to him.'[10]

4 The Conscripted 'Cruiser'

ON a morning near the end of August 1939 in an office on Leadenhall Street in London's shipping district, one of Shaw Savill's managers picked up the telephone. A demanding voice said, 'Where is your steamer *Jervis Bay*?' The tone was pure Admiralty.

'She's in London preparing for a voyage to Australia.'

'Has she commenced to load?'

'No, not yet.'

'Then she is not to do so. We are requisitioning her for service as an armed merchant cruiser.'[1]

Armed merchant cruisers (AMCs) were an ancient tradition. For thousands of years, cargo ships had been used as auxiliary naval vessels. In World War I the Germans had fitted them with modern guns, disguised many of them as freighters under Allied or neutral flags, and attacked unsuspecting cargo vessels supplying the British. The Royal Navy, short in combat ships early in that war, too, had half-heartedly armed large cargo liners to protect trade routes from the enemy.

That these makeshift vessels accomplished little did not affect British naval policy between the world wars. The Royal Navy, which had been cut back severely in the 1920s and 1930s, was short on convoy-escort vessels that were proper warships. Once again, at the beginning of World War II, it had no choice but to invoke the AMC alternative. By the end of 1939, fifty cargo liners, which should have remained freight and troop carriers, had been converted into jury-rigged 'cruisers.'

During their construction as commercial ships, many potential AMCs were stiffened under Admiralty supervision so that if needed in wartime, they could be fitted with as many as nine 6-inch guns. Generally the guns were old and worn, removed from Royal Navy ships of previous wars. Due to their aged mountings, most of them could not be elevated more than 15 degrees. This shrank their range to about 12,000–14,000 yards. The upper levels of the ships were altered to increase the guns' fields of fire. But their fire-control mechanisms were primitive. Magazines were fitted into the lower holds, some of them protected by wooden enclosures. Ammunition had to be hefted manually. Bridges and wheelhouses, needing protection against shell splinters and machine guns, were surrounded by concrete slabs. These converted vessels, with no cargo and passengers to weigh them down, rode high. They presented a huge freeboard to enemy guns, and their thin-plated hulls gave no protection to critical systems that were above the waterline, such as boilers and steering gear.

At least one AMC, the *Jervis Bay*'s sister ship *Esperance Bay,* had a full-scale *Hunt*-class destroyer painted on both sides of her hull. No one could say for sure whether the fake destroyer ever achieved her purpose of scaring off an edgy U-boat commander.[2]

The need for the inadequate AMCs disturbed many naval and maritime people. Commander W B Rowbotham reflected their feelings in a 1947 issue of the *Journal of the RUSI* (Royal United Services Institution):

> It is well known that the shipping firms and also the Ministry of War Transport did not like this large number of the finest cargo carriers being taken away from their proper functions to masquerade as warships at a time when the heaviest demands were being made for their normal services...For this state of affairs neither the Admiralty nor the shipping firms were to blame. Rather it must be laid at the door of those responsible for the London Naval Treaty of 1930 (which limited the tonnage and number of Britain's and other nation's warships)...It may be doubted whether, in any future war, these armed types of Auxiliary will ever be resurrected.[3]

Most AMCs were assigned to the Northern Patrol to control neutral traffic and to intercept enemy merchantmen or engage their better armed German counterparts. They made minor contributions as the Royal Navy quickly cleared the seas of the small German commercial fleet, except for some coastal and Baltic Sea traffic. The fragile ex–cargo liners were not expected to survive in battle against real cruisers, U-boats, enemy AMCs, or other warships—and most did not. A few of them were assigned escort duty at a time early in the war when virtually all convoy trips were perilous and were expected to remain so until swift, dedicated escort ships, equipped with improved asdics, radars, guns, and depth-charge gear, began sliding down the ways.

After World War I, the Australian government retained a fleet of cargo carriers, some of them interned German ships. With a mind-set of 'we've got them, so let's use them' and an infusion of cash, it established the Australian Commonwealth Government Line and ordered five new cargo liners and two refrigerated ships. The *Jervis Bay* was the last of five *Bay*-class liners—all built in Britain and stiffened for later installation of guns—to go to sea.

She entered service in 1922.

The *Jervis Bay* was named for a cove that housed a naval station about 80 miles south of Sydney. The harbour itself was given the name of Admiral Sir John Jervis, who saved England by destroying a Spanish fleet in 1797. Jervis's protégé, Captain Horatio Nelson, later fought off Napoleon's fleet at the Battle of Trafalgar and invented the 'engage the enemy more closely' tactic that inspired Royal Navy battle leaders for the next century and a half. When Captain E S Fogarty Fegen took command of HMS *Jervis Bay,* which soon would confront the *Admiral Scheer,* he stirred his crew with a promise to fight like Nelson if presented the opportunity.

Viewed at the time as a handsome ship, the *Jervis Bay* stretched 549 feet from stem to stern and displaced 13,839 tons. Her colours were dark green hull with a white line around it, white fo'c'sle and bridge deck, and yellow funnel. Three main decks, the two lower ones divided by ten bulkheads, ran her full length over her double-bottom hull. The engine crew lived on the boat deck, which carried two motor boats and twelve lifeboats—six 28-footers stowed within six 30-footers. Her fo'c'sle accommodated the deck crew on the upper level of the bow. Beneath the fo'c'sle and forward sections of the three long decks, an orlop deck provided additional hold space. The bridge deck stood forward of the funnel and commanded about 300 degrees of visual field.

The *Jervis Bay*'s holds, some of them insulated for storage of perishables, contained 378,000 cubic feet of space. Cargo was handled by two electric cranes and twenty-three derricks, one of them capable of raising thirty-five tons. She also carried lower deck, multi-berth, third-class cabins: tight, stifling quarters for 732 passengers, mainly immigrants or emigrants.

Twin screws powered by two oil-fuelled Parsons compound turbines drove the ship. At the maximum 90 rpm, she reached fifteen knots. Her propulsion system was so efficient that a full load of 3,400 tons of oil gave her a top-speed endurance of 14,500 nautical miles. At convoy speed, about nine knots, she could cross the Atlantic between Halifax and Britain at least fifteen times before refilling her bunkers—nearly 39,000 miles.

The *Jervis Bay* started her maritime career with trips between Southampton and the Australian ports of Brisbane, Sydney, Melbourne, Adelaide, and Fremantle, and with additional calls at Malta, Port Said, Aden, and Colombo. Her cargoes generally were factory and mill products from Britain and meats, wool, fruits, and wines from Australia. She sailed under the Australian flag until threadbare post-war economics forced the government to sell the

Bay ships in 1928 to the Aberdeen & Commonwealth Line, managed by Shaw Savill & Albion.[4]

Just after her privatisation, the *Jervis Bay* became newsworthy for the first and next-to-last time when eight men stowed away at Fremantle. They were immigrants disenchanted with life in Australia. They wanted to return to Britain. Four of them huddled in an empty piano case on the boat deck, two hid among potatoes in a musty storage locker, and two roamed freely among the six hundred passengers. After a few days they were discovered, but they sneered at an order to work their way home. They were manacled and locked in the brig and the security guard's cabin. They slipped the cuffs, broke through the wall between the rooms, and set fire to their beds. The crew hosed down the two rooms, while the stowaways raucously sang, 'It ain't gonna rain no mo', no mo'.' At this point Captain Frederick Daniel, whose ship was heading to the Ceylonese (now Sri Lankan) port of Colombo, transmitted a panicky call: 'Mutiny. Threatening set ship on fire. Send immediate assistance.'

News flashed around the world that mutiny had broken out on an Australian liner. With no warships immediately available, the

The Jervis Bay before her conversion into an Armed Merchant Cruiser(AMC). *(Source unknown)*

Royal Navy put twenty marines aboard the oiler *Slavol* and met the *Jervis Bay* at sea. The scruffy stowaways put on a bravado display and laughed at the marines in their tropical shorts, but they behaved themselves. They were arrested and tried in Colombo and served five and a half months in a local jail. It is not known if they ever got back to Britain.

From that bit of excitement until 1939, the *Jervis Bay* led an uneventful, three-round-trips-per-year existence. This all changed when she was conscripted by the Admiralty.[5]

On 30 August the former Aberdeen & Commonwealth cargo liner was delivered to the Western Albert Dry Dock in London for her speedy conversion by Harland & Wolff into an armed merchant cruiser. The firm removed some of the flammable peacetime fittings, though deck planks and other wood trimmings stayed in place. Some wooden magazine compartments were added. She remained a potential bonfire. Cabins were retained for officers and petty officers. Dock workers ripped out passenger cabin walls to provide large spaces for messes and crew quarters in order to reduce the response time to calls to action.

The *Jervis Bay* was transformed into a 'fighting' ship with the addition of seven Mark VII breech-loading, 6-inch guns, the oldest of which was stamped '1895' and had seen action in the Boer War. The most modern artillery fastened to her decks was manufactured just after the turn of the century. Armourers mounted guns P.1 (port side) and S.1 (starboard) on the fo'c'sle. P.2 and S.2 were positioned on the well deck between the fo'c'sle and the bridge. On the poop deck the X gun covered the stern and the after sides of the ship. Between the poop and the superstructure, P.3 and S.3 overlapped the fields of the guns fore and aft of them. (Months after the original refit, steel shields were fixed to the 6-inchers, giving the gun crews a modicum of protection from foul weather and enemy shell splinters.)

Their short range, no more than eight miles, together with their want of accuracy and the World War I fire-control apparatus, gave the makeshift 'cruiser' fire power that was little to be feared by the Germans with their speedy well-armoured ships and advanced gunnery. She was now one of what many AMC crews called 'Admiralty-made coffins.'[6]

By the time her refit was completed on 23 September, the *Jervis Bay* had put on some weight and now displaced 14,164 tons. However, minus the bulk of her normal cargo and passengers, she rode too high, stiff, and unsteady. Like other AMCs, she was filled with thousands of tons of ballast—it is not clear whether the packing was stones, timber, pig-iron, or a combination—and she settled a bit more deeply into the sea and regained a little stability. But her hull, newly painted a menacing dark grey, remained a side-of-a-barn target.[7]

Chatham Barracks, about fifteen miles down-river from London, was jammed with thousands of young men, and many not so young, who had been called up or had volunteered for naval duty a few days before the war started. Most of the *Jervis Bay* crew were there. Few of them knew each other. They had been preselected and issued *Jervis Bay* cards. They endured probing physical examinations, eye tests, and vaccinations. Gas masks were stuffed into their duffel bags. A short course at gunnery school acquainted them with obsolete 6-inch and anti-aircraft weapons like those fitted to all AMCs. Much of their conversation was about their ship-to-be. After a few weeks at Chatham, they boarded a northwest-bound train and began speculating on where they would find her. A half-hour into their musings, the train pulled onto a siding at the Royal Albert Dock alongside the *Jervis Bay.*

They were met by their commander, Captain H G Harris, a long-retired officer who had been called back into service. At a nearby dock they saw the *Rawalpindi,* another armed merchant cruiser that fate soon would link to them.

The landlubbers among them were struck by the *Jervis Bay*'s size. But others who had seen wartime naval action were concerned that she was an easy target for torpedoes and gunfire. 'Too much freeboard' was Fred Billinge's quick observation about the looming rise of her hull above the sea surface.

'Anyway, she's a ship,' said Tom Davison, a long-time seaman who was happy to get out of Chatham and back to a maritime regime.[8]

In early October the *Jervis Bay* sailed out the Thames under orders to Scapa Flow. On the way, her crew got their first taste of gunfire in a practice session off Sheerness. The shields were still missing, as were the fire-control circuits. Directions had to be bellowed down 2.5-inch tubes into big brass earphones worn by the communicators for each gun crew. Jack Barker, one of the young, inexperienced ratings, was on the mess deck when the guns opened fire. Flatware and dishes jumped in their trays. Cork particles, stuck on the ceiling to absorb galley moisture, drifted down over his head, shoulders, and beef sandwich.

The shock of the cannonading wore off quickly as they headed out of the Channel into the North Sea. Newcomers to rough weather—as many of the crew were—found out what instability was on a big, nearly empty ship. Riding high on the heavy sea, with the freeboard catching air like a giant sail, the *Jervis Bay* immediately tested her crew.

Barker was so seasick he didn't know what to do. He craved shelter, but below it was stifling and he felt worse there. He had to keep watch by his 3-inch anti-aircraft gun on the boat deck, four hours on and four off. The queasy recruit saw a ventilator shaft jutting up from the deck near the gun. Down the flue he saw a strong protective mesh about 6 feet from the top. In desperate need of isolation, confinement, and cover, he squeezed between the ventilator top and its hood, lowered himself down the shaft, and stood on the mesh. He was just tall enough to keep his eyes level with the opening. If needed, he could quickly get to his gun. He lived in the narrow shaft on his feet for three miserable days, catching vertical catnaps against its sides. The rest of his gun crew, relaxed Scottish fishermen with hearty appetites, tried to comfort him and brought him food, the sight of which made his stomach lurch.

On the way to Scapa Flow, the speculation on their assignment narrowed down to one possibility: Northern Patrol. The North Atlantic, especially in the wintry half of the year, was one of the world's roughest, stormiest, coldest stretches of sea. Not choice duty! On 6 October they arrived at Scapa. Several other AMCs were anchored there, all of them scheduled for the patrol.

Five days into their stay at the Orkney Islands base, the *Jervis Bay*'s anchor fouled a bottom cable during a gale. After several attempts were made to hoist the anchor free, the capstan broke down. The ship swung around and came within yards of colliding with another AMC, the *Aurania*. She was considered a menace to the rest of the fleet in the harbour and was ordered to Newcastle-on-Tyne for repairs and for further refitting. The *Rawalpindi* replaced her on the patrol schedule.

The *Jervis Bay* made a halfway stop for minor repairs at Rosyth on the Firth of Forth. The destroyer HMS *Sabre* led her through the mine fields. It was night-time and because the anchorage was blustery and foggy, Captain Harris decided to move the ship to a safer mooring. *Sabre* crewman Frank Purcell was 'awakened by the sound of something like steam blowing.' 'I jumped out of my hammock,' he said, 'and went on deck to investigate the cause....I thought we were still alongside the jetty when I heard the order to abandon ship. What I thought was the jetty was the bow of the *Jervis Bay* sticking in our port side amidships.'[9]

When the *Jervis Bay* cleaved into the *Sabre* her disabled 5-ton anchor, still hanging from the bow, rammed through the destroyer's plates and into the engine room. The *Sabre* quickly settled. Steam

rushed out of her safety valves and filled the engine room with a
thick fog. Her funnel ejected sparks. Lieutenant Commander K M
Morrison of the *Jervis Bay* got a lifeboat manned, but by then the
other ship's stern was under water. The *Sabre* was kept from sinking
by a combination of some watertight compartments and the
impinging anchor, which was hooked onto the destroyer's
framework. She was like a caught fish. No crewmen were lost.

Following the *Jervis Bay*'s series of misadventures, she finally
reached the Tyne and was tied fore and aft to big mooring buoys.
However, just as the off-watch party landed for shore leave, they
turned back and looked on with dismay as their ship blew off her
moorings and drifted toward the mud flats. Tugs immediately
chugged out and got her back to midstream to be tied up again. The
next day she was nursed along to Hebburn and put into dry dock,
where Murphy's Law was less likely to take effect.

Hebburn was an impressive place, as described by Adrian
Thorpe, who served aboard the *Jervis Bay* before she escorted the
HX 84 convoy: 'An orgy of shipbuilding was taking place on all
sides, and all day long we were deafened by the drumming of
pneumatic riveters and blinded by the flickering violet-white glare of
electric welders. Within 500 yards of where we lay there were, in
various stages of construction, a battleship, four cruisers, a destroyer
and two corvettes.'[10]

By this time, many of the *Jervis Bay*'s men felt that they were
ship's company to a jinx. They envied the crews of 'real' warships,
especially the men of the destroyer HMS *Kelly,* which had come in
for repairs after sea duty. The destroyer's captain was the
aristocratic Lord Louis Mountbatten, who had already started
making a legend of himself. *Wouldn't it be jolly to sail under Lord
Louie's command,* they mused.

The *Jervis Bay* was still in dry dock when they heard about the
Rawalpindi: sunk in the first naval battle of the war, in the grey, sub-
Arctic sea southeast of Iceland.[11]

Captain Edward Coverley Kennedy of HMS *Rawalpindi* pressed the
binoculars into his eyes until they hurt. His mouth was a tight line.
'It's the *Scharnhorst,* alright,' he muttered. He sent his crew to their
action stations as the new German battleship sliced toward them.

The *Scharnhorst,* at 35,000 tons and thirty-two knots, was the
next higher class of capital ship commissioned after the
panzerschiffe. The heavily armoured (two to fourteen inches of steel)
warship approached to about four miles, swung into a parallel course,
trained her nine 11-inch guns on the AMC, and signalled, 'Heave to.'

Kennedy was a square-jawed, tough, sixty-year-old pensioner who had volunteered for sea duty at his former rank. He came from a seafaring family that had served in the Royal Navy continuously for nearly two hundred years. He swung his ship around toward a nearby fog bank and ordered full speed (fifteen knots) ahead. The German vessel raced to intercept the *Rawalpindi* before she could reach the protection of the pea soup. Kennedy again altered his ship's course, aiming at an iceberg about four miles distant. A German shell buzzed across her bows and sent up a geyser some two hundred yards ahead.

'Heave to,' signalled the German captain, Kurt Casar Hoffman. He was growing impatient.

A *Rawalpindi* lookout reported another ship off the starboard bow. Kennedy turned straight at her, hoping she was a British warship, but as the new arrival swung about, he realised she was the *Gniesenau,* the *Scharnhorst*'s sister ship.

'Abandon your ship.' No more nonsense for Hoffman.

No response from the *Rawalpindi*.

An engineering officer hurried to the AMC's bridge. He told the captain the firemen and gun crews were ready. The *Rawalpindi* rode between two of the most powerful battleships in the world. But by Royal Navy tradition, surrender was not an option. Though chafing at the British silence, Hoffman gave them the courtesy of two more abandon-ship signals. Still no response.

'We'll fight them both,' Kennedy said. 'They'll sink us, and that will be that.' He grasped the engineer's hand: 'Goodbye.'[12] He ordered his gunners to open fire.

One of the *Rawalpindi's* shells hit the *Gniesenau* amidships, resulting in a moment's elation.

The crew were silenced by the *Scharnhorst*'s answering salvo, which struck the boat deck and killed most occupants of the bridge. Kennedy survived the blasts. The *Gniesenau* put her first salvo into the main fire-control position, killing everyone there, and destroyed one of the starboard guns and its crew. The merchant cruiser's captain ordered all remaining guns to fire independently. One *Rawalpindi* gun captain claimed three hits before his weapon jammed. The German report on the battle allowed that only a single shell struck the *Gniesenau*.

In the next few minutes, Captain Kennedy and 238 of his men were killed as the *Rawalpindi* became a blazing, foundering wreck. The Germans stopped firing. They sent boats out to pick up survivors, each of the warships rescuing a single boatload totalling twenty-seven British sailors. Just as the *Scharnhorst* secured another lifeboat, her lookouts sighted the British heavy cruiser *Newcastle*.

They could easily do away with the smaller warship, but the time it would take would heighten the Royal Navy's opportunity to hunt them down. On orders from Berlin, the lifeboat's line was cut (its eleven survivors were later picked up by HMS *Chitral*), and the two speedy battleships left wakes toward the Norwegian coast. Although spotted once early in their retreat, they disappeared into fog and returned to Wilhelmshaven four days after the encounter.[13]

The news of the *Rawalpindi's* sinking quickly reached the Hebburn dry dock. Tom Davison, at home on leave in Dover, told his wife Bessie: 'That was the patrol that we were due to go on. We would have been done, too, if we hadn't had to go back to the Tyne.'

One of the men aboard the *Jervis Bay* tried to be offhand: 'Well, she's bought it.'

Another piped in, 'Yes, you've got to expect it.'[14]

The crew's deeper feeling was that fate had played a hand in their favour. In spite of their recent run of bad luck, they were thankful that their conscripted ship had behaved like an awkward recruit. But the very thing that saved them also touched off a simmering apprehension about the competence of the ship and her officers.

Not long after the *Rawalpindi* sinking, Commander J A P Blackburn boarded the *Jervis Bay* as second in command. Another volunteer out of retirement, the fifty-year-old Blackburn was a slim, straight-backed, vigorous leader who had served on a battleship and on cruisers, and as commander of a training ship. In World War I he had won the Distinguished Service Cross for his role aboard a Royal Navy submarine that sank a U-boat. He also had led a morale program for petty officers. Just the exec the *Jervis Bay* crew needed.

Blackburn quickly perceived that his first task on the AMC was to raise spirits and keep them high. His main concern was the crew's anxiety about the early performance of the ship. Morale was crucial on extended, hazardous patrol missions. First, he scrounged a projector and screen for a ship's cinema. Then he started learning each of the crew's names. The few times he could not match a face with a name, he feigned some reason to talk with the man and get him innocently to reveal it.

By 19 December the work at Hebburn was completed, and the crew were given winter uniforms, consisting of jerseys, sea-boot stockings, mittens, and balaclavas, and also a tropical kit. The mixed issue confused them. After slipping out the mouth of the Tyne, the *Jervis Bay* headed north. It seemed they were rejoining the Northern Patrol. Then the ship swung around the top of Scotland, turned south down the Irish Sea into the Channel, and pulled into Portsmouth, where she was outfitted with additional equipment. The men's perplexity increased and they grew rather glum. Blackburn had to do something to perk them up. With his support, they identified shipboard talent and organised a successful concert, something of a morale booster. It was the beginning of the coalescence of individuals into shipmates.

On New Year's day, off Portland, they had their first gunnery practice since the original refit three months before. Blackburn worked the men hard. He organised a variety of crewmen, such as stokers and stewards, to heft ammunition and fight fires. For gunnery-control tasks, he chose men with good enunciation who could relay instructions clearly. He knew the limitations of the *Jervis Bay* as a fighting ship, and after the *Rawalpindi*'s demise, so did the crew. He was determined they would be capable of putting up a good fight.

They developed into a well-oiled crew. Furthermore, they saw that Blackburn was a grade-A officer and a superb seaman. Their respect for their executive officer grew. After the gunnery drills, the *Jervis Bay* sailed southward to her first station as an armed merchant cruiser. The destination was Freetown, Sierra Leone, on the west coast of Africa.[15]

Freetown was a port of assembly for convoys whose ships came from eastern South America, the bottom of Africa, and from sources of supply around the Indian and South Pacific Oceans. It was the southern version of Halifax. More than 150 ships could fit into the magnificent harbour. However, shore facilities were inadequate. Bunkers of the many coal-fuelled ships had to be loaded by ragged local labourers shouldering lumpy sacks from barges alongside. With that quality of help in some critical operations, the task of bringing the cargo carriers to 'in all respects ready' status was painful.

The convoys usually comprised about ten ships. The *Jervis Bay* was one of their escorts. She took them to the English Channel, then came about and returned to Freetown for the next convoy. She never paused in Britain for even a day's shore leave. With a welcome one-time exception in Dakar, the Paris of the upper west coast of Africa, Freetown was the only place to get ashore, but there was nothing to do there. The climate was steamy, with an annual rainfall of about 180 inches. It was one of only two stations (Hong Kong was the other) where uniformed Royal Navy officers were allowed to carry umbrellas.

The *Jervis Bay* ship's cat. *(Rainsbury)*

The navy decided to make the *Jervis Bay* less conspicuous as an armed merchant cruiser by changing her colour from dark grey to the green-white-buff of her commercial days. While anchored in Freetown on clear days, the crew painted her from platforms slung over the sides. It was duty that was never welcomed. In this equatorial harbour, the intense sun and thick humidity saturated with the stench and taste of the heavy enamel made it unbearable. Some of the painting contingent devised a way of bringing a little fun and relief to their hated task. They took advantage of a ship's rule that if a brush dropped in the water it had to be retrieved. Diving after paint brushes soon became standard operating procedure. Until someone shouted, 'Shark!' No brush hit the water after that.

In February Captain Harris was taken ill and carried off the ship. None of the crew ever saw or heard of him again. Blackburn was appointed acting captain. His first command assignment was a break in the escort routine: find the British freighter *Hartesmere,* which was foundering in the South Atlantic with a broken propeller shaft. A long, six-inch tow cable was laid around *Jervis Bay*'s main deck inside the railing. With an old fix on the now silent grain carrier's whereabouts, navigation officer Lieutenant Commander George L Roe estimated her position, taking into account the known currents and prevailing winds. Cutting along Roe's prescribed southerly bearing at her maximum fifteen knots, the *Jervis Bay* sighted the *Hartesmere* in a few days, straight on. Blackburn shook his head admiringly and smiled at Roe: 'Congratulations. That is excellent navigating.'[16]

The commercial liner *Queen of Bermuda* had just started towing the damaged ship. The *Jervis Bay* took over and headed to Freetown. She was held to six knots by the heavily laden vessel. Her engines laboured for ten days in the equivalent of low gear, and she was about a half-day out of Freetown when the cable snapped. Tom Hanlon went over the side in a bo'sun's chair to splice the parted ends of the line. Before he completed the job, a trawler delivered a new cable. A few more hours of groaning turbines and they reached the harbour.

The crew had completed what turned out to be the longest tow of World War II. They were pleased with their performance. The admiral in command of the region came alongside in his barge and gave them a 'Well done!' through his bullhorn. The ship they had come to regard as an error-prone orphan now was *their Jervis Bay.* They were happy to be Blackburn's crew.

The acting captain led them on one more hard-working, uneventful, monotonous escort cruise—ten days to Britain, U-turn in the Channel, five days back to Freeport. Then on 1 April 1940, their new commanding officer took over. Blackburn stood on deck as Captain Fegen boarded the *Jervis Bay.* The two men, who knew each other from years before, clasped hands. Fegen said: 'I wonder whose April Fool's Day this is, yours or mine?'[17]

5 The Captain

EDWARD Stephen Fogarty Fegen was the son of Mary Catherine and Vice Admiral Frederick Fogarty Fegen of Ballinlonty, County Tipperary, born on 8 October 1891. He descended from two illustrious Irish families. The Fogartys traced their history back to the fourth or fifth century, to Fergus Carrbheal, the 123rd monarch of Ireland. Fogertagh, the 157th monarch, was assassinated in 719. William O'Fogarty, physician to King Charles I, was imprisoned in the Tower of London and died there in 1665. The Fegens and Fogartys became connected in the marriage of Frederick James Fegen and Mary Rose Amelia Fogarty in 1848.

Capt E S Fogarty Fegen, commanding officer of the Armed Merchant Cruiser HMS *Jervis Bay*.
(Barbara Fegen)

The Fegen association with the Royal Navy began with James, identified in the old Admiralty lists as a lieutenant with seniority in 1778. From then until World War II, almost every male in the family chose a naval career, most of them attaining the rank of commander or captain. Frederick James Fegen served as secretary to several admirals and retired from the Royal Navy as paymaster in chief. His son, Frederick Fogarty, was cited for bravery in an 1887 battle with an Arab dhow off Zanzibar in which he was wounded as he led a seven-man launch (off the cruiser *Turquoise*) in a pitched battle and rescued fifty-three slaves. For this action, he was promoted from lieutenant to commander. Appointed aide-de-camp to King Edward VII in 1904, he reached the rank of vice admiral in 1910, a year before his death.[1]

By that time, the admiral's son Edward (called Ted in the family and Fogarty, only out of earshot, by his future crews) had finished five years of schooling at the Royal Navy College at Osborne and Britannia (ranking eighth of fifty-seven graduates). Starting in 1909 he served as a midshipman on two battleships, a cruiser, and two destroyers. Promoted to sub-lieutenant three years later, he was assigned to another battleship and then, in typical swift Royal Navy rotation, was stationed on a small torpedo-gunboat-minesweeper as second in command. Near the end of this short assignment in 1914, he was raised to full lieutenant and transferred to the light cruiser *Amphion* on which he participated in the first naval gun battle of World War I.

On 5 August, the day after Germany and Britain declared war on each other, the year-old German passenger liner *Königin Louise* was sailing off the English North Sea coast. The skipper of a British trawler signalled the *Amphion* that the German ship was behaving suspiciously, throwing things off the stern. A few days earlier, the *Königin Louise* had been converted into a minelayer, painted and marked like a hospital ship, and loaded with two hundred of the weapons.

The *Amphion,* under Captain C H Fox, and two destroyers took up the chase. Captain Biermann of the *Königin Louise* steamed to the southeast hoping 'that this would draw my pursuers over the

Lieutenant Fegen served aboard HMS *Amphion* when she engaged in the first sea battle of World War I on 5 August 1914. A German minelayer was sunk, but the next day the *Amphion* struck two mines and went down with half her complement and some German prisoners. *(Imperial War Museum)*

minefield.' The destroyers followed her wake into the array of mines at such speed—over thirty knots—that their bow waves probably pushed any subsurface explosives aside long enough to pass through safely. They brought the German to bay, with HMS *Lance* firing the first shot. The slower *Amphion,* which somehow also eluded the mines, finished off the *Königin Louise* with her 4-inch guns and helped rescue forty-six German sailors. The role Fegen played in the action is not documented.

Heading to Harwich the next day, the *Amphion* struck one of her victim's devices. A large hole was blown in her bottom, her bridge was destroyed, and fires broke out in several areas. As she began settling, her forward magazine exploded. The cruiser's still-turning engines pushed her in an uncontrollable spiral. She hit another mine. When she sank, she took 147 men (about half of her complement) and 24 German prisoners with her. Fegen, apparently no more than slightly hurt, was picked up by one of the destroyers, and with hardly a pause to recover his wits, he was reassigned to a flotilla leader.[2]

All told, from his first station as a cadet aboard the cruiser HMS *Cornwall* until his last in 1940, Fegen was given thirty-three shipboard assignments. His early career was a mixed bag of praise and admonition (normal, in the Royal Navy's scheme of things):

1910: Fegen was considered partly to blame for loss of a target and hawser and was ordered to pay for them.

1911: 'Painstaking and able with fair command—fine physique…Should do well.'

Later in 1911: 'Untidy & slovenly. Lethargic but improving & fine physique.'

1912: 'Slow but trustworthy.'

1913: 'Good & reliable officer. Maintained a proper tone in gunroom. Can box & play football.'

1914: 'Very hard-working, careful, zealous, and energetic. Good at games.'

1916: Commended for work in salvaging a wrecked airship.

1918: Judged in error in collision of HMS *Paladin* under his command.

Later in 1918: Awarded Lloyd's Medal for saving lives on a burning tanker.

1919: Removed from command of torpedo boat for 'lack of responsibility' in allowing a 'shortage of spirits' to occur.

SOME OF "THE KING'S NAVEE."

Ward Room celebrities on HMS Valiant. Fergen, then a lieutenant is in the middle of the top row. *(Battleship magazine 1919-1921)*

1924: Committed an error in judgement as commander of a destroyer that led to a collision and was 'warned to be more careful.'

From then on Fegen received only positive assessments. His longest tour anywhere was his only extended stretch of land duty in 1927–1929, when he was promoted to commander and made commandant of the Royal Australian Navy College in Jervis Bay. (The double coincidence here is startling: not only was his final appointment as captain of HMS *Jervis Bay,* but his final wartime adversary, Captain Krancke of the *Admiral Scheer,* headed the German Naval Academy ten years later.) Fegen's performance rating for those two years was portentous: 'Excep gift for gaining confidence of young offrs' and 'Makes right conduct his aim.'[3]

One of his most notable deeds came in 1929 as commander of the light cruiser *Suffolk,* when he responded to a distress call from the Dutch trading vessel *Hedwig.* On her way back to Hong Kong from a South Pacific venture, the *Hedwig* had grounded on Patras Reef in the South China Sea during a monsoon and could not work herself free. Fegen quickly reached the scene, brought the *Suffolk* about, and took charge of some motor launches. They approached the fourteen Dutch sailors in heavy seas, picked them off the reef in the face of crashing breakers, and brought them back to the cruiser. Holland awarded him a life-saving medal, and the Admiralty expressed 'their appreciation of the good work.'[4]

During the early and mid-1930s, Fegen commanded several light cruisers. In 1939 he was transferred to the heavy cruiser *Emerald,* on which his reputation rose like a helium balloon. His captain, Augustus Wallington Shelton Agar (awarded the Victoria Cross in 1919 as a secret service agent who helped sink a cruiser under Bolshevik command), later wrote: 'We had as our Executive Officer Commander Edward Fegen ('Fogarty' as he was known to some), my right-hand man and a born seaman...I was very lucky to have him.'[5]

Lieutenant B J Morgan (later to be a rear admiral) said, '[The exec] ran the ship.'[6]

Fegen's leadership and courage shone like the gold the *Emerald* carried in the second month of the war when the British began transferring their bullion treasure to the safety of Canada. The North Atlantic was acting up during that vital passage. Agar's observations about the man and the moment are revealing: 'I shall never forget the biting cold [and]...the hail and snow blizzards [during that crossing]...When boats were either stove in or washed overboard, he was always first on the scene and invariably in the most exposed

HMS *Emerald*, the heavy cruiser aboard which Commander Fegen served as Executive Officer before being promoted to Captain of the *Jervis Bay*. *(Imperial War Museum)*

position...I have met few officers with less regard for their personal safety or more for their men, and he was universally loved and respected by all on board.'[7]

Leading Seaman Bob Smith, who occasionally worked under Fegen on the *Emerald,* said: 'I'd never seen weather like it...Once we lost a shackle on a paravane [anti-mine] line and Commander Fegen and I went over the side on life lines to put on a new one. He was the Executive Officer and would never ask a man to do anything he wasn't prepared to tackle himself. Our hands were so frozen that they stuck to the metal and we were absolutely drenched by the freezing waves that came right over the bows.'[8]

On 28 February 1940 Fegen was promoted to acting captain and given command of HMS *Jervis Bay.* 'He was like a schoolboy who had just been awarded his first prize,' Agar said, 'and we were all as pleased as he was and gave him a great send off.'[9]

By the time Fegen boarded his new armed merchant cruiser in Freetown, his 'schoolboy' excitement had been replaced by a commanding officer's demeanour. The *Jervis Bay* crew were introduced to a physically imposing, broad-chested, six-footer who still had the bearing of the athlete he was when he boxed and played rugby as a young officer. The captain was a handsome man, whose thick dark brows shaded his deep-set eyes and emphasised a straight, well-shaped nose. His black hair was parted on the left side and plastered flat across his head in the Art Deco style of the time. Though his prominent cheekbones and compressed lips gave him a certain grimness, the corners of his mouth often curled up slightly with what could be viewed as irony or wit. A strong jaw added to the confidence his men were soon to feel under his command.

The navy was Fegen's life. He was imprinted by his family's tradition of service in the Royal Navy, spread continuously across three centuries, and he spent most of his adulthood literally at sea. Reticent about himself, he revealed little about his beliefs, thoughts, and life. Admiral Sir Morgan Giles, a gunnery lieutenant under Fegen on the *Emerald* who respected him as executive officer, described him as 'an entirely unintellectual man.' On duty, he was totally focused. 'A bulldog of a man,' said Giles. 'A salt horse.'

Fegen ran a tight ship and expected his officers and ratings to maintain uncompromising sailing and fighting standards at all times. Although he tended to be laconic at sea, he was unstinting with words of encouragement; thirty-two years as a Royal Navy officer had taught him that a 'Well done!' and a 'There you go, lad!' were what the men needed to hear from their commanding officer.[10] Yet he was no stickler for protocol.

In the view of George Pollock, author of *The Jervis Bay,* published in 1958, Fegen was quite prepared when the occasion arose, to be completely informal. 'He did not insist…on being piped aboard,' Pollock wrote. 'He realised the *Jervis Bay* was not a typical ship of the Royal Navy and therefore it would have been inappropriate to expect all the details of traditional naval etiquette.'

Ashore, Fegen usually shed his naval bearing, engaged in good-natured banter, and openly enjoyed himself. Pollock wrote: '[At] a big ship's dance at the Admiral Beatty Hotel in St. John, New Brunswick, the Old Man went up on the stand and took a few turns at the drums. …He attended the ship's 'operas' and boxing matches…because he thoroughly enjoyed joining his men in their off-duty entertainment. He got on well with his engineering officers, none of whom was Royal Navy. They liked his lack of side when he met them over a glass of gin.'[11]

Little documentation exists on Fegen's lifestyle outside the naval environment. He was a bachelor and a practising Roman Catholic. If he had close male or female friends, it is not clear who they were. He visited acquaintances at various ports, played cards with them, and often played with their children like an uncle. His niece Gillian (née Fegen) Cooper remembers: 'He was very good with children and tremendous fun to be with. We loved any visits we were lucky enough to get.'[12]

Shortly after he took command, Fegen called the crew together. He said he was pleased the Admiralty had assigned him their ship. Then he relayed the navy's praise of the *Jervis Bay*'s past performance and complimented the company for their good work. So far, it was a conventional greeting from a new captain. Listening politely, the men

In August 1940 Captain Fegen visited the fishing lodge of Frank and Rachael Dunn on the Renous River in Central New Brunswick. Left to right, unknown, Lt Commander Keith Morrison, Captain Fegen, Pat Whelan their fishing guide. *(Courtesy: Betty MacKenzie, Saint John, New Brunswick)*

Jervis Bay officers: (front, left to right) Wireless Operator Donald Curry, Midshipman Richard F Owens, Midshipman Ronald A G Butler (DSC), Midshipman C C T Latch, Midshipman W B Thistleton; (middle row) Paymaster Commander E W White, Lt Commander K M Morrison, Commander J A P Blackburn (DSC), Captain E S F Fegen (VC), Engineer Commander J H G Chappell, Lt Commander A W Driscoll; (back row) Gunner E R Stannard, Lt Richard Shackleton, Surgeon Lt H St. J Hiley, Paymaster Lt A W Stott, Wireless Lt Hugh Williamson, Lt A H W Bartle, Lt Norman E Wood, Lt Walter Hill, Lt Commander George L Roe, Lt H G B Moss, Paymaster Lt J G Sargeant. *(Courtesy of #53 Jervis Bay Branch, Royal Canadian Legion, Saint John, New Brunswick)*

already knew they were a good ship's company; Commander Blackburn, in his short acting captaincy, had brought them to a high level of competence and spirit. Fegen knew they were somewhat bored with his ceremonial address, even though he kept it brief.

He paused. For a long moment, he looked out over the crew. The silence and his piercing gaze caught their attention. Then, Captain Fegen's voice took on an impassioned resonance. Expectant now, the men were ready to absorb his words:

'So far, we haven't seen any real action, but I promise you this much: If the gods are good to us and we meet the enemy, I shall take you in as close as I possibly can.'

The terse, Nelsonian declaration lit a fire in the officers and the ratings. Those who survived the *Admiral Scheer* battle never forgot that promise of courageous action, nor the confidence Fegen displayed in them, nor their instantaneous respect for their new skipper. It was the beginning of the kind of powerful relationship Fegen had constructed with his men on other ships. By his leadership and example, he soon instilled extraordinary spirit and discipline in the *Jervis Bay*'s company. He also won their affection, not as a good fellow or a pal, but as a confident, fair-minded, trustworthy commander.[13]

HMS *Jervis Bay* transferred from Freetown and on 30 April 1940 arrived at her new base in Hamilton, Bermuda. The channel into the berthing area had clearance of about five yards on either side to the rocks. The service of a tug was offered. Fegen good-naturedly waved it off and took the cumbersome ship in under her own power. It was a tricky manoeuvre. As the ship drew closer to the quay, one of her officers grew agitated. 'Don't shout so loudly, Mister...,' Fegen murmured. 'We'll be all right.' This display of seamanship, risky though it was, accelerated his endearment to the crew. It was not long before one of the experienced ratings said, 'I think we'd follow old Fogarty anywhere.'[14]

Bermuda was a feeder assembly port for delivering ships to underway convoys out of Halifax, Nova Scotia. A week after her arrival, the *Jervis Bay* sailed as escort with her first Bermuda convoy, BHX 41, to a rendezvous with HX 41 about six hundred miles east of Newfoundland. As was to be her routine, she returned to the tranquil British resort island after dropping off her ships.

Just before embarking on his fourth and final Bermuda escort cruise in mid-July, Fegen spent a quiet weekend at the home of his old schoolmate, Commander Guy Ridgway. Ridgway had other friends over, and Fegen, as always a changed man ashore, entertained them with his repartee over the bridge table. But, as always, he kept his own counsel on his naval life and his private affairs.

After the *Jervis Bay* handed the ships of BHX 58 over to convoy HX 58, she sailed on to Saint John, New Brunswick, on 22 July for a complete refit and degaussing. The dockside was piled high with 24,000 sealed, empty 45-gallon steel drums, which were packed into her holds and 'tween-decks for buoyancy. The men understood the drums were intended to keep her from sinking rapidly in event of an enemy attack. They called them 'ping-pong balls' to soften the impact of that realisation. The *Jervis Bay* and her officers and crew were prepared to sacrifice, if need be.[15]

During the sojourn in Saint John, the captain flashed one of his occasional losses of temper. According to John Crosse, a Canadian naval historian: 'I had a friend called Paul Ledoux whose father was a sergeant on the dockyards at St. John…This big guy in civilian clothes [came] up to him and demanded to be let in, but [the sergeant] just shoved his bayonet towards his gut and told him that he wasn't getting in unless he showed his ID. At this, the big guy got real mad and started jumping up and down yelling, 'Don't you know I'm the captain of the *Jervis Bay*?' And Paul Ledoux's dad just shoved the bayonet closer to his gut and told him he didn't know him from Adam, and that he wasn't getting past the gate unless he produced his identification.'[16]

Fegen finally gave in and showed his Royal Navy ID. As soon as he passed through the gate, the storm dissipated. He smiled to himself. He knew he'd behaved badly and he admired the guard for having stood up to him.

Following her refitting, the *Jervis Bay* arrived in Halifax; two days later, on 9 September, she sailed as sole escort with convoy HX 72. One night early on the crossing the tanker *Frederick Fales* gave six blasts on her whistle, indicating she had sighted a U-boat. Fegen ordered some guns trained on the only suspicious-looking object in sight, only to find that it was one of the ships of the convoy that had strayed out of formation in the dark. The next morning the tanker signalled that she had sighted what looked like the wake either of a submarine or a torpedo pass just ahead of her. Fegen's deeply tanned cheeks flushed red: 'God damn it!' he bellowed. 'Why the devil didn't he ram the bloody thing?'

On 20 September, they heard by radio that the *City of Benares*, with 90 children aboard being evacuated to Canada (77 of whom died), had been torpedoed and sunk on the way to Britain about a half-day's steaming ahead. That night, in accordance with orders, the *Jervis Bay* reluctantly left the convoy and set course back to Halifax. Within four hours two of HX 72's ships had been sunk.

Later that night, according to crew member Adrian Thorpe, a lookout spotted a torpedo wake crossing the merchant cruiser's bows with a few yards to spare.

On their return to Halifax, Fegen and his men learned that HX 72 had been attacked by a pack of five U-boats and twelve of the forty-one cargo ships had been sunk. The news devastated them. Although they obviously had not deserted the convoy, it must have taken a good dose of convincing by the captain and his second-in-command Blackburn to overcome their frustration and self-blame and to prepare them for their next trip.[17]

The crossing with HX 78 was the scene of another of Fegen's rare outbursts. It occurred on the bridge during a night of some cold, dirty weather. At such critical times, the captain never left the bridge. On this occasion, he was dozing

On September 4, 1940, while the *Jervis Bay* had just finished her refit at the Saint John Drydock, His Excellency the Earl of Athlone, Governor General of Canada, and HRH Princess Alice, Countess of Athlone, were given a tour of his ship by Captain Fegen. *(Courtesy: #53 Jervis Bay Branch, Royal Canadian Legion, Saint John, New Brunswick)*

in a deck-chair he had set up in the wheelhouse. A bo'sun's mate brought up a jug of hot cocoa. It was lights out and black in the wheelhouse as he groped his way to the cup shelf. Unaware of the deck-chair, he stumbled over it and dumped the steaming drink onto the captain's lap. Fegen vaulted out of the chair and sprayed him with invective, and then gave his ancestry a going over. When the Old Man's motor finally revved down, he breathed in deeply, then out, and without rancour he said, 'If you have any cocoa left in that jug, you'd better pour me out a cup.' Without further incident, the *Jervis Bay* arrived back in Halifax on 20 October.[18]

6 In All Respects Ready

BRITAIN adopted the already-ancient convoy system about eight hundred years ago when shipping on its trade routes became vulnerable to attack by the French, who had just taken Normandy from King John. Cargo ships were ordered to sail in groups with armed escort. The system worked well. But by the next century, an overriding competitiveness enticed many ship owners into sailing independently to make port ahead of their commercial rivals in the slow convoys. This rebelliousness led to serious shipping losses until it was put down in 1336 by Edward III. The value of herding cargo vessels under man-of-war protection was fully recognised by then, and the system was used by most seafaring nations.

In the early nineteenth-century wars against Napoleonic France and the United States, convoys were obligatory, and Lloyd's did not insure ships sailing alone. During the remainder of the nineteenth and into the twentieth century, Britain engaged in no major naval campaigns and needed little merchant ship protection. By the onset of World War I in 1914, the Admiralty had pretty much forgotten how effective the escorted-and-insured clusters had been. Reestablishment of the convoy system was undermined by its negative attitude. Most naval leaders claimed that merchant vessels could not maintain their stations in a prescribed formation and could not manoeuvre properly when an array of ships had to change direction as a single organism. Another grumble was that large, slow-moving flotillas would be easy, juicy targets. Old-school officers insisted on using their fighting ships for patrolling the ocean, engaging in pitched battles, and hunting down U-boats rather than passively escorting cargo ships. Finally, the government took over the insurance risk, cutting off Lloyd's natural function of warning the Admiralty when shipping losses were getting heavy.

The bureaucracy's foray into the indemnity business turned out to be a costly, inefficient blunder. Not until mid-1917—with the loss by then of nearly sixteen hundred lone cargo ships to U-boats and hundreds more to the Germans' disguised merchant cruisers— did the Admiralty find itself forced, under protest, to reinstate the convoy system.

From the moment convoys were introduced, shipping losses to U-boats and surface raiders dropped spectacularly. None of the old school's objections was validated. Most merchant ships performed as tactics demanded. The Germans discovered that convoys, despite their huge dimensions, were in effect no more than dots in the vast ocean and no easier to spot than independently sailing prey. When raiders managed to find and attack convoys, they had to deal with effective warship escorts, and they began taking a beating. June 1917 marked the beginning of the end for *das Boot* in World War I.

What the British had learned, and then forgot early in World War II, was that escorting convoys was as much an offensive as a defensive tactic. It was a kind of counterpart to the German disguised surface raider, which looked like an Allied or neutral merchant vessel until she closed enough to drop a hinged hull section that masked her guns and blast the unsuspecting victim out of the water. The slow convoy likewise was a lure to the U-boat, which upon revealing itself became a quarry for Royal Navy destroyers and other escorts.

It should have been evident that the escorted convoy was crucial for the British at the onset of the war in 1939. Winston Churchill, first lord of the Admiralty, told the House of Commons in late September that the best ways of dealing with the German trade-warfare menace early on were the convoy system, the arming of merchant ships, and anti-submarine warship teams. However, in accord with the navy's dominant belief, he was sure that the new asdic device for detecting U-boats would 'enable two destroyers to do the work that could not have been done by ten last time.' 'Nothing can be more important in the anti-submarine war,' Churchill told First Sea Lord Sir Dudley Pound, 'than to try to obtain an independent flotilla which could work like a cavalry division...systematically [searching] large areas over a wide front. In this way these areas would become untenable to U-boats.' Here again, reflecting the temperament of the admirals, and in keeping with his own warrior instincts, Churchill urged the aggressive action of hunters as opposed to the passive role of convoy escorts.

U-boat commanders quickly learned how to evade early asdics, and the cavalry approach failed almost completely. The result was heavier convoy losses than might have been the case had they been strongly escorted. It created the situation that was to place the *Jervis Bay's* next convoy, HX 84, in extreme jeopardy: attacked by a pocket battleship that probably would have hightailed it away from the scene had the cargo carriers been escorted by conventional warships. (Not until 1942 did Churchill fully accept the convoy system as a potent offensive tactic.)[1]

Halifax was bursting at its seams. Its population swelled from 68,000 in 1939 to nearly 100,000 by the end of the war. Because it was an ideal convoy assembly port, thousands of construction workers, shipyard workers, stevedores, merchant and Canadian Navy sailors, and their families and girlfriends had poured into the Nova Scotia city by October 1940. A scattering of German informers also roamed the port area. Commander Frederick B Watt, director of the Naval Boarding Service in Halifax, called it 'an overcrowded hellhole.' 'Every scrap of living space was filled,' he wrote, 'the hotels, the private homes, the boarding houses, the tenements and the slum rooms. Some enterprising newcomers resorted to makeshift shacks thrown up on the city's fringes and into the woods.'[2]

And everybody nervously remembered the 1917 collision/explosion of the munitions carrier *Mont Blanc* that had levelled two square miles of the city's North End.

The port area was a double harbour. One anchorage was a 4-mile long, 1-mile-wide calm ocean inlet with facilities for merchantmen and naval ships. It narrowed into a channel leading into the virtually land-locked Bedford Basin, 3 miles by 1.5 miles, where more merchant vessels were anchored and wharfed. The port probably was the busiest of its size in the world during the war. It was a key to the survival of Britain. Nearly all cargo traffic from North America and parts of South America funnelled through Halifax. There the ships were processed, organised, and sent out in convoys supplying the beleaguered island nation.

The Canadian Naval Control Service, directed by Captain Richard Hibbert Oland, managed all shipping into and out of the port. It plotted and was responsible for every detail of convoy assembling and routing. Watt, who had served under Oland in the navy in the 1920s, was appointed by his former commander to head the Naval Boarding Service (NBS), whose function was to make sure every merchant ship was 'in all respects ready' before she sailed.

One of the critical functions of NBS was to uncover any sabotage devices and to assure safe stowage of munitions and volatile chemicals. Watt's predecessor had little enthusiasm for the job. He and his men boarded the ships wearing wrinkled, dirty clothes of their own choosing, and displayed little discipline. They went through half-hearted inspections and left their slipshod attitudes behind with the merchant crews. After Watt took over, the senior member of the team, Able Seaman Al Oxner, who had been at odds with the desultory operation of NBS, became the new chief's adviser, supporter, and unofficial second in command. Through him, another key problem was revealed: low morale among a large number of ships' companies.

Seamen from many nations laboured aboard convoy ships with little recognition, minuscule pay, and fear of a sudden torpedo in the ribs. Most British merchant crews understood they were struggling for national survival, and they faced the raider and U-boat danger with a fighting spirit. Some crews represented other maritime nations and sailed disciplined ships; many of them sympathised with the British, though some favoured Germany. Other convoy vessels were operated in a slovenly manner; their crews were ill-treated by their officers—many of them incompetents—and they were scared to death of being blown to hell in the freezing North Atlantic. Many of them deserted in ports like Halifax, and sometimes ships were held at anchor for weeks until full crews could be signed aboard. Watt and Oxner met the sabotage and morale problems head-on.

The NBS men willingly, even eagerly, accepted Watt's new discipline. They now wore uniforms. They conducted their searches in a crisp and thorough but friendly manner. They talked to the crewmen, listened to their suggestions, and spotted problems in working conditions. Watt passed this information to appropriate parties aboard ships and ashore, and if need be to Captain Oland. As a result, beneficial changes were made, and crew members began feeling that NBS men were trustworthy and cared for them.

One of them, a seaman with a hacking cough, whose bunk and blankets were wet from a leaking hull, couldn't get the ship owner to authorise repairs. Watt told Oland, who called in the balky ship's agent and broke the man's resistance with a voice that roared like an incoming 15-inch shell: 'Get the plates sealed!'

Some of the most effective morale boosters were packages of cookies, cakes, magazines, winter woollens, and mufflers provided by women's organisations. Just before departing with convoy HX 84, Captain Fegen wrote a letter of thanks to the New Brunswick Division of the Canadian Red Cross: 'May I ask you to convey...our deep appreciation for the magnificent gift of winter comforts that arrived safely on board yesterday afternoon. From my own experience in the North Atlantic last winter I know [they are] going to be of the greatest value in the months to come.'

One especially useful NBS service was the provision of accurate information and the scotching of destructive scuttlebutt. The port of Halifax was a perfect incubator for the hatching of metastatic rumours. Watt's staff spent much of their time dealing with concocted and passed-along stories that foretold disasters. One such rumour placed the *Admiral Scheer* in the North Atlantic. The pocket battleship actually was undetected from the time she left her berth on October 23 until she confronted HX 84. While the tale of her breakout was one of many wild harbour-side stories that were neutralised by NBS, this one happened to be true.[3]

On the morning of 28 October, several months after he took command of the boarding service, Watt found time to attend his first convoy conference. 'As it turned out,' he later wrote, 'I participated in a meeting which no one who was there would ever forget. The convoy was HX 84, whose mid-ocean escort would be the armed merchant cruiser *Jervis Bay*.'[4]

Oland chaired the meeting at the head of a T-shaped table with twenty-nine merchant ship captains gathered round. Sailing orders were laid out at their places, with charts showing each ship's station in the convoy array. Oland's staff discussed the details of the crossing—navigation, station-keeping, communications, blackout, radio silence, emergency procedures. Then he introduced retired Rear Admiral H B Maltby, the convoy commodore. Slender, every inch Royal Navy in bearing, with a high, clipped voice, and an outdated salty vocabulary, Maltby smiled reassuringly and laid out the rules of the road:

'Lights are bugaboo. For the love of Peter, tell old cooky not to open the galley door when he lights the fire at five in the morning. That sort of thing can be seen for miles. Old Fritz just loves to see a light. Post extra lookouts in the fog. Exercise your gun crew regularly. Keep 'em trim and ready for action. Don't break wireless silence under any circumstances. If a torpedo is spotted, take avoiding action by turning. You can all recognise a torpedo? You've seen 'em, haven't you? (Uneasy chuckles from the captains.) And, for the love of Mike, be on time.'

Maltby grinned broadly and slowly settled onto his Victorian cushion.

Oland next presented the escort commander: 'Gentlemen, Captain Fegen of the *Jervis Bay*.'

Of course, when the escort captain rose before the convoy masters and Naval Control Service officers, no one around the table knew they were witnessing the beginning of one of the memorable heroic naval actions of World War II. Unlike his awkward, vulnerable ship, Fegen was an imposing, commanding presence. He stood straight, tall, and rugged in his inevitable charcoal-grey peacoat. The crow's feet at the corners of his deep-set blue eyes radiated a blend of experience and wit. All together the captain's demeanour projected leadership and efficiency. Fegen broke a small smile and glanced around the table. His deep, confident voice, free of the brogue of his Irish heritage, radiated through the room:

'In past convoys, I've noticed a tendency on the part of some masters to regard the escort as very reliable. So much so that they'd just leave everything to us. Well, gentlemen, we are reliable, but we do like to be backed up. Now, I ask you to take careful note of the silhouette of the *Jervis Bay*. I'll circle around a couple of times so you can familiarise yourselves with the appearance of my ship. She's pretty big, and sometimes, when I want to check vessels, we loom up out of the fog and they all put their helm hard over and run like hell.'

That gave the masters a good laugh.

'I think I can assure you that if we run into any routine unpleasantness, such as one of the enemy's armed merchant cruisers, *Jervis Bay* will be able to attend to it. Should we have the unlikely bad luck to cross the path of a pocket battleship, I can only promise to do my best. Under that circumstance there will be a good deal you will want to do for yourselves.'

Fegen discussed the signals he would use in case of a German attack and the escape responses of the convoy ships. All questions were answered fully. The meeting broke up with Commodore Maltby's benediction: 'Good sailing, gentlemen.'[5]

HMS *Jervis Bay's* crew had returned to Halifax a few days before the masters' conference, and they had some time to spare in the city. Though they were all in uniform, a considerable number of them were ex-merchant sailors. They were fond of drink, some of them overly so, but they acquitted themselves rather sedately compared to Royal Navy regulars and reserves. Actually, discreet shore-leave behaviour was easy in wartime Halifax, a bleak and undemonstrative city that did not attract or welcome roisterers.

There was one exception. A tough stoker had got fighting drunk and wrecked the cafe he was in. Fegen ordered him to the brig for two weeks and reduced his leave and pay for six months. The other engine-room ratings (crewmen) were surprised by the captain's leniency.

'Is the Old Man going soft?' said one of them.

'It doesn't make sense, letting him off like that,' another commented.

After a time they understood the logic to the captain's sentence. The loss of ten pence a day didn't seem like much, but for a poorly paid stoker it added up to a sizeable chunk in 180 days. More than that, the hooligan was allowed to go ashore once every three months, but only if a volunteer accompanied him. 'Aye,' said one of the men, 'can you see anyone going ashore with that bloke.' Fegen had given the stoker's shipmates final say on the term of his punishment.[6]

Sam Patience, a twenty-one-year-old who had already experienced an unfair share of naval encounters, had arrived in Halifax aboard the liner *Duchess of Richmond* a few weeks earlier. He was transferred to one of the newly acquired ex–US World War I destroyers, the Lincoln, renamed HMS *Sherwood*. The British were loosening up the creaky joints and gears of that mothballed flotilla and accustoming themselves to the controls, engine rooms, guns, galley arrangements, and the strange sleeping accommodations. The Royal Navy ratings were used to hammocks, which gently damped the ship's pitch and roll in heavy seas; American bunks rode like broncos.

As one of the more experienced ratings on the *Sherwood*, Patience reached his coveted goal of steering a ship as quartermaster. However, nearly two weeks aboard the top-heavy, unstable, uncomfortable old destroyer in her working-up and compass trials were enough for him. After the trials, the ship was back in Halifax readying to sail for Britain.

On Sunday evening, 27 October, Patience was in the *Sherwood's* mess under the scissors of an Irish seaman who was trying to sell his barbering skill to the crew. Not sure whether to trust the man, he tightened up and grimaced. Then he saw the ship's first lieutenant coming down the companionway with a man he didn't know. The lieutenant introduced him as the *Jervis Bay's* leading seaman quartermaster. He said the man's wife, who had a very young baby, was ill, and he wanted to get home to Lancashire as fast as he could. But the *Jervis Bay*, after delivering her convoy to the Western approaches, would come about without stopping and sail back to Halifax. Would Sam be willing to exchange places with him? The *Jervis Bay* was sailing in the morning.

The young Scotsman masked the abhorrence he felt about crossing the North Atlantic on the old American tin can. At the same time, he tried to suppress the joy that coursed through his veins at the prospect of being a quartermaster on an armed merchant cruiser. Patience put on what he hoped was a thoughtful face, hesitated a long moment, then calmly allowed that he could manage the switch. Waiting for the two men to leave and for the barber to snip his last lock, he sauntered out of the mess, then dashed to his quarters grinning and singing to himself, threw his gear into his duffel, and within ten minutes he sprinted aboard the *Jervis Bay*.[7]

Captain Fegen admired his executive officer. He and Blackburn had got to know each other at several training sessions, but it had been more than fourteen years since they last met. As acting captain of the *Jervis Bay* for several months before Fegen took over, he had raised the efficiency of the ship's company to such a high level that the new commander had little more to add to the running of the escort vessel than his style of command.

'They're a damn good crowd of lads,' Blackburn said. 'I'm very fond of them, very proud of them.'

Blackburn's feelings about the ship were deeply personal. 'I loved the *Jervis Bay* as I loved no other ship in my long service,' he later commented. 'I sweated out my soul to turn her into an efficient fighting unit.'[8]

He was disappointed in being relegated to second-in-command when the forty-eight-year-old Fegen, two years his junior, came aboard. The new captain understood his feelings. He quickly made it obvious to Blackburn that he depended on the exec for the highest levels of performance, counsel, and support. Both men were highly professional and Royal Navy line-officers to the core. In spite of differences in temperament, they were a superb team. They ran a happy and efficient ship. And, together, they were ruthless about the only thing that mattered: security of the convoy. They would have used force, for example, to silence a ship that was jeopardising the convoy by carelessly emitting radio-receiver oscillations. In general, they made sure the convoy's ships followed the rules and kept in formation.

Fegen was dismayed, shortly before the *Jervis Bay* sailed out of Halifax harbour as protector of convoy HX 84, when he got the news that he was losing Blackburn, who was promoted to captain and given command of his own AMC, HMS *Voltaire*. At the same time, of course, Fegen and the entire crew were happy for their respected and well-liked executive officer, who deserved the elevation in rank and his new command. Under Captain Blackburn, the *Voltaire* left port on 5 November as escort to HX 86. Late that afternoon, while on the bridge, he received a radio message. His heart sank as he read that HX 84 was under attack by a pocket battleship, and he was to return his convoy to Halifax.[9]

7 The Fifth of November

ON the clear, cold afternoon of 28 October 1940, all but nine of the thirty-eight merchant ships of convoy HX 84 and their armed escort HMS *Jervis Bay* started moving one by one out of the harbour at Halifax. The first of them, the commodore's freighter *Cornish City*, carrying steel and general cargo, was visible from the parade grounds as she rounded the shipyard corner. She disappeared behind waterfront commercial buildings, then re-emerged against the trees of the Dartmouth hills across the inlet. Slipping behind some red-brick tenements for a minute or two, the ship poked her starboard bow into view again and slowly faded into the smoky haze at the mouth of the harbour. From then until the procession ended about an hour and a half later, three of the meticulously spaced ships almost always were in view through the three waterfront 'windows.'

About four miles outside the harbour, after reaching a marker buoy, they settled into a temporary array under direction of the escort and the commodore's ship, and headed eastward. The next day the convoy was joined by the last nine ships from Sydney (Nova Scotia) and Bermuda. They slipped into prearranged positions, giving HX 84 four long ranks in nine short columns. Six hundred yards separated the columns, except the fourth and fifth, which, to accommodate the *Jervis Bay*, had 1,200 yards of manoeuvring space between them. In the columns, the ships followed each other by 400 yards.

Ten ships made up the first rank, with the *Cornish City* in position five and the *Jervis Bay* by herself between positions four and five. From these places they controlled the course and pace of the convoy and at the same time served as markers to help the other ships keep to their stations. To the right in columns six, seven, and eight, were *Rangitiki*, *Trewellard*, and *San Demetrio*, all of which were to be major actors in the coming battle.

Among the second ten vessels, which also played significant parts in the drama a little more than a week ahead, were *Stureholm* in the fourth column, fellow Swedes *Vingaland* (fifth) and *Delphinula* (sixth), and *Maidan* (eighth). The third rank of nine included *Fresno City* in position two and *Beaverford* (eighth). Three of the final nine that were to be singled out were the Swedish *Delhi* (first), *Trefusis* (fourth), and *Kenbane Head* (ninth).

While they were an ungainly fleet—about three miles wide and two-thirds of a mile long—British convoy experience had established that the long-edge-forward rectangular array was the

Convoy HX84

Column No / Rank	1	2	3	4	5	6	7	8	9
1	Erodona (Tanker)	Andalusian	Hjalmar Wessel (Norway)	Empire Penguin	Cornish City (commodore's ship)	Rangitiki	Trewellard	San Demetrio (Tanker)	James J McGuire (Tanker)
2	Emile Franqui (Belgium)	Persier (Belgium)	Cetus (Norway)	Stureholm (Sweden)	Vingaland (Sweden)	Delphinula (Tanker)	Sovac (Tanker)	Maidan	Aethol Telalar (Tanker)
3	Danae II	Fresno City	Castilian	Briarwood	Aethel Empress (Tanker)	Pacific Enterprise	Beaverford	Cordelia (Tanker)	Anna Bulgari (Greece)
4	Delhi (Sweden)	Lancaster Castle	Oil Reliance (Tanker)	Trefusis	Puck (Poland)	Saint Gobain (Sweden Tanker)	Solfon (Norway)	Varoy (Norway)	Kenbane Head
5			Dan y Bryn	Morska Wola					

HMS Jervis Bay

← Direction of convoy

Convoy HX84 attacked by *Admiral Scheer* 5th November 1940. *(Courtesy of #53 Jervis Bay Branch, Royal Canadian Legion, Saint John, New Brunswick)* most efficient anti–U-boat geometry. It made signals from the commodore and the escort visible to all ships. If under attack, the whole convoy could turn—say, 45 degrees—simultaneously. Since U-boats generally approached from the flank, the rectangular target was smaller and the ships with more valuable cargoes in the interior columns were better protected.

The convoy soon was joined by two Canadian destroyers, but not by some of the hoped-for ex-American destroyers. None of these fifty old four-stackers, which had been acquired in the trade for British bases, could be made ready in time to meet the convoy. The Canadians would turn back to Halifax after two days. This procedure was routine in the early months of the war, a result of the Royal and Canadian Navies not being equipped to escort all convoys with potent warships all the way home. HX 84 would be met by naval escorts and aircraft two to three days out from Britain. For the middle ten days or so of the crossing, the convoy would have no more protection than the old guns and guts of ex–cargo liner *Jervis Bay*.

The AMC was responsible for cargoes consisting of 126,469 tons of petroleum products; 42,352 tons of steel; a total of 20,863 tons of copper, brass, chemicals, butter, evaporated milk, cheeses, refrigerated meats, flour, and canned foods; 12 fighter planes; 1.5 million cubic feet of timber; 3,414 bales of wool; and 4,566 linear feet of pit props (wood supports for mine roofs).[1]

Sailing went smoothly for the ships of HX 84. They moved at a sluggish nine knots (top speed of the slowest member), stations were kept, and for the first four days the trip was uneventful. That is not to say it was easy for the engine crews of the thirty-eight freighters and tankers.

Station-keeping for them was not merely maintaining the required knots. The engineers made constant adjustments, a far more difficult task on a multi-thousand-ton ship than it is for motorists on a crowded road. Deep in the engine and boiler compartments, they were blind to what was happening on the surface except for orders telegraphed down from their bridges for increases or decreases in revolutions. They were always busy and sweating: ratcheting engines, shovelling coal or maintaining the flow of fuel oil, checking steam valves and boilers, greasing gears, and lubricating other moving parts.

The chief engineer of the *Jervis Bay*, Commander J H G Chappell, a tall, heavy-set man, knew his ship well, having served for many years with the Shaw Savill Lines. A polished and urbane disciplinarian, he drove his men even harder. They had to respond immediately to Captain Fegen's oft-changing orders as the escort raced off here and there, poking into suspicious areas, prodding laggards, and searching for the sources of radio-receiver oscillations that could attract German hunters to the ripe cluster of cargo vessels. Up to the day of the attack, the captain kept warning certain ships to 'stop scraping on the air.'

At night, the ships were darkened, except for a small navigation light that looked like a dim star that had drifted down onto each stern. The vessels in the second, third, and fourth ranks steered by the tiny blue hazes ahead. This kept the quartermasters squinting at the barely visible markers and making frequent tiny adjustments at the helm, while the officer-in-command on the bridge called for rpm changes.

The chief engineer of the *Jervis Bay*, Commander JHG Chappell. (Mike Chappell)

The *Jervis Bay*'s above-deck crew endured a different kind of strain. Continuous vigilance (looking for straying convoy ships and possible U-boats and surface raiders) was maintained by watches at several stations: on the bridge, in the crow's nest 40 feet up on the foremast, on either side of the lower bridge, on either side of the after part of the boat deck, on the fo'c'sle, and on the poop. The ship investigated every patch of fog for potential trouble. The guns were constantly manned. Sometimes the gun crews slept by their weapons with little weather protection and none from the cold, except for their pea jackets and balaclavas. (Some of the *Jervis Bay* survivors suffered permanently impaired health as a result of their watches and gun stations.)

As on all the escorting runs, Fegen ran daily defensive exercises: gun drills, practice shoots, ammunition handling, fire fighting, and responses to breakdowns in weapons and communications. The crew had to be prepared as a warship to engage the enemy. During the shoots, he moved from gun to gun, offering tips and encouragement, and reminding the men of their duty with a fusion of wit and authority.

No actual threats or untoward events marked the crossing until 1 November, when the last ship in the last rank, the little Polish freighter *Morska Wola* carrying general cargo, dropped back with engine trouble. By 5 November, she was 120 miles behind the convoy. The tanker *San Demetrio* also fell behind with a malfunctioning power plant. Her engineering officer, not anxious to sail alone in the North Atlantic during the German submariners' 'happy time,' urged his men to speedily correct the problem, a cracked piston. They succeeded, and the tanker, carrying more than 11,000 tons of aviation fuel, caught up to the convoy and reoccupied her position in the first rank on the morning of the fateful day.

The morning of 5 November dawned cold, calm, and clear for HX 84's now thirty-seven cargo ships and their sole protector *Jervis Bay*. The sun slanted down from the cloudless southeastern sky and glanced obliquely off the surface, leaving patches and streaks of gold and silver on the long, low swells and colouring the approaching broken overcast to the north. The convoy was more than seven days out of Halifax, halfway home. Through late morning, Captain Fegen's order of the day for all ships continued to be what it always was: Maintain stations. Maintain radio silence. Maintain 360 degrees of vigilance.[2]

8 Out of Nowhere

AFTER the 9:40 am catapult launch, as recounted in chapter 3, Lieutenant Pietsch circled his Arado once around the *Scheer*. The ship's company, anticipating he would spot a British convoy, cheered and waved him on. Pietsch waggled the wings of his 'parrot' and flew off to the south. He climbed to about 10,000 feet, where the scout plane was little more than a dot as seen from the surface. The first triangular reconnaissance sector was a sweep 115 miles wide and 80 miles out from the pocket battleship.

Through the large Perspex dome, Pietsch and his observer Gallinat scanned overlapping fields of view covering a full 360 degrees. Pietsch was keenly aware of the captain's warning not to allow the Arado to be seen by the enemy. He kept the seaplane above the increasing clouds for invisibility from the surface. Of course, it worked both ways—while they were hidden, the flier and his observer could not see the entire British merchant marine if it were a single convoy spread out below them. Pietsch's way of stealthily spotting ships was to slip into breaks between clouds for a few seconds of observation and then duck back to cover before shipboard watches could see or identify the Arado.

The fliers reconnoitred the area for about an hour and returned to their ship at 11:20 am, indicating to Krancke they had found nothing. Then they swung out to the second sector. Before noon, Pietsch dipped into an opening. His face lighted up. He sucked in a breath. Ships!

The observer strained at his safety straps and peered over the pilot's left shoulder. He confirmed the sighting. They quickly counted eight ships and raced back into the clouds. Radio communication was forbidden. The excited pilot flew back to the *Admiral Scheer* at top speed (190 mph). He arrived twenty minutes earlier than expected and happily waggled the wings. He signalled with the code light, 'Eighty-eight sea miles.'

A wave of elation rolled through the bridge. Some observant crewmen noted the change in bearing of the officers through the plate glass of the command post and immediately inferred that a convoy had been sighted. The rumour radiated throughout the ship almost instantaneously.[1]

H C Fellingham, third mate on the *Trefusis*, reckoned she was the slowest ship in the HX 84 convoy. Nine knots was all she could pull out of her straining engines. She was located fourth in the fourth rank. Her wheelhouse was not much larger than a telephone booth and accommodated only the helmsman. Normally, on most merchant ships, the officer on watch was stationed close to the helm. Because of the tight squeeze in the *Trefusis*'s wheelhouse, Fellingham stood his 8:00 am–to-noon watch on the open bridge and, consequently, was better able to see and hear what was happening outside the ship than were enclosed watches on other ships.

Fellingham later said: '[Between 11:00 and 11:30,] I heard the sound of an aircraft...to the rear of the convoy and on our starboard side...[I] took up the binoculars and [scanned the area the whine was coming from]. I caught a brief but positive sight of a small seaplane passing...through a small break in the clouds.'[2]

There is little doubt that Fellingham spotted the Arado on its second sweep, although the time in his recollection was about an hour earlier than that reported by the *Scheer*. It is likely the Germans used Central European Time and the British GMT. He reported his sighting by Aldis lamp in Morse code to Commodore Maltby straight ahead in the first rank of ships. Maltby asked him to confirm that it was a seaplane. He did. No other convoy watches reported hearing or seeing an aircraft.

In all the documentation of the *Jervis Bay* convoy, there is no mention of Fellingham's observation being passed along to Captain Fegen. The report might have been deep-filed because it was not confirmed by other watches. However, it is hard to believe that Maltby may not have relayed it to the escort.[3]

After the convoy sighting, the *Scheer*'s first task was to recover the Arado. With the sea swell and chop becoming noticeable, the helmsman manoeuvred the ship into a sharp turn that swept out a momentarily calm 'duck pond.' Pietsch brought the plane's pontoons neatly down onto the surface after a single bounce. He idled over to the ship's port side and stopped under a deck crane. The pilot pushed back the dome, climbed out of the cockpit, then, after several tries, with some crewmen playfully hooting at his misses, he caught the crane's swaying coupler and hooked it to the Arado's lifting ring. The crane operator pulled the slightly rocking aircraft out of the sea and swung it delicately onto the catapult rails.

Pietsch leaped to the deck carrying a map that had a big red X on it, enough evidence for nearby crewmen to confirm the convoy rumour. He scrambled up to the bridge where Krancke, in contrast to his excited officers, calmly heard him out and examined the map.

'Thanks, Pietsch,' the captain said. 'Good work.'

Krancke immediately ordered the navigator to plot a course to meet the convoy in the shortest possible time, about three hours. That done, he put the ship on the calculated heading at top speed, twenty-seven knots.[4]

The captain then lit a black Brazil cigar and began to consider the facts, the risks, and the alternative actions. With the Arado secured by 1:00 pm, the pocket battleship could reach her prey no earlier than 4:00 pm. The position would be about 52°47N by 32°32W. On the one hand, dusk would be coming on. It would not be the most advantageous time to approach the convoy. Some of the cargo ships could escape into the night. On the other hand, the captain felt, the *Scheer*'s new radar could be useful in finding and targeting ships in the dark and behind smoke.

An alternative was to wait until the next morning before attacking. The Germans could sink many more ships by using the Wheel Principle. First, they would destroy the escort or escorts, and then, with about nine hours of daylight available, they would sail at high speed in an ever increasing spiral around the slowly dispersing convoy vessels and pick them off. By then, however, the convoy would be about 120 miles closer to the Western Approaches, the zone where Royal Navy warships would be waiting to meet them and accompany them to home ports. German intelligence did not know exactly where the zone began. Krancke suspected that by 6:00 am British naval units probably would be about two hundred miles to the east, some six hours away. He felt this would allow the *Scheer* less time to create havoc and evade the inevitable and intensive Royal Navy search.

Hours before, the meteorology officer had forecast a low in the general region around the projected battle site. The clouds were advancing southward, and the spaces between them were pinching shut. The swells, which made Pietsch's landing a bit tricky, were gradually increasing.

'If it's not a professional secret, Defant,' the captain asked, 'what does the clerk of the weather have to say this morning?'

The meteorologist predicted a steady worsening and several days of dirty weather. By dawn, the ship would be riding on a much heavier sea. Although the *Scheer*'s weapons were technologically advanced and her gunnery was as good as any in the world, the rocking and yawing and poor visibility would cut into the precision of her 11-inch and 5.9-inch guns. On the other hand, the storm might conceal her from British pursuers.

A third consideration was to wait for convoy HX 85 to reach the area a few days later. That would mean riding out the expected storm, 'grounding' the Arado, possibly meeting the convoy under difficult sea conditions, and giving the Royal Navy more of an opportunity to spot the ship.

Krancke weighed the alternatives quickly. For him, there was only one decision. He ground out his cigar and ordered an attack.

As the captain's mind was occupied with strategy, the ship's company crowded into the mess to a fast lunch. Experienced sailors ate heartily; they knew they could face a battle better with full bellies. Many of the younger crewmen were too keyed up to eat. After lunch, without waiting for orders, the men began clearing the decks. They removed railings, clamped the portholes tight, covered hatchways and other openings, and secured all boats and exposed fittings. Below, everything that could roll or slide with a 'loose cannon' effect or could become a dangerous projectile (dishes, hanging photographs, etc.) was stowed or tied down.

The *Scheer* sliced through the undulating sea at flank speed on a collision course with her still invisible prey. It wasn't long before her radar screen began showing a sequence of peaks: the ships of HX 84.[5]

SS *Mopan,* a refrigerated banana carrier, was stricken by a fate which brought her face to face with the *Scheer* but which stalled the raider's confrontation with the convoy. In mid-October, the *Mopan* had been cruising empty from Britain to Jamaica, where she was to pick up a cargo for delivery to the besieged people at home, when one of her twelve passengers fell sick and required land-based medical assistance. A long way from their Caribbean destination, Captain S A Sapsworth called for his ship's full speed of fifteen knots and reached Kingston harbour far ahead of schedule. Rather than allowing her to lie idle for several days, the shipper Elders & Fyffes loaded her with seventy thousand stems of bananas awaiting another vessel that had not yet arrived. Thus, with her substitute cargo, the *Mopan* set out earlier than originally slated.

Elders & Fyffes had a pool of seamen who were allowed to choose their ships. Urban Peters selected the *Mopan,* because 'banana boats are good little ships to sail on. They're clean and conditions are good. A fortnight at sea, a week in Jamaica, and back again.' It seemed a pretty cushy job for a merchant seaman. The worst problem he could remember, until the encounter with the German raider, involved a mealtime passenger who wanted a banana. 'On being told there were no bananas,' Peters said, 'he blew his top. 'What! A banana boat and no bloody bananas in the galley!'"[6]

The *Mopan* was a sleek 5,400-ton vessel with comfortable accommodations for a dozen passengers and about seventy crew. Near her maximum speed, she could make the Jamaica-to-Britain crossing in as little as ten days—fast enough to outspeed the ripening of her cargo. Her ability to move twice as fast as most convoys led Elders & Fyffes to sail the *Mopan* and others like her independently, against Admiralty wishes.

Late in the morning of 5 November, the *Mopan* overtook the convoy from the southwest and crossed in front of it. Hailed by the

Jervis Bay for identification, she was invited to join the cluster.

Captain Sapsworth signalled back, 'No, thanks, I have a valuable refrigerated cargo.' He also was anxious to move along at a pace that could help his ship avoid submerged U-boats. The *Mopan* sailed ahead, and HX 84 soon receded below the horizon.[7]

About two hours after the encounter, the banana boat's lookout sighted a mast. The captain soon was convinced it was a warship, bow first and difficult to identify, but most likely British. The stranger was moving very fast. On closer approach , she seemed to resemble a Royal Navy battleship. Sapsworth ordered the British Merchant Marine's red ensign hoisted up the stern mast.

Peters, listed as an assistant steward, was gunnery-trained and served as a member of the *Mopan*'s gun crew. About 2:30 pm, as he was relaxing below, he heard one of the cooks say, 'Hey, there's a funny-looking warship out there.' Peters joined his mates rushing to the gun deck.

'It's all right, it's one of the *Royal Oak* class,' the gun-crew chief said.

Another voice reported, 'She's flashing a Morse signal to us.'

As it turned out, the flashes came from guns, and loud geysers erupted off the port bow. Splinters shattered a lifeboat. Everyone was shocked into silence, except the refrigeration engineer, who whispered, 'It's a bloody Jerry.'

In the moments after the explosions, the gunners scattered, a cook took the chickens out of the ovens to keep them from burning, another cook raced to his locker and put on his raincoat and soft-felt trilby hat, and Peters collected his raincoat and put cigarettes and his razor in the pocket. Then came the 'abandon ship' command.[8]

The spikes on the *Scheer*'s radar monitor now were fairly well defined. It was a good-sized convoy, certainly more than the eight ships the Arado's pilot had observed. But the technology was not refined enough to indicate that one of the spikes was not part of the presumed HX 84.

At 2:27 pm, earlier than expected, the *Scheer*'s lookout reported smoke on the horizon at 50 degrees.

The alarms sounded, and the men raced to their action stations. Only a smudge, it puzzled Captain Krancke. It could come from no more than a single ship. 'Either it's the…cat that walks alone,' he mumbled to no one, 'or a British auxiliary cruiser [scouting ahead of the convoy].'

As the pocket battleship raced toward the smoke, Krancke's binoculars reduced it to an ordinary freighter. 'It doesn't look much like an auxiliary cruiser,' he said. 'What do you make of her, Budde?' he asked the chief of the Wireless Interception Service.

'As far as we know, the British haven't used anything as small as that for an auxiliary cruiser.'

'But it doesn't do to under-estimate the enemy's intelligence. Just because we wouldn't expect a small ship like that to be an auxiliary cruiser might be the very reason the British turned it into one.'

Although she did not look like much of a fighting ship, at that still considerable distance, one could not be sure. 'Warn all posts to be on the alert for torpedo tracks,' the captain ordered.

It did not take long for the ships, moving together at a combined forty knots or so, to close to less than a mile. Krancke ordered the big guns trained on the other ship, making sure the radio shack would be the first target. Then he ordered the signalman to hoist 'stop at once' flags. This was followed immediately by the *Scheer*'s blinker lamp warning her not to use her radio.

Krancke saw some of the *Mopan*'s crew hurry to man the lone gun on the aft deck.

'Warning shots ahead,' he snapped.[9]

Three of the starboard 5.9-inch guns fired in quick succession, and three shells exploded close to the freighter's bow. Her gun crew scurried back toward the boat deck. Krancke's next signal to the cargo ship was, 'Take to your boats at once.' Budde was instructed to call for gunfire at the first hint of a radio signal. The *Scheer*'s immediate response would be to silence their transmitter with an 11-inch shell and sink the fully crewed ship.

Anxious to get to the convoy, the German captain quickly grew impatient. He watched as the first boat was lowered. Two more were carefully winched down to the water, and the British crewmen began rowing toward his ship—much too slowly for Krancke. He was tempted to get under way, destroying the *Mopan* as he went and leaving the crew to their lifeboats in what promised to be a heavy sea. However, he was a humane man. He moved the *Scheer* a little to one side for a clean bead on the other ship and battered her with his 4-inch anti-aircraft weapons and 1.5-inch rapid-fire guns, setting her afire while her crew gradually approached and boarded the barking, crackling warship.

Captain Sapsworth was brought to Krancke, who, upset at how sluggishly the *Mopan* was sinking, ordered an increased rate of fire.

The cargo ship's captain yelled, 'Not in the stern. Munitions!'

The German did not understand Sapsworth's anxiety, but he complied with the plea. He later found out that the Briton was afraid the red ensign would be blown off the stern; he wanted it flying proudly when the ship went down. By the time the *Mopan,* her intact ensign, and all her bananas disappeared below the surface, a precious hour had passed. The time was now about 3:30 pm[10]

Abandoned refrigerator ship *Mopan*, carrying 70,000 stems of bananas, is hit at her waterline by a 4.1-inch shell from one of the *Scheer's* anti-aircraft guns. (*Bordkameradschaft* Admiral Scheer)

As the *Admiral Scheer* sped toward her rendezvous with the target convoy, the captives were put in quarters two decks below the main forward turret. The principal topic of discussion was the behaviour of their captain. Mainly, they wondered why he had refused to send out a radio message, which could have warned the *Jervis Bay* convoy of the

Mopan crewmen being brought aboard the Admiral Scheer while the Germans were sinking their ship. (*Bordkameradschaft* Admiral Scheer)

The *Mopan* sinking after being shelled by the *Admiral Scheer*. All her crew were taken aboard the pocket battleship as prisoners. *(Bordkameradschaft* Admiral Scheer*)*

Scheer's presence in the area. The captain did not fare well in the early assessments. Many crewmen, perhaps stirred up by some angry shipmates, disapproved his purported behaviour. The grumbling continued through four and a half years of imprisonment and into the post-war decades, with no definite conclusion.[11]

Peters had two bones to pick with Sapsworth. In a taped interview, he said: 'The biggest thing that bothered me was that the radio operator [James Macintosh]…said the captain wouldn't let him send a message out, because he was afraid. All he had to do was send the letter 'R'. Jimmy said he asked him two or three times. [He said the captain] was panic-stricken, he was laying on his face on the bridge. He should have sacrificed the ship.'

Quoted in *The Battle of the North Atlantic,* Peters also said: 'We never got the abandon-ship order. But, there was the skipper, away in his boat with his suitcase…Somebody in our boat shouted, 'Women and skippers first.'' (In an article in the British maritime magazine *Sea Breezes,* Peters reverses himself, admitting the abandon-ship order was given.)[12]

Quartermaster Gerard Riley said he overheard the radio operator ask Sapsworth whether he should send out a distress message and the captain reply, 'For God's sake, no! She'll blow us out of the

Mopan Captain SA Sapsworth (2nd from left) talks with a German officer after being brought aboard the *Admiral Scheer*. (*Bordkameradschaft* Admiral Scheer)

water if you do.' Then, Riley said, the captain gave the order to abandon ship.[13]

Third Mate Hedley Jones said: 'The abandonment was conducted in a calm and orderly manner despite intermittent shelling by the *Scheer*...Captain Sapsworth was an efficient shipmaster. However, he was a secretive and lonely man, and, sometimes, he assumed an overbearing attitude toward the ship's crew.'[14]

As recently as May 1993 *Sea Breezes* rehashed the Sapsworth issue in an article by the still bitter Peters. Since the captain was not known ever to have publicly explained his action, the editor felt compelled to insert a possible 'other side of the story':

'The *Admiral Scheer* would undoubtedly have had her guns trained on the *Mopan,* one of them at least aimed directly at her wireless room. At the first squeak of a transmission the warship would have opened fire and at such close range would have blasted the *Mopan* out of the water before any sensible signal could have been made, possibly causing great loss of life. By refusing to let his radio officer send the 'Raider' signal the master ensured that the ship was abandoned in what appears to have been a safe and orderly manner.'[15]

In addition, by taking their sweet time in leaving the *Mopan* and rowing almost languidly over to the *Scheer*, the British sailors helped bring the cover of night an hour closer to the convoy.[16]

9 Ranging In

THE *Rangitiki*, the convoy's largest ship at 16,698 tons, had come a long way from Wellington, New Zealand. The handsome cargo liner carried seventy-five passengers, thousands of bales of wool, and thousands of tons of refrigerated meats and cheeses. At about 3:45 pm, her lookout reported a smoky smudge on the horizon at a bearing of 020 degrees, close to that of the *Mopan* after she'd passed in front of the convoy. A report was signalled to the commodore's ship and the escort, both of which confirmed the sighting. Although no official reports or accounts make the connection, it is likely that the *Rangitiki, Cornish City*, and *Jervis Bay* were seeing traces of the destruction of the *Mopan*. (Several witnesses later reported no smoke was ever seen coming from the *Scheer's* funnel.) The *Jervis Bay's* Captain Fegen informed his watch officers of the sighting and instructed the quartermasters to remind them to pay special attention to the 020 direction at five minutes before every hour. Then he moved to the exposed port wing of the bridge.[1]

After the *Mopan* distraction, the *Scheer's* radar continued spiking near the edge of its range. A visual sighting of the convoy was imminent. The raider's twin propellers rotated at top speed, pumping foaming, churning wakes behind them. As her sleek stem cut through the softly swelling surface at twenty-seven knots, water rode up her bows and curled away in continuous breakers. The men were excited and ready. The officers of the bridge appeared composed, but even Captain Krancke's mind swirled with images of exploding British merchant ships. The jangle of the telephone startled them. It was the fire-control director near the top of the fighting mast. Smoke. Lots of smoke. It was their quarry.

The captain climbed to the foretop with his binoculars. He saw a long grey smear at the southern horizon. There seemed to be at least a dozen ships. The navigation officer, Lieutenant Petersen, who had pre-war service with the Hapag Line, estimated more than twenty. At 4:30 pm, a profusion of masts began growing against the blue-grey-gold of what remained of the lighted sky. Then the first silhouetted hulls appeared.

After scanning the array for any sign of warship escorts, Krancke mused aloud, 'Have they got no protection at all?'

'There's only one ship there with what strikes me as an unusual deck structure for a freighter,' said Petersen, with binoculars raised and pointing at the escort with his free hand.

'Looks like some sort of auxiliary cruiser,' said the captain.

'She's turning out of line now. I should say they've spotted us.'

'She's an auxiliary cruiser, all right,' said Krancke. 'She'll give her recognition signal in a moment. Whatever it turns out to be, repeat it once as though we are calling her.'

The German commander wanted the convoy escort to be in doubt about the *Scheer's* identity as long as possible so that he could close before opening fire. The distance now was about fifteen miles.

The auxiliary cruiser flashed 'M A G' in quick succession. According to Krancke, the *Scheer's* signal officer immediately sent an 'M A G' out as if he, too, were requesting an identification. 'But,' he said, 'the bluff failed.' (This exchange with Petersen, as recounted by Krancke in his book *Pocket Battleship*, may be partly fiction, since none of the convoy crews, *Jervis Bay* survivors, or *Scheer* sailors reported Morse flashes from the German ship.)[2]

Able Seaman Sam Patience took his quartermaster station at the wheel of the *Jervis Bay* at 4:00 pm The helmsman he relieved told him to make sure of the five-minutes-to-the-hour reminder to the officer of the watch.

Patience was a fairly big man, six-foot-one, and two hundred pounds. His long, boyish, blue-eyed face projected an assured, instinctive intelligence. Though barely twenty-one years old, his seafaring experience and action outmatched all but that of the oldest salts. He was born in the fishing village of Avoch on the northeastern coast of Scotland, the youngest of seven brothers, all of whom fought in the war (one was killed), and two sisters. His early life was dominated by the hard simplicity of Calvinist discipline. He left school at age ten, and at thirteen he followed the path of his father and brothers aboard a fishing boat. After several years of hazardous, low-paid toil, he foresaw a bleak future in fishing. Since he loved the sea and knew little else, he joined the naval reserve in 1938 and then the merchant marine. He served aboard cargo liners plying mainly between Britain, New Zealand, and Australia. Following a rare trip to South America, he was called up by the Royal Navy in August 1939.

Keen on winning a quartermaster rating, which would net him more pay and prestige, and which would give him the opportunity to get his hands on the wheel of a big ship, Patience was disappointed in being rated as an able seaman and sent to Chatham for training. He was assigned to the old battleship *Resolution*, and was aboard and out to sea before his uniform arrived. His ship participated in the Britain to Canada gold runs and twice returned from the dominion escorting the earliest empire troop convoys.

In April 1940 the *Resolution* was dispatched to Norway, and Patience was assigned to handle cordite charges in a magazine five decks below, where the men were required to wear felt slippers as a spark preventive. He had the good luck that none of the available slippers fit his size-twelve feet, followed by bad luck in being sent to an even lower deck in the shell room to work the hoists that carried fifteen-inch projectiles up to the guns. Still out of uniform, Patience experienced a string of bomber attacks, shell fire, and machine gun strafing.

In June Patience's well-travelled duds caught up to the ship after months of trailing him back and forth across the Atlantic, 'in a more bedraggled state than I was.' He laundered the duffel-full, donned his dress whites,

Able Seaman Sam Patience.
(Andrew Patience)

and for the first time felt 100 percent Royal Navy. His shipmates applauded his change from scruffy 'civilian' to crisp rating.[3]

Nautical to the bone, Patience regarded the 29,000-ton ship as a 'creaking old tub,' commanded by Victorian throwbacks with their style of harsh discipline. Once he was given seven days' punishment for griping about burnt potatoes. In addition to the Norwegian campaign, Patience was on the *Resolution* in a battle against an Italian fleet off the Balearic Islands and in the heart-breaking attack against their defeated French ally's ships at Oran. In late September, during a British assault on French ships in the harbour at Dakar, the 'old tub' was torpedoed by a submarine and seriously damaged.

Surviving all the *Resolution's* actions intact, the young able seaman finally transferred to Halifax and joined the breaking-in crew of the old, former American destroyer renamed *Sherwood*. He hated the unstable tin can and felt lucky two weeks later on being invited to join the *Jervis Bay* as an able seaman/quartermaster.

On his debut at the helm, Captain Fegen came over and asked where he'd been and what he'd done. The captain was especially interested in the new quartermaster's Norway experiences and in the actions against the French ships. 'He was a very alert man,' Patience said, and one who 'always seemed to be on the job.'

As the young helmsman stood at the wheel, confidently guiding the ship into that late afternoon of 5 November, he wiggled his toes and rocked to and fro, breaking in new, unlaced size twelves. The small, glass-enclosed wheelhouse was directly below the watch-officer's station on the open fore bridge. Communication between the two stations was through a speaking tube.

Patience noticed from the moment he took the wheel that the captain was on the port side of the bridge. Fegen wore what he had always worn on wintry North Atlantic duty: his charcoal-grey pea jacket, binoculars dangling on his chest. He appeared interested almost exclusively in the northern horizon. Occasionally, he'd raise the glasses, concentrate on a point for a few seconds, then sweep and resweep the confluence of sea and sky, and return to naked-eye scanning. Fegen had moved to the northern wing of the bridge because of the smoke report. His extreme level of alertness hinted that perhaps the seaplane sighting by Fellingham on the *Trefusis* four hours earlier had been relayed to him by Commodore Maltby. Patience had never before seen the captain's attention so fixed. He suspected something was up.[4]

The rest of the *Jervis Bay's* company were unaware of the subtle drama on the bridge. The officers and ratings tended to routine duties, taking care of personal things, trying to relax, or musing about possible U-boat and surface-raider attacks.

Able Seaman Fred Billinge, dark-haired and thick-eyebrowed, with a compact, deep-chested body that warned off any would-be troublemakers, went up to the wireless-relay room several times a day and caught the BBC's news broadcasts. He kept his shipmates informed about the blitz and other aspects of the war. The tide of the Battle of Britain had just begun to turn in favour of the RAF, but it was not an unambiguous fact at the time. The Luftwaffe continued bombing London and other cities. Although Hitler had secretly called off the invasion until spring, in Britain it was still believed imminent. Of more immediate concern was the horrendous rate of merchant ship sinkings; no one knew the U-boat packs' first 'happy time' was about to tail off. Billinge's report on 5 November, reflecting the BBC's minimisation of enemy action, was that few bombs were dropped and fighting continued in Greece.

Twenty-seven-year-old Tom Davison worried about his wife and daughter in Dover, right in the middle of the war. Tom Hanlon, a thirty-seven-year-old steamroller driver, felt lucky his wife had returned to her family in Wales with their daughter. Men from the especially hard-hit south of England and London spent continuous days and nights worrying about their wives and children, girlfriends, and other family members.

One seaman, a navy reservist, who was called up before the war started, was extremely apprehensive. The solidly built, laconic former policeman had told some of the crew that he had been involved in the arrest of some fortune-tellers shortly before his call-up. One of them had told him, 'You'll never see your twenty-eighth birthday.'

As his twenty-seventh year passed into its final days, he grew increasingly anxious. Now, just over seven hours were left. He was strung out despite the reassurances of his mates, who paid little attention to the possible effects of the prophesy, if fulfilled, on themselves.[5]

Visibility remained excellent. The clouds had not yet reached the southwestern horizon, and the late sun struck golden highlights off the sea surface and illuminated a grey curtain of precipitation far to the north. It was the calm before two storms: the onset of a North Atlantic low and the appearance of the *Admiral Scheer*.

Shortly after four o'clock, the *Rangitiki's* lookout, who was at the highest elevation among the HX 84 ships, sighted a mast at 328 degrees bearing. The sun set at 4:31. One hour of twilight remained. By 4:45 Captain Fegen and several officers who had joined him on the bridge identified the stranger as a warship humping down on them. But whose warship? Her superstructure and refitted control tower initially convinced some of the *Jervis Bay* observers that she was a *Rodney*-class battleship. Lieutenant Commander N L Pisani of the Royal Navy, a passenger on the *Rangitiki*, also recognised *Rodney* characteristics. But as the vessel drew closer, he reckoned she was not big enough to be a British battleship. Fegen and his officers, too, were weighing the significance of the size of the approaching warship. The captain decided not to wait for a positive identification.

The clock was a second or two before 4:55. He ordered, 'Sound action stations.'[6]

In the wheelhouse, Patience was aware of the increased activity on the bridge, but he did not know a warship had been sighted. The time was seconds before he was to give the watch officer his 020-degree-bearing reminder. As the clock reached 4:55 pm and he leaned ahead to the speaker tube, alarm rattlers rocked him back and jolted the ship alive. Some of the men immediately groused about another drill, but they were their captain's men and they broke into a controlled stampede to their action stations. Within moments, Petty Officer Walter Wallis stepped into the wheelhouse. Patience hollered: 'Quartermaster relieved. Chief quartermaster at the wheel. Course North, 82 degrees East.'

In his unlaced shoes, he slid down the ladder to the boat deck, dropped to the promenade deck, down to the well deck, ran to the fo'c'sle, and climbed to his position at the P.1 gun.[7]

Tom Davison. (Chris Davison)

Petty Officer Walter Wallis, RNR.
(Walt Wallis via Trevor Reeve)

Tom Davison and Jack Barker had decided they'd have *dhobi* sessions (a word for 'launderer' stolen from the Indian branch of the Empire). Davison finished his load, stepped into a bath, heard the alarm, pulled on his trousers and jersey, ran minus shoes to his mess locker, contorted into his pea coat on the run, still barefoot, and made it almost as fast as his mates to the P.3 gun between the aft part of the superstructure and the poop deck. His duty was to take deflection and elevation information from the transmitter and set the numbers on two dials.

The athletic Barker, washing his clothes in a V-necked football shirt, snatched up his duffel coat and raced up to the boat deck to his place at the starboard anti-aircraft gun. One of his crew realised they had no water buckets to flush down the deck in case of fire. Barker and two others ran to the bucket locker. No one had the key, and the petty officer in charge of that area was nowhere in sight. 'No time,' one of the men said, and he kicked in the door. Barker was shocked at the precipitate 'vandalism.' *There'll be hell to pay,* he thought. But they got their buckets and lugged them back to the gun.[8]

Able Seaman Everett Morrow, one of the nineteen Canadian crewmen, was at his job in the officers' mess. 'The first thing I did was shut the [watertight] doors to the engine room, to the galley, and to [our sleeping quarters],' he said. 'The last job I had was bringing in the injured from the outside deck to the sick bay.'[9]

Titch Appleyard was lounging in his bath, soaking off a stretch of deck duty, when the alarm sounded. The able seaman leaped out of the tub, water cascading off his body, and pulled on his coveralls and boots. His first destination was the mess deck for clean, dry clothes he had stored in a locker. Too late! The area's doors had already been sealed. Dressed appropriately for an arduous task, though soggy from bath water, he made it down to a sweaty after hold where he was in charge of five stewards manhandling 6-inch shells.

Quartermaster Wallis had no time to retrieve his inflatable life-belt from his cabin. The slim, dark-haired thirty-year-old with a finely drawn face dashed to the wheelhouse and took the helm from Patience. Big Hugh Williamson, the senior radio officer, thundered up from his quarters to the radio shack. The navigation officer, Lieutenant Commander George L Roe, had already manned the adjacent chart room. He beckoned Williamson through the connecting hatch and handed him a piece of paper marked with coded letters and numbers. 'Hold on to that,' he said, 'till you get the word to go.'

Williamson set himself up at the high-frequency transmitter. Richard Shackleton took over the medium-frequency radio. Two naval coders stood at the coding table. The four men were ready to respond instantly to a 'transmit' order.

Petty Officer Charles Castle entered the generating room, his battle station. It was just aft of the radio room under the bridge. Castle, one of the few active-service men on the ship, switched on the two generators that delivered power to the guns' fire-control system. He hooked up a 24-volt battery to each generator as an alternative power supply. Then Chief Gunner's Mate William Jervis and his five men took charge of setting up and testing all the fire-control instruments and links. That done, the gun crews were ordered to 'follow director,' meaning now they were responsible to the fire-control director. Using information from the director's and the range-finder's crews, they were to manoeuvre their vintage guns to the given elevations and bearings. Co-ordinated for each salvo, the guns were fired electrically by the director. The gun crews had to load and aim their weapons manually. The men knew the drill well. But the system was primitive.[10]

One man on the *Jervis Bay* did not hear the alarms jangling. Fred Billinge, the self-appointed ship's war correspondent, was in the wireless relay room catching the BBC news. When it ended at five o'clock, he tuned in to dance music for a few minutes. Stepping outside, he nearly was bowled over by a group of running men. He shouted: 'What's the panic?'

On hearing 'action stations,' he rushed to the S.2 gun. He then called to a nearby petty officer: 'What's the matter?'

'Don't worry about it now. It's only the *Ramilles* [a World War I British battleship] over there.'

Thus began the crew's orgy of ship identification guesses and anxious reassurances. Over on the P.1 side, one gunner declared it was the *Resolution*. Patience, who had just arrived breathless at his station, looked through a telescope fitted to the gun and, reminding his mates that he had served on that battleship, said: 'That's not the *Reso* [no 'tiddly top' on the funnel]. It's one of another class.'

The P.3 gunlayer, sighting through a telescope, said, 'It looks like the *Revenge* or another one of that class.'

A Fleet Reserve man, at the X gun on the poop, who was an experienced range-taker and user of warship silhouette charts, comforted his crew: 'It's all right. It's one of the 'R' class or the *Barham*.'

One creative anti-aircraft gun crewman decided the captain of the *Mopan* had changed his mind and was coming back to join the convoy.

No enemy ships were among the 'identified.' The 'R' class won the speculative competition hands down. All, of course, were wrong.[11]

Fegen leaned over the rail of the open fore bridge and bawled: 'Chief yeoman, make the challenge!'

Dennis Moore and three of his signalmen immediately Morse-flashed 'M A G.' While signalling, Moore tossed in his opinion: 'It looks like the *Ramilles* class, sir.'

The captain needed no more guesses. 'Does he reply?'

'No, sir,' said Moore.

'Give him the challenge on the 10-inch.'

The chief yeoman switched to the larger lamp, opening and closing its shutters. 'No reply to your challenge, sir.'

'All right, yeoman, give it to him on the 36.'

Moore laboriously resignaled the challenge on the big searchlight, which was mounted at the top of the bridge. Still no response.

By this time the *Scheer* had approached close enough for Lieutenant Commander A W Driscoll in the after gun control, binoculars to his eyes, to say unequivocally:

'That is a pocket battleship.'

Captain Fegen was born and nurtured to come to the decision he then made. As the men recalled—for many of them, more than a simple memory, it was seared into their beings—he had told them on taking command of the *Jervis Bay* that, if confronted by the enemy,

'I shall take you in as close as I possibly can.' He had no David-and-Goliath delusions. He knew his armed merchant cruiser was no match for a pocket battleship. He also knew his men trusted him. They were duty-bound, well-trained, and high-spirited, and on his orders they would accept whatever was in store for them. They would make up for the ship's limitations. Each man was important to Fegen. He was not one who took his authority over them lightly.

His concern for his own ship and crew, nevertheless, was second to his responsibility for the safety of the convoy's thirty-seven ships. Their survival was the *Jervis Bay's* paramount mission. Their cargoes were crucial to the only country standing up to the onslaughts of Hitler and his Axis partners. The future of a free Europe depended on Britain's success.

'Full speed ahead,' Captain Fegen barked into the voice tube.[12]

His command rolled down to Wallis in the wheelhouse. The quartermaster echoed the order to his assigned midshipman, who pulled the engine-room telegraph lever to full speed. As her twin screws turned up to their top rpms, the *Jervis Bay* began accelerating out of her first-rank central position up to her full fifteen knots. During the manoeuvre, the captain ordered a signalman to hoist the white/red/yellow/white flags for 'prepare to scatter.' Once clear of the convoy, he asked Commodore Maltby to have the convoy make a 40-degree turn to starboard. The *Jervis Bay* turned to port and bore straight at the enemy. Two minutes later, for an unknown reason, Fegen cancelled his request, but the emergency turn had already been completed.

The officers and petty officers on the port wing returned to their bridge stations. Fegen issued the 'commence firing' command. With the *Jervis Bay's* bow cutting directly at the *Scheer*, only four guns had a clear shot at the German warship, which was at least four miles beyond their range.

Roe poked his head through the hatchway between the chart room and the radio room and said: 'Get that [signal] off on the double.'[13]

At eighteen words per minute, Williamson and Shackleton filled in the missing numbers and began tapping out in code the message Roe had given them earlier (thirty wpm was possible, but the radiomen made sure they'd be received correctly):

TO: Any British Man of War

One battleship bearing 328, dist. 12 miles, course 208 from position 52 degrees 45 minutes North, 32 degrees 13 minutes West

Chief Yeoman Moore was on the bridge watching the intruder through the ship's telescope. At 5:15 pm, he saw flashes. He gulped and reported in a thin, tight voice: 'Gunfire, sir.'[14]

When the distance between the *Scheer* and the convoy's escort had closed to about ten miles, Krancke swung his ship to port so that both eleven-inch turrets and the starboard secondary guns were facing her adversary. The captain ordered the big guns trained on the auxiliary cruiser and the medium 5.9-inchers on what appeared to be a tanker close to her. Then he noticed that the convoy escort's captain had put his ship in front of a large two-funnelled cargo liner, begun generating smoke, and was heading straight at the *Scheer*. Likely, Krancke thought, the big ship (the *Rangitiki*) was the most valuable vessel in the convoy, possibly even a troop carrier. He'd get to her later. For now, his priority was the escort. He ordered a ranging salvo from the forward turret.

At 17,000 tons the MV Rangitiki was the largest ship in convoy HX84. *(via Mike Chappell)*

The recoil from the three stabs of flame and thunderclap jolted the pocket battleship back and sent unprepared men staggering. Twenty-three seconds later, Krancke saw 150 to 200-foot spouts appear almost simultaneously near the target and then erase themselves down to the surface.[15]

Just after Patience reached his P.1 gun, the order to make smoke came to his crew and to the S.1 position on the opposite side of the fo'c'sle. He and several others of the gun crew began preparing the dozen or so smoke floats lining the fo'c'sle rails. They had to battle rusty caps on the chemical tubes that emerged from the centres of the floats. When the men finally opened the tubes and lighted the contents, they hefted the fifty-pound floats to the rails and dropped them over the sides. Dense grey clouds rose, spread, merged, and streamed out behind the ship, providing the beginnings of cover for the convoy ships. The *Jervis Bay*, in front of the screen, couldn't have been more visible to the German fire controllers.

Patience returned to his gun, where he was the ramming number of the crew. His job, after the loading number put the one-hundred-pound, 6-inch shell in the breech, was to shove the shell home with a six-foot, cushion-topped pole. He was followed by a third man who placed a fifty-pound charge of cordite behind the shell and closed the breech. The gun was elevated and aimed by other crew members. After the firing, they had to lower the gun before reloading. Just as he picked up his ramming pole in readiness, a thought struck him about his family*: What a silly mug I've been. I haven't let them know what ship I'm in, and here I am in a fix like this.*

His brief reverie was interrupted by one of his gun crew shouting, 'Look, the bastard's firing!'[16]

As flashes appeared against the starboard silhouette of the warship, Commodore Maltby on the *Cornish City* raised signal flags (as Fegen had requested) calling for the 40-degree turn to starboard, away from the approaching enemy.

The anxiety of the *Jervis Bay* crew lasted exactly twenty-three seconds, when, with a sound like Samson tearing a canvas tarpaulin, three shells came down about fifty yards short of the bow and exploded just under the surface. Black-and-white-streaked geysers erupted as high as the top foremast. Heavy spray carried over to the P.3 gun crew. Their drenched faces turned inky black from particles of charred matter suspended in the water.

At the P.1 position, a sharp splinter from one of the shells created the first horror of the battle. As Patience stood at ready next to one of his gun's loading numbers, he heard a 'thunk.' He turned toward the sound and saw the man's blood-spouting torso and severed head fall simultaneously to the deck. Fighting off shock and revulsion, the young quartermaster turned away and fastened his attention on the breech of the gun.

Maltby then launched a series of Very rockets that signalled the convoy ships to 'scatter and proceed with the utmost speed.' R L McBrearty, second officer of the *Lancaster Castle*, later wrote: "'Scatter' meant just that. You were now on your own and had to find the best way out.' The only prescription in the scatter procedure was: deploy smoke floats as you go.[17]

10 Rain of Steel

WHEN Captain Krancke saw signal rockets rising from the *Cornish City*, he wondered who they were intended for. Were they a command for the ships to scatter? A signal to escorting warships on the out-of-view starboard side of the convoy? He wasn't sure, but risk or no risk, he would continue the attack.

As another, corrected, salvo roared out of both turrets, he saw small spurts of gunfire on the British merchant cruiser. They were feeble compared with the *Scheer's* discharges. But, the captain thought, the enemy's response was rapid and showed that they were ready for action and their gun crews were well trained. Their first two or three shells fell several thousand yards short, the probable maximum range of their guns. This helped Krancke to determine his first tactic: Pound the escort from beyond her range until she sinks or is beaten into impotence, and then execute his mission and go after the convoy ships.

A few seconds later, the deck of the *Scheer* was sprayed from a near miss. A freak charge of cordite in one of the *Jervis Bay's* old guns had given its shell a prodigious ride. Krancke was concerned and puzzled. Maybe the British ship had one longer range gun. Or she had no central fire-control and the guns were managed independently. Perhaps her gun crews would adjust their aim and soon range in on his ship. Then he saw the billows of smoke spreading and starting to merge, and he realised a scatter was under way. A random pattern of splashes no closer than two miles from the *Scheer*, apparently from the guns of the convoy ships as well as the escort, relieved the captain's anxiety.

The *Scheer's* second salvo hit just behind the on-coming escort. It was good bracketing. The British vessel was about 18,000 yards away, well within the range of the 11-inchers. But, at that distance, bows first, she was a very small target; to the naked eye, she looked like no more than a bell buoy at the horizon. Not only was the escort moving, but the pocket battleship was cutting perpendicularly across her path and, at the same time, rocking on the developing swells. It became quite tricky for the *Scheer's* gunners to put the shells where they wanted them. However, her fire-control and ranging systems were the best then in existence. Her third salvo hit the target. (In his 1956 book Krancke said the first strike was scored on the fifth salvo. None of the convoy observers remembered it that way.)[1]

In the radio shack, Williamson and Shackleton continued broadcasting their under-attack signal to 'any British man-of-war.'

The position of the *Jervis Bay* was hopeless. Captain Fegen prayed that the message might ultimately bring the Royal Navy down on the German raider. After a number of iterations, Williamson turned to Shackleton: 'Will you get my life-jacket, Dick? I've left it down in my cabin.' He continued transmitting as Shackleton went to their quarters below. The round trip took about two minutes. In that time, the third German salvo found their ship.

Chief Quartermaster Wallis in the wheelhouse was guiding the merchant cruiser straight at the enemy when his eyes filled with the flash and smoke of an explosion on the fore deck. He gritted his teeth and hunched his shoulders as he watched the steel fore topmast fall toward his station. At that moment, another shell came down behind him. The mast hit the deck heavily just short of the helm. In the split second before Wallis could finish thanking his stars for his lucky escape, he realised that the second shell had blasted the bridge just aft of him, but somehow left nary a crack in the wheelhouse windows. The two almost simultaneous close calls left Wallis with a sudden dread of being cut up by flying glass in the next salvo.

A largely accurate painting (by Montague Dawson) of the *Jervis Bay* early in her battle with the *Admiral Scheer*. The three starboard guns are visible, as are the P.1 on the fo'c'sle and the X gun on the poop. Actually, the *Jervis Bay* had only four lifeboats on each side. *(reproduced with the kind permission of the Furness Withy Group)*

In spite of the miracle of the windows, the second explosion did serious damage, putting the director, range-finder, and fire-control equipment out of action. On returning to the radio room with Williamson's life-jacket, Shackleton found that its port wall had disappeared, the transmitters and cables were gone, and, to his extreme distress, his long-time shipmate and the two naval coders were dead. Behind that carnage, Petty Officer Castle, who had witnessed the Japanese bombing and burning of Canton, choked through a thick swirl of dust and smoke in the generating room and discovered both generators were wrecked. The backup batteries were upended and leaking acid onto the deck. That left the ship's key instrumentation without power.

The worst of the damage from the first hits was that several officers were killed or wounded. Captain Fegen's left arm was nearly torn off at the shoulder. It stayed attached by virtue of his holding it in place with his right arm.

Shackleton climbed the ladder toward what was left of the upper bridge. As he reached the next to last rung, he saw Fegen above him, pain contorting his face, clutching his arm, blood spilling off his sleeve. Trying to appear calm, he reported, 'Wireless room is out of action, sir.' The captain acknowledged and groaned, 'Thank you...' His eyes glazed. He teetered momentarily and braced his hip against what was left of the railing. No more words came.[2]

As the commodore's Very rockets released the ships from convoy discipline, they began scattering to avoid the German guns. All thirty-seven of them revved up to top speeds varying from nine knots to sixteen knots. (A few captains removed piston rings— though it was unhealthy for the cylinders—and managed to eke two to three knots more out of their power plants.) At first, most of them headed for the smoke that light air from the southeast was wafting between them and the pocket battleship.

Captain W Fraser of the *Erodona* got the best view of the beginning of the attack. His 6,200-ton tanker, carrying a cargo of benzene, was in the convoy's most vulnerable position, the first ship in the first rank, closest to the approaching raider. While the *Jervis Bay* put herself in harm's way and drew most of the initial gunfire, the *Erodona* joined her sister ships in executing the co-ordinated 40-degree starboard turn away from the *Scheer*. On sighting the scatter signal, she immediately moved toward the comparative safety of one of the smoke screens being laid throughout the convoy. Before reaching cover, she, like several other ships, fired a few bravado rounds from her 4.7-inch gun. The captain steered her west, then

north, hoping that the pocket battleship would not go back to where
she had come from after concluding the attack on the convoy. (From
his ship's initial position, Fraser was able to provide the Admiralty
with an accurate account of the early action.).

The combination of independent manoeuvring by thirty-seven
captains, impairment of their vision by the smoke, and the gathering
dusk created chaos in the scatter. Several near collisions occurred. R
L McBrearty, second mate of the 5,200-ton *Lancaster Castle*,
carrying lumber and steel, said the captain and his officers decided
that every time they saw a gun flash they would turn the ship's stern
to it and make as much speed as possible. This and similar tactics by
other ships came close to producing an amusement-park bumper-car
effect. 'One ship,' McBrearty said, 'came so close to us going in the
opposite direction that we could hear them shouting to us as she slid
down our starboard side...I believe she was the *Rangitiki*.'

As the lumbering *Trefusis* was overtaken extremely tightly on
the starboard beam by a big, deeply laden tanker, H C Fellingham
expected his ship's plates to be ripped off. He could do nothing but
hang onto a railing and gape. P J Davies of the oncoming *James J
Maguire*, a 10,500-ton tanker filled with gasoline and kerosene, later
said: 'I was detailed to manoeuvre the ship, pick our way through
the scattering mass of ships. I had a few escapes from collision
which in workaday navigation would have taken my breath away.'[3]

In spite of the confusion and the German menace, many of the
ships' officers were awed by the sacrificial action of their escort. At
the first flash of the *Admiral Scheer*'s big guns, Davies started
looking around for the *Jervis Bay*. In a report, he wrote: 'At the sight
of her steaming in to sure slaughter to save the rest of the convoy I
felt...a glow of inspiration and defiance.'

Captain Fraser told an Admiralty hearing: 'What saved us from
the force of the shells in the first place was the *Jervis Bay* going into
action against the enemy.'[4]

The Williamson-Shackleton attack signal was picked up at Whitehall
in London. The initial response, as recorded in the Admiralty's War
Diary 'Situation Report' on 5 November 1940, was:

> At 2006 today [London time] JERVIS BAY escorting HX 84
> in mid North Atlantic signalled that an enemy battleship
> (ADMIRAL SCHEER) was in sight and reports that the
> convoy was being attacked were received. RENOWN,
> BARHAM, and destroyer escort were ordered to raise steam.
> AUSTRALIA was ordered to RV [rendezvous]...[with

HOOD, two other warships, and screening destroyers] who proceeded to cover the approaches to Brest and Lorient against enemy's return. 5 town class destroyers on passage to UK were ordered to spread to locate the ADMIRAL SCHEER, and three of which were nearest the position of attack were ordered to close Convoy HX 84 to rescue survivors and to attack the raider by night if opportunity offered. REVENGE was ordered to the Clyde and ROYAL SOVEREIGN to Halifax.[5]

None of the British warships named in this first response was close enough to the action to interrupt the *Scheer's* assault on the convoy.

One of the *Scheer's* first three broadsides resulted in a jolt to Captain Krancke. The violent recoil cracked the ship's radar crystal and put her key spotting and ranging device out of action. Now the Germans would have to depend on their stereoscopic range-finders and bearing directors. Though their fire-control system was degraded without the radar, it remained superior to anything the British had at that point in the war. With the smoke screens spreading and dusk deepening, the *Scheer's* ability to detect the convoy's ships was diminishing, and by dark it would be reduced to luck and searchlights. The opportunity to devastate the convoy now was problematical.

Nevertheless, the first hits on the British escort encouraged Captain Krancke. The merchant cruiser had to be neutralised without delay. He needed time to severely hurt the convoy before nightfall in order to achieve his mission of discombobulating the Royal Navy and disrupting convoy traffic in the North Atlantic. The *Jervis Bay* was a large ship and would not be easy to sink quickly, unless a shell entered one of her magazines and blew her bottom out. He ordered all of the *Scheer's* big guns to concentrate on the already burning merchant cruiser. Every six-gun broadside delivered nearly 2.5 tons of projectiles.

The sweltering 11-inch-turret crews, staggering from the roar and kickback of their weapons, had settled into a jouncing cadence. No sooner was a salvo on its way than the retracted guns sprang forward to their loading positions. Hydraulic lifts raised the 780-pound shells from the magazines into the turrets. They were shoved mechanically into the firing chambers, the breeches were closed, and another salvo was discharged before the previous one hit its mark. The gunners took as little as thirteen seconds between salvos. (The Mopan's captive crew, in a compartment just under the forward turret, were shaken and deafened by the cannonading.)

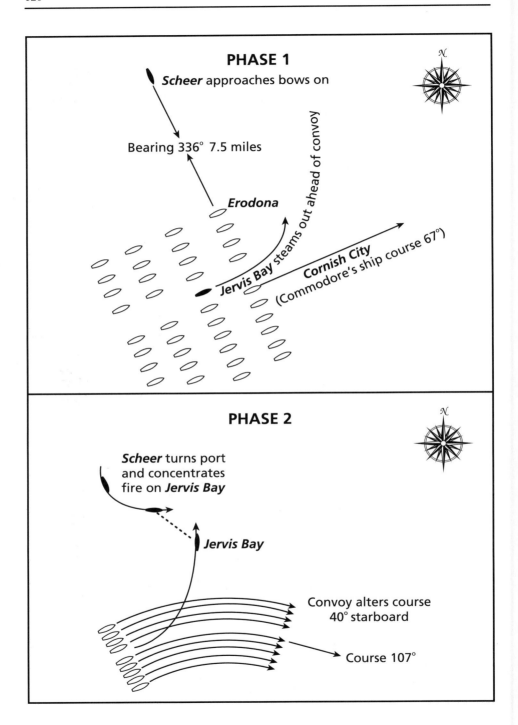

Four-panel sketch of ships' courses in the first ten to fifteen minutes of the battle.
(W Fraser/Chris Robinson)

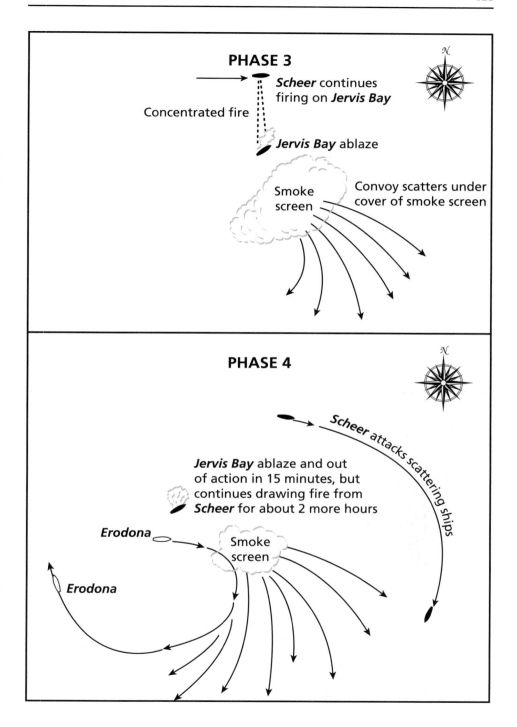

These four film frames were taken from film shot by a *Scheer* crewman with a 16-mm camera through a telephoto lens. They cover no more than the first fifteen minutes of the engagement: (a) Just before German shells hit her, the *Jervis Bay* (far left) is turning at full speed toward the *Scheer* as HX 84 convoy ships begin scattering and laying smoke. The fountain raised by a maximum-range convoy shell is at best two miles from the *Scheer*. (b) Burning and apparently out of control (since she is no longer bearing straight at the pocket battleship), the *Jervis Bay* is struck on her stern by an 11-inch shell. (c) Moments later, a three-projectile salvo explodes amidships on the merchant cruiser. (d) More hits and near misses and smoke obliterate the forward section. Some convoy ships continue their scatter in front of the early smokescreen. (*Bordkameradschaft* Admiral Scheer)

Brownish yellow smoke from the rapidly firing guns drifted back over the ship. Those not under cover had difficulty breathing, and only the fire-control crew and men at bridge level and higher could see the convoy. Information Officer H J Brennecke gave a running commentary on the course of the action over the ship's speaker system. The men heard that the British escort was heavily damaged and burning from the bombardment of the big guns and that the medium artillery (5.9-inch) on the starboard side had zeroed in on a tanker behind the merchant cruiser. The tanker (*Delphinula*) seemed to have been hit several times and was trailing flames and smoke. Obviously finished, she was allowed to disappear into a smoke screen.[6]

As the big shells crashed down on the *Jervis Bay*, a seaman on the fo'c'sle suddenly remembered it was Guy Fawkes night. 'I've always looked forward to the bonfires,' he told a shipmate. 'Not like this, though.'

Shortly after the first hits on the ship, the dark-haired, stocky Commander Roe, one of the few surviving officers of the shattered bridge, limped into the wheelhouse gripping his left thigh. Blood was streaming through his fingers. 'I've been hit,' he said. Wallis tied Roe's handkerchief to his own and, while keeping the helm steady on course closing the *Scheer*, he twisted them into a tourniquet and stopped the navigator's bleeding.

After Roe returned to the fore bridge, Wallis felt the wheel go loose in his grasp. A shell had smashed the hydraulic tubes leading from the helm to the motor that operated the rudder. The ship, with her engines racing, was out of control. He called up the voice tube to the bridge: 'Steering gear out of action.'

A decisive voice responded: 'Man the after steering position.' It was the sorely wounded Captain Fegen, who had mustered enough energy for the moment to regain his tone of command.

Wallis hurried out of the wheelhouse and descended to the lower bridge. The ladder down to the boat deck was gone. He took a breath, bent his knees, and dropped the twelve feet to the deck...no bruises or sprains. Some of the port-side lifeboats were burning. Shells kept exploding on and near the ship. The quartermaster heard zings and cracks and clangs of flying shrapnel. He presented as low a profile as he could, crawling to the end of the boat deck until he found a ladder to the well deck. Then he raced to the alternate steering position, located in a housing under the X gun on the poop deck.

The wheel he sought was in the forward part of a twenty-four-foot-wide compartment, whose curved after end conformed to the shape of the ship's stern. Wallis took hold of the helm and prepared to steer by the gyro and magnetic compasses in the space. But the bulkhead in front of him was blank and the side walls had no ports. He had no way of knowing where the enemy ship was. He called down the tube to the steering-engine room and asked the engineer-in-charge to connect to the after wheel. That done, Wallis called to the after control position, which would have to serve as his eyes. No response. Twice more. Not a squeak back up the tube. In all the racket of systematic destruction, the quartermaster did not realise the position had been hit and all its occupants were dead men. All he could do was steer blindly as straight ahead as he could...until Roe limped into the compartment and sized up the situation. The navigator stationed himself out on the poop and, with the ship's burning superstructure blocking his view ahead, he did the best he could to call course corrections to Wallis.[7]

Chief Engineer Commander Chappell, on hearing the primary steering was out of action, ran to the bridge, where he was killed by another German hit.

The guns, minus their central controls, now were the independent responsibility of each of their crews. Their rate of fire was slow because they had to go through a cycle of maximum elevation (45 degrees) for maximum range to nearly zero elevation for reloading, and back to maximum for firing. And it all seemed useless because the enemy ship remained far beyond the reach of their Boer War weapons. One of Patience's fellow crewmen on the P.1 gun cried out: 'We might as well stand here and throw bloody spuds for all the good we're doing.'

The truth was that as long as the *Jervis Bay* kept firing shells at the *Scheer*, Captain Krancke would focus his attention on her before going after the convoy.

The *Scheer* picked up speed and continued cutting across the *Jervis Bay*'s bow in order to concentrate the broadside of six big guns and four starboard medium-calibre guns against the escort. Krancke's course also was the beginning of the Wheel Principle's high-speed, ever growing spiral aimed at corralling and sinking the much slower convoy vessels.

In order to close the *Scheer*, Fegen now had to maintain a constantly shifting bearing to starboard that kept the ship's bow pointing several degrees ahead of the speeding raider. This skewed position of his ship made the *Scheer* visible only to the P.1 and P.2 guns and the X gun on the stern. The three old 6-inchers fired as fast as they could but still fell hopelessly short. The gun crews counted on the captain getting their slower ship close enough to reach the attacker. But the *Scheer* stayed out of range. For each futile, 100-pound shell they put into the air, two or three 2,340-pound German salvos reached their ship.

Early in the projectile exchange, the forward port side of the *Jervis Bay* caught most of the fury of the big guns. From bridge to bow she was a mass of twisted girders, bent and jagged plate, dead and wounded sailors, and flames.

Amid the fo'c'sle wreckage, Leading Seaman Tom Hanlon kept his P.1 gun banging away. The P.2, under Crackers Rushall, managed about ten or fifteen minutes of firing before its recoil mechanism overheated, jammed, and refused to spring back into the loading position. By then, the *Jervis Bay's* steering was out of control. Her bows slipped into a slow rotation to port, moving the P-guns out of firing position and bringing the ship's starboard side to bear on the *Scheer*. As the shift occurred, the gunner's mate on the fo'c'sle shouted: 'Port crews take cover! Starboard crews close up!' The starboard guns that still functioned picked up the firing.[8]

Hanlon went down to the sickbay with a splinter embedded in the left side of his jaw. He saw Surgeon Lieutenant Commander Tyrell George Evans, with a bloody bandage around his head, tending the casualties, calling for more supplies and pain-relievers. After Hanlon's wound was treated, he headed back to his gun. Able Seaman Everett Morrow, delivering a wounded man to the bay, paused next to the doctor and was sickened to see that 'half of his face was blown away.'

Before Hanlon returned to the P.1 station, Leading Seaman Tiddly Bonney, in the well deck below the silent gun, called to its huddled crew: 'How about the poor blighters in sick bay! Let's try to get them out.'

Patience and Tom Storey joined Bonney. The sickbay was under the port side of the remains of the bridge in what had been the *Jervis Bay's* passenger salon. They entered and were almost driven back by smoke. The sickbay had taken a hit and was burning. The doctor was bending over a seriously wounded man. Others in bunks lining both sides of the bay were shouting. Bonney told Patience and Storey to get a hose. They ran out the door, found a hose, and screwed it onto a hydrant on the well deck. Patience paid out the line from its reel, and Storey carried the nozzle to the sickbay. As he entered the compartment, the area lit up in a brilliant flash and the door slammed shut. Patience was left holding a severed hose. The door was impossible to open.[9]

It was like one of today's special-effects movies: so many horrendous things happening so fast...no time to understand them...no way to respond in a compassionate way...feelings come later, if you survive. Patience turned and hurried back to his P.1 gun on the fo'c'sle. Moments later, a shell glanced off the anchor winch that had broken down the year before and saved the *Jervis Bay* from the fate of her Northern Patrol replacement, the *Rawalpindi*. Somehow it released the anchor. Men on the well deck below heard the anchor chain begin clattering out the hawsehole. The ricochet hit under the S.1 mount and blew the gun and all but one of its crew clear off the ship. Patience, about twenty to thirty feet away, felt a searing pain just above his right hip and lost consciousness.[10]

In one madly courageous moment during the rain of steel, after the white ensign of the Royal Navy was blown off the top of the main mast, Midshipman Ronald A G Butler, a handsome, lively, enthusiastic young man, helped an unremembered seaman climb the rigging and nail up a replacement ensign. It was to be one of the last traces of the *Jervis Bay* as she later disappeared below the North Atlantic surface.[11]

Just after sending Wallis to the stern steering position and somehow defying several more hits on and near the bridge, Captain Fegen gathered what vigour was left to him and, aided by Dennis

Moore, descended the last remaining ladder from the starboard side of the bridge. Still grasping his nearly-severed left arm, he started back with Moore along the boat deck toward the after control position. He ignored the shell blasts and hail of splinters, and concentrated on placing one foot ahead of the other. As Fegen was passing an anti-aircraft gun station, Jack Barker got a close look at the captain's terrible wound. Fegen glanced at the young gunner. Unable to smile, he squeezed out the words: 'Keep at it, lad. Keep at it.' (To Barker, for the rest of his life, these brief words of encouragement were a branded confirmation of the strength and spirit of the captain and the *Jervis Bay* crew.)

The captain reached the after control compartment, but his wound prevented him from climbing into it. A God-damned ladder was undermining his authority. Looking about in extreme frustration, he saw that some cordite bags laid out for the aft guns had caught fire and were close to exploding under the poop deck. He called down Midshipman Butler—who had moved into the after control—and directed him to throw any loose cordite in the stern area off the ship. One of the men whose help Butler had enlisted picked up four 25-pound bags of the volatile powder and was staggering to the railing when a flaming fragment hit his burden. He disappeared in the explosion. The young junior officer, stupefied at first, then in a daze, returned to dumping the bags.

Still focused on protecting the convoy, Fegen chuffed out an order (to whoever could hear him) to drop more smoke floats off the stern. Petty Officer Castle, who had come aft following the destruction of his generators, took charge of the task. He gathered several men whose battle stations had been blown away and put them to work making smoke. Despite the rusty caps on the smoke canisters and the intrusion of exploding shells and shrapnel, they got twelve of them into the water.

'Good smoke screen, boys,' said Castle.

He looked back toward the captain...no sign of him. Nor of the control room. It had been blown out of existence just before Wallis called them from the aft steering position. While struggling with the smoke floats, Castle was unaware of the destruction behind him.[12]

Butler had got rid of most of the remaining cordite, and as he neared the after control, there was a 'blinding flash' and a sound 'like a thousand gongs.' As the only survivor of that explosion, he saw 'the man beside me literally burst into pieces.'

'I felt my face warm and wet, and looking down I saw my hands...red...with blood, and stuck on [my coat were] some utterly revolting pieces of flesh and gristle.'

The midshipman saw Fegen near the wreckage of the after
control room. The captain held his left arm 'cranked slightly across
his body with blood running over the four gold stripes on his sleeve.'
Again escaping a shell that almost had his name on it, Fegen was
now left with no control stations. He decided to see what he could
do forward. Then his luck ran out. He and Moore never made it to
the burning bridge. Second Radio Officer Shackleton saw them on
the deck, dead.[13]

Most of the *Admiral Scheer*'s men who could see the fires and
black smoke rising out of the British escort marvelled at the courage
and discipline that kept her crew fighting desperately to the end. The
German captain, probably without realising what it was at the time,
silently delivered the first eulogy to Captain Fegen: *That man has
the authentic Nelson touch,* Krancke mused. *He must be a
commander with such authority over his men that they're prepared
to follow him to certain death in a hopeless fight.*[14]

11 The Lower Depths

THE black squad in the engine and boiler rooms were tugged by two conflicting feelings. Their action station was below — hemmed in top, bottom, and sides by steel plate (thin as it was), grinding engines, roaring furnaces, and hissing pipes. The steel, the massive machinery, and the din filled them with a deep, irrational sense that they were protected from whatever was happening above. Yet they knew a penetrating shell could create a lethal hell in their compartments. Their only connections to the outside were a telegraph line from the bridge and four flimsy ladders to the upper decks. It was the self-deceptive comfort of their armoured womb that kept the black squad level-headed and efficient, while in a corner of their minds lingered the understanding that some ladders had to survive a shelling if they were to have a way out of a sinking ship.

Lieutenant A J Robertson was in his cabin when the alarm sounded. Twenty-seven years old, he had spent the last six years at sea with Shaw Savill, the *Jervis Bay* manager. His station was in a narrow passageway on the port side of the mess deck at the watertight hatch above the engine/boiler area. His team — two other engineering officers, three stokers, and a greaser — quickly joined him. Three such groups worked the *Jervis Bay* routine, alternating four-hour watches below. When the clanging started, the team that happened to be tending the engines and boilers remained there for the duration of the action. Robertson and his men, scheduled below on the next shift, took their places on the mess deck. Their job was to keep station unless and until they were needed in the propulsion area below. The third team took over fire-fighting duties throughout the ship.

Like virtually all of Fegen's men, Robertson's team was reliable and disciplined. But, having gone through many practices and several false alarms, they felt rather mellow. Unaware of the approach of an enemy ship, they thought they would be back in their bunks within five minutes. In less than that time, however, they were shaken by a great muffled roar. The ship shuddered, and the mess deck went black. They felt the *Jervis Bay* heel over and return to upright. Water washed over their shoes. It seemed to them the ship was sinking rapidly.

In a few minutes, an electrician brought them torches, and they were relieved to see it was only a hydrant that had opened and covered the floor with a few inches of water. They were not sinking. The engines were still running. Then the torch bearer, who had come from the deck, told them they were under attack by a pocket battleship.

Ever since the *Rawalpindi* was sunk by German battleships, Robertson had felt that the *Jervis Bay* would meet the same fate. He tried not to pass his heightened anxiety along to his team, though each of them surely had his own dire thoughts. While they were cut off from what was happening on the outer decks, at least they were above sea level. They were extremely frustrated waiting at the engine-room hatch while the ship was taking shell fire. More than for themselves, their concern was for the men in the bowels of the ship tending the two turbine engines and the ten chambers firing the six large boilers.

They understood what damage a shell could do to the ship's propulsion system and to the men in the lower depths. An explosion near the network of pipes could release scalding steam and cut power to the turbines. Holes opened in the furnace exhaust pipes or the funnel could obstruct the draft and produce blow-back—jets of burning oil and clouds of black smoke. A furnace struck by a shell would behave like an oversized flame-thrower. One hit on a boiler could cause a succession of boiler explosions, instantaneously destroying the propulsion rooms and everyone in them.

Among the black squad, such fears were held in check not only by the steel womb fantasy, but also by the continuous demands on their time during an action. Through the one-way telegraph, they were told what to do, not what was happening above. The bridge had no time for a blow-by-blow narration. The engineering crew's duty was to react to orders at once. In reality, their prospects were dismal.

After about a half-hour, during which Robertson's team on the mess deck had become aware of the pounding their ship was taking, the boiler-room officer opened the door and appeared in the passageway. Just after he told them, 'It's a shambles down there,' a shell penetrated the engine room and exploded inside the condenser. Sea water began flooding the entire propulsion area. It was a lethal hit to the machinery but, luckily, not to the men. The black squad clambered up the ladders, and all of them escaped.

When it became obvious to Robertson that there was nothing his team could do below, he went to a higher deck. There he got his first look at the destruction, raging fires, and bodies of shipmates. On the boat deck, as he crossed a grating above the engines and below a skylight, he paused to look down. Nothing was visible under what he estimated was thirty feet of water. Except for the two guns still functioning—neither of which could reach the enemy—all of the parts that made the *Jervis Bay* a warship were gone. Robertson overheard the captain's coxswain tell the senior surviving officer, Commander Roe: 'It looks like we've had it, sir.'[1]

The six men in the after hold's magazine were so insulated from the action outside that they did not know the ship was under fire. Titch Appleyard, the able seaman who had launched himself out of a bathtub upon hearing the action-station alarm, was in charge. He was a tough, five-foot-four, forty-three-year-old farm worker. He had a youthful face, and his skin and colour glowed with the freshness of a man half his age. Dripping water and dishevelled, he had met his crew of five stewards, whose job was to supply one-hundred-pound shells to the P.3, S3, and X guns. Appleyard had led them through trapdoors in the hatch that covered the after hold, down through three decks using pigeonholes in the bulkheads, into a small-arms magazine, then through a hatchway into their station, which was just over the bilge and the keel. It was as low as one could descend in the ship without inhaling sea water.

The space was fifteen feet square and seven feet high. Unlike those in some other armed merchant cruisers, its walls, floor, and ceiling were protected by steel plating. The walls were lined with four-foot-high steel racks holding the 6-inch shells. An electric hoist carried the shells up the full height of the hull to the well deck. The job for each steward was to place a shell in a cylindrical canvas bag and carry it to the hoist. When the hoist held five bags, Appleyard clipped their handles together for stability and fastened them to a hook on the hoist cable. He then telephoned Able Seaman Frank R Mallon, who manned the hoist motor, and told him to pull up the load. Mallon pushed the up button, and the hoist ground slowly through the three decks, pushed past two trapdoor covers, which automatically shut to prevent shells from falling back on Appleyard's crew, and onto the well deck. He unfastened the shell bags and separated their handles. Shell carriers lugged the individual bags to their gun crews. When they returned for another shell, they dropped their empty bags by Mallon's feet. He sent the empties down to the magazine on the hoist's return trip.

Appleyard and his five stewards had sent up about fifty shells when the lights went out and the trapdoors refused to open. He tried telephoning Mallon. 'Don't you want any more bloody shells?' There was no answer. The line was dead. So was Mallon.

Without torches or standby lighting, the men in the magazine were stone blind. They ruminated on what malfunction might have cut their electric power. They heard some deep, muffled sounds, which could have come from practice shots or a heavy sea or some loose equipment in another part of the ship. But the hull was not rocking much. Appleyard finally said: 'We'll have to get a move on. There's something wrong. We'll have to get out.'

They felt their way in the dark to the small, watertight door between the magazines. One by one they passed through the opening, entered the small-arms space, and climbed its ladder through the steel cover. It was still pitch black when, again in single file, they began using the precarious series of pigeonholes to climb through the three decks and reach the trapdoors above the small-arms hoist. It was a good forty feet up. Appleyard, the first to arrive, found that the trapdoors would not budge. Apparently they were locked from the outside or jammed by something heavy. Nobody responded to his pounding and shouts for help. Appleyard turned face down and called into the dark: 'All right, boys, we'll have to go down again. We're doing no good here.'

The first man into the small-arms magazine stopped and yelled up: 'Hell, we're taking water.'

By the time the sixth man, Appleyard, entered the magazine, they were over their hips in the rising flood. It finally dawned on them that the shells they'd been feeding to their three gun crews had been used in anger and that the *Jervis Bay* was in trouble. Although one of the ship's rules of action was, 'Do not leave the magazine by way of the shell hoist,' Appleyard said the hoist shaft was their only chance. With the hatch between the two magazines now under water, he led the way, holding his breath and ducking into the shell room.

Again they felt for pigeonholes, carefully picked their way up, and reached the hoist trapdoors. This time their banging and shouting were heard, and the doors were pulled open. They had been below for nearly an hour, about three-quarters of it in rumbling blackness. On deck, the five stewards, inexperienced sailors all, did not survive the battle.

Appleyard, a veteran gunner, went forward to lend a hand. The first thing he found was the holed deck where the S.1 gun and its crew once were. The P.1, on the wrong side of the ship now, aimed across the bow with its crew firing blindly toward where they hoped the *Admiral Scheer* would be. Then Appleyard reported to Commander Roe that the aft magazines and guns were out of action.[2]

12 Someone Else is Getting Away

CAPTAIN Krancke admired the grit of the merchant cruiser's captain and his men. Less than a half-hour after the *Scheer's* 11-inch artillery opened the one-sided duel, the *Jervis Bay* was blazing wreckage. Yet, or so it appeared to the German commander, one of her guns continued firing. Flashes on the stern apparently caused by explosions of the few remaining cordite bags suggested to him that the gun on the poop deck was still operating. He could not feel free to concentrate on the convoy ships until he was satisfied that the *Jervis Bay* was no longer a threat. The hope of a lucky hit must be spurring the British captain on.

Krancke believed that if his ship were hit in a vital area, slowing her down, her chance of surviving a Royal Navy hunt would be severely compromised. Therefore, he kept his big guns on the tormented escort. He did not know that the enemy captain was dead and all his weapons had been silenced.

Krancke directed his 5.9-inch guns to a freighter whose small-calibre weapon was popping wildly and who was laying much of the smoke that was slowly spreading in front of the convoy. After a few near misses, the captain ordered all armaments—heavy, medium, and light—to zero in on the drifting *Jervis Bay* whose stern was still 'firing' at the *Scheer*. The crushing salvos to her port side opened new holes in the hull and shattered what was left of her superstructure. Fires now covered nearly the full length of the convoy escort. Though she was in a decided list, she was not settling. *What in heaven's name*, Krancke wondered, *was keeping her afloat?*[1]

The *Jervis Bay* began leaving a trail of forty-five-gallon barrels. They popped up to the surface from some of the big holes the *Scheer* had opened below her waterline. They were the first to leave the hull from among the thousands that had been loaded into the merchant cruiser's many empty spaces during her refit five months earlier. While the ship was torn, mangled, split, and burning, most of her interior holds were sufficiently intact to retain their buoyant 'cargoes.' It almost looked as if the only way the *Scheer* could put her under was to blow her apart compartment by compartment. She should have sunk in less than thirty minutes, but the empty, watertight barrels served their purpose and kept her afloat for over two hours, more than half of that time under heavy or medium fire from the German warship. Krancke's concentration on the moribund ex–cargo liner could have been redirected more effectively to the slowly scattering ships of convoy HX 84.

As long as the *Jervis Bay* continued trying to close the *Scheer*, her port side faced the enemy ship while her starboard guns were forced to remain silent. Fred Billinge and his S.2 gun crew amidships on the well deck were frustrated and angry. They could do nothing but crouch and huddle for protection while their ship was being destroyed systematically. Unfortunately, they were vulnerable, since their gun shield was no barrier to shell splinters.

In the periphery of his vision, Billinge saw his sight-setting crewman slide down from his platform and become a lifeless pile on the deck. He looked about and found that the entire gun crew had been killed. His attention had been focused on the incoming shells, most of which were hitting the forward port side of the ship. In the terrible racket around him—the explosions, the almost continuous hits of flying splinters, and the shouts from other stations—Billinge had not heard any sounds from his stricken men even though some of them were within arm's reach. Why in hell was he still alive, untouched? He got out of the S.2 area in a hurry. He had no time to mourn the loss of his men or even to pass into a state of shock. Like other motivated *Jervis Bay* crewmen whose stations had been put out of action, he went to see if he could help out elsewhere.

He found several men fighting a fire under the bridge. The clothing of one of them was in flames. Danny Bain, like Sam Patience a youthful Scottish ex-fisherman, began tearing off the victim's clothes. Bain's uniform caught fire. But he kept on trying to save his shipmate. Billinge knew the man was beyond help. He dragged Bain away to a gun tub—a wooden half-barrel filled with water for soaking the head of the ramming rod—where he doused the burning sailor with handfuls of water, then rolled him on the wet deck to squelch any smouldering material. The entire upper part of Bain's body, including his face, was scorched. Billinge thought about the pain the slightly built youth would have to endure if he were to go over the side into salt water.

Leaving him to the care of the remaining fire-fighters, the sole survivor of the S.2 gun crew headed aft with three other men. Another crewman whom they met while moving sternward told them Paymaster Ernest V White had taken hundreds of pounds of currency out of the ship's safe and laid it out in his cabin. As they approached the paymaster's quarters, Billinge felt heat from fires under the deck plates passing through the thick soles of his boots. The door was locked. One of the men, a stoker, asked for a lift to an open porthole so that he could see what all that money looked like. Billinge and the others boosted him, and as he inserted himself into the opening, the cabin became an inferno. He was sucked into the space. The others had no way to retrieve him.[2]

Sometime after the drifting *Jervis Bay* came about, while her starboard side was being hacked away by the *Scheer's* artillery, Patience had returned to the P.1 gun following his and Tom Storey's aborted attempt to drag a fire hose into the burning sickbay (see Chapter 10). The ricochet that blew the S.1 gun and its crew off the ship nearly put an end to the young able seaman at his post on the other side of the fo'c'sle.

Patience regained consciousness with water splashing on his face. The first thing he saw was Crackers Rushall kneeling in front of him, saying: 'Come on, come on. You'll be all right.' He felt his neck. There was blood. Patience wondered what had happened to him and how badly he was wounded. He didn't know where he was. At first, he did not recognise the man helping him as the crew leader of the jammed P.2 gun. He carefully moved his head, then touched his neck again. He was relieved to find that the wound was no more than a nick and the blood was only oozing. Another half-inch or so and the sliver would have severed his carotid artery. He reached up and got an assist to his feet.

A bit woozy, Patience held on to the remnants of a pipe for support. Looking around, he was puzzled to see that he was on the well deck. Rushall told him that his body had suddenly dropped alongside the P.2 gun. After a moment's thought, Patience realised the explosion that had knocked him senseless had blown him aft and down fifteen feet to the steel well deck. The ex-fisherman had no memory of any of it. But he could imagine himself vividly on that unconscious flight. What he could not understand was how he survived with only a scratched neck, a headache, and, as he later found out, splinter wounds in his head and his hip.[3]

Tom Hanlon, in charge of the P.1 gun, which was impotently facing away from the German raider, moved about his distressed ship to help anywhere he could. He discovered that all the guns were silent. Some, like his own, were now on the wrong side of the ship and had no target. Others were incapable of firing or their crews were dead. Hanlon noticed that the starboard side of the boat deck was less maimed than the port. By then, Krancke had shifted the *Scheer's* big guns to fire on convoy ships but kept the medium and smaller artillery trained on the stubborn merchant cruiser. The starboard was beginning to experience direct hits. Already, the lifeboats on that side were thoroughly punctured or burning and unseaworthy.

The *Jervis Bay* was being pounded by 5.9-inch explosive

Certificate for Wounds and Hurts

These are to Certify ~~the Honourable the Minister of National Defence of the Dominion of Canada~~ that

(Name in full)	(Rank or Rating)	(Official No.)

SUTHERLAND PATIENCE   A.B. R.N.R.   X 19818 A
SAMUEL

belonging to His Majesty's ~~████~~ Ship "JERVIS BAY"

being then actually upon His Majesty's ~~████~~ Naval Service in

Here describe the particular duty. HAMMER P1

"Injured" or "Wounded." †Date. was* Wounded on† Nov. 5" 1940 by

Here describe minutely the nature of the injury sustained and the manner in which it occurred—as required by articles 1207, 1318, 1354 of the King's Regulations.

the explosion of an 11" shell from the enemy which landed on the forecastle as she was putting a smoke float over the bow. He was blown on to the well deck. He sustained 2nd degree burns on the left hand involving the dorsal and palmer surfaces. Also a puncture wound in the Right abdominal wall by a piece of shrapnel 2. Loss of entire lower denture

‡"Sober" or "not sober." He was‡ ~~Sober~~ at the time.

Age about 21 years. Born at or near Avoch, Scotland Height 6 ft. 4½ ins.

Personal Description. Hair Brown   Eyes Blue   Complexion fresh

Particular marks or scars. { Rear right hip about 2" long —

Date 7/ Nov. 27.   19 40

Senior Surviving
Signature of ~~Commanding~~ Officer of Ship.   N E Wood

Rank Lieutenant RNR (T-124)

Signature of person who }
witnessed the accident. }

Rank

Signature of }
Medical Officer. }   R. Webster

Rank Surg. Lt RCNVR.

NOTE:—The grant of a Hurt Certificate to a Petty Officer or Man is to be noted on his Service Certificate.

C.N.S. 3435
5m—2-40 (4133)
N.S. 815-9-2455

Sam Patience's certificate for Wounds and Hurts. *(Andrew Patience)*

projectiles, fragmentation shells bursting over the ship, and fire shells meant to ignite anything flammable that was not yet afire. Wooden fittings that had not been removed in her first refit, remaining timber deck planks, and thick layers of paint provided fuel for the incendiaries. Every overhead explosion produced a vicious spray of splinters that, on hitting the ship, sounded like a clangourous string of Chinese firecrackers. The 'light' bombardment intensified, and Hanlon squeezed himself into a bulkhead partition for protection against flying debris and shrapnel. He couldn't understand how he had escaped injury or wounds in his meanderings around the ship.

To the right of his shelter, the gun chief saw Lieutenant Commander Keith M Morrison limping along the deck, also passing miraculously unscathed through the barrage. Morrison, a former chief officer for the Orient Lines, was a kind of utility officer on the *Jervis Bay*, charged with a variety of duties including crew morale. Though he was a fatherly forty, he had an open, boyish, handsome appearance. His hair was blond and his eyes a vivid blue. Now his face was grim and grimy. A bloody rag bandage with long, loose ends was tied around his right leg. Hanlon, an experienced seaman, stopped him and brought up a matter that had increasingly nagged at him and other crew members over the last half-hour: 'What's the sense of them banging away at us like this, sir? They know we're finished.'

Morrison gazed at the gunner for a moment. Then he said, 'Well, while we're getting it, someone else is getting away.'

The laconic response to Hanlon's anguished question was not a brush-off. It reflected the officer's deep understanding of the reason for Captain Fegen's pledge to take his ship as close to the enemy as possible. It renewed his desire and strength to live through the unmerciful pasting the *Jervis Bay* was taking. He realised that in his own small way he was contributing to the escape of many HX 84 ships, every one of them needed desperately at home. The loss of any cargo ship or tanker would be felt in Britain's fight for survival against Hitler.[4]

Before Morrison had started forward to the boat deck, he, Commander Roe, and Quartermaster Wallis had met outside the destroyed aft control station. The ship was without propulsion, steering, communications, and operating guns. Her entire superstructure was burning. There were fires below. Many holds and compartments were filling with sea water. The battered ship was kept from sinking only by the remaining barrels. However, the longer she stayed afloat, the more men were being killed; God knew how few were left alive. The two officers and the chief agreed that saving men was the most urgent, and indeed the only, thing left to do. The *Jervis*

Bay probably would stay afloat for some time, and she would continue to distract the Germans and draw fire. Roe, in command since Fegen's death, said: 'Pass the word...Abandon ship.'

Each of them made his way forward to different areas of the ship. Roe took the port side of the boat deck. Patience, still at the silent P.2 gun with several other men, looked up to the fo'c'sle and saw the acting commander lean down and shout: 'It's every man for himself now, boys.'

Morrison, after reminding Hanlon about Fegen's convoy escort philosophy, told him of Roe's decision and moved on to pass the 'abandon' order to anyone he could find. The time was about 6:15 pm The destruction of the *Jervis Bay* had been going on with occasional interruptions for an hour.[5]

13 Every Ship for Herself

THE tanker the *Admiral Scheer* had targeted with her 5.9-inch guns, just after she began drilling the *Jervis Bay* with her heavy artillery, was the 8,100-ton *Delphinula*, carrying a load of gasoline. When the first few ranging shells straddled her, the tanker captain devised a ploy that deceived the Germans into stopping the attack on her. Like many other HX 84 ships, the *Delphinula* dropped a smoke float that drifted behind. Then the captain had a second float lashed to her starboard quarter and ignited. It glowed intensely red and produced a heavy stream of smoke from the deck, giving the impression the ship was burning. Three more floats were tied to the port side and lighted at short intervals. As the 'flaming' tanker passed behind the *Jervis Bay*, the shelling ceased. When she reappeared, still 'afire,' Captain Krancke decided to waste no more shells on her. The *Delphinula* soon entered the convoy's spreading smoke screen; ultimately, she escaped to the north, as did several other vessels.

A few minutes after firing some desultory misses at an annoying gun-popping freighter and then returning all of the *Scheer's* armament to the *Jervis Bay*, Krancke swung the main turrets to the largest convoy ship while continuing to jab at the escort with the other batteries. The new target was the *Rangitiki* with her seventy-five passengers. At the beginning of the scatter, the German commander had seen the *Jervis Bay* race between the big cargo liner and the *Scheer* — obviously, he reckoned, singling her out for protection. Suspecting the *Rangitiki* was a troop carrier, he now selected her as the most urgent target. In the gathering dusk, he had to leave off the other ships for a time and sink her immediately.[1]

Some of the *Rangitiki* passengers were helping as lookouts for U-boats. Dr. Firth (given name missing) had just finished his watch and was in the lounge when he 'heard two sharp cracks.' He thought it was a follow-up to the *Jervis Bay's* anti-aircraft practice earlier in the day. He went out on the deck for a look and saw dirty geysers rise out of the sea between his ship and the escort. For a moment he believed it was an air attack, but suddenly he realised the nearest enemy airfields were far out of bomber range. A nearby steward gasped: 'Good Lord, it's a naval action.'

Then he saw two flashes on a low grey shape near the northern horizon. Firth and other onlookers saw the *Jervis Bay* draw ahead and turn toward what obviously was an enemy ship, firing as she went. People were shouting: 'Go at 'im, boy!' 'Give it to 'im!' 'That's the stuff!'

Then the raider scored some hits, and the *Jervis Bay* slowed down, although she kept firing. Moments later, Firth saw an 'enormous [blue-crimson] spout of flame...and a huge column of black smoke' blow out of the escort. He 'knew then it was a hopeless fight.'

After Commodore Maltby's scatter signal, Captain H Barnett rang for maximum revolutions, but a cracked piston held the *Rangitiki* down to thirteen knots. He manoeuvred her through a gradual starboard turn in an effort to keep the raider astern. Unlike many other HX 84 captains, Barnett told his 4.7-inch gun crew to hold their fire. While a few out-of-range shots might have raised the spirits of the crew and passengers momentarily, gun flashes on the *Rangitiki's* poop surely would draw the enemy's attention to their ship. Instead, he ordered two smoke pots dropped and moved at all available speed toward the screen laid by ships ahead. Just before the *Rangitiki* reached its cover, the *Scheer* sent over a ranging salvo. It fell about five hundred yards short on the starboard side. As the *Rangitiki* began dissolving like an apparition into the outer smears of smoke, a second flight of three 11-inch shells straddled her amidships. The next salvo got within fifty yards, showered the bridge with blackened sea water, and sprayed splinters into forward areas of the cargo liner. The concussion lifted a formation of dishes off the pantry shelves; they all came down together with a shattering crash that gave the cooks and stewards a start.

Firth, who had gone below to be with his wife and the other passengers, heard 'a terrific bang and a thud which shook the whole ship.' It was on the starboard side, prompting them all to move to the port alleyway. Firth guessed it wouldn't be of much use if the next salvo hit the *Rangitiki*, but it might give them a bit of extra chance. Waiting was a strain. Somebody started them singing, with 'Roll Out the Barrel' as the first of a medley.

Captain Krancke believed the *Scheer's* ranging salvo had exploded on the presumed troop transport's stern. (Several of the convoy's captains also thought the *Rangitiki* had been hit.) Chief Gunnery Officer Alfred Schumann fired again at the fading target, hoping that she would not alter her course behind the screen. The smoke lit up in a way that convinced the Germans they had scored another hit. Though they suspected the 'wounded' ship by then must have changed her bearing, Krancke ordered a final salvo for good luck before they stopped firing at the ghost.

The *Rangitiki* increased her arc to the starboard once she entered the smoke until she was heading northwest to safety. When the flashes of gunfire, which looked like heat lightning in the black southern sky, ceased later that night, Barnett set her course to Liverpool. Without the distraction of the *Jervis Bay*, he later said, the raider 'could have picked off the ships of the convoy ships one by one.'[2]

The *Scheer* then turned her attention to some of HX 84's slower ships. But it was after 6:00 pm, and little more than the last faint day glow remained at the southwestern horizon. Her spotters found two, barely visible dark grey silhouettes in the twilight. Her big guns sought the larger, unidentified ship and the medium artillery took on the 3,000-ton *Andalusian*. No hits were observed on either target.

Krancke climbed down from the upper command post on the fighting mast and returned to his bridge. The overall action had been under way for more than an hour, yet he could claim no confirmed sinkings, not even the tortured escort ship, which by all logic should have gone down a half-hour before. The captain's attention continued to be diverted by the blazing hulk of the *Jervis Bay* and the occasional flash of exploding cordite charges. He betrayed an irrational anxiety about the impotent ship. He wanted her out of his sight. The *Jervis Bay* was the most visible object in the darkened battle zone. Krancke sporadically ordered his gunners to pepper her, while at the same time increasing his attention to the scattering cargo vessels. Had Captain Fegen lived to assess the effect of his close-to-the-enemy tactic, his severe face surely would have broken into a slightly crooked grin.[3]

When the German commander finally decided to concentrate on other targets, he dropped the 'wheel' tactic in view of the ship's dysfunctional radar. His intent was to race southward where many of the slowly dispersing merchantmen were, charge into their midst, and pick them off as he found them. Spotting in the dark required men with extremely sharp senses, animal-like instincts, and searchlights. The scheme presented a double risk, increasing the possibility of a collision (crashing into a tanker could be a disaster) and putting the raider within range of the convoy's guns. Despite the small calibre of these weapons, and as ill-trained as their gun crews probably were, a lucky hit could damage a critical function on the *Scheer*.

At 6:11 pm, a dim shape loomed up at short range. It was the heavily laden, 7,900-ton *Maidan*, with Captain C L Miller in command of a crew of seventy-one Indians and nineteen Europeans. Under a dead-weight cargo of iron, steel, copper, brass, solder, and trucks, she had no chance. All the *Scheer's* starboard armament opened up on her. Krancke gave the freighter no opportunity to return fire. Almost at once explosions occurred along the length of her hull and superstructure. She was smothered in flames. Within moments her fiery bow rose, and she sank with all hands like a cast-iron anchor, issuing an intense hiss and a huge, evanescently red cloud of steam. The *Maidan* disappeared with all hands like a full moon behind an advancing storm.[4]

Early in the scatter, the 5,200-ton *Trewellard* had reached the most easterly position of the convoy ships and was the closest to the raider. She was bound for Liverpool with nearly twice her weight in essential goods: 5,400 tons of steel, 3,000 tons of pig iron, and twelve American-made fighter planes. Her captain, L Daneil, swung her around to the southwest and had the gun crew ignite five smoke floats and throw them overboard. Then he made the mistake of ordering them to open fire on the enemy warship. The *Scheer* now was on a twenty-knot course, southsouthwest, about four miles off the freighter's port side, beyond the range of her old 4-incher.

The Germans at first did not notice the popgun freighter. They had been focused primarily on the *Rangitiki*, which quickly took cover in the Trewellard's smoke screen, and they were still distracted by the *Jervis Bay*. It was after finishing off the *Maidan* that they turned to the other iron and steel carrier, locating her by the gun flashes on her poop. Daneil's men had got off nine shots before Krancke's first salvo struck her after hold, blowing pig iron into the sea and silencing the gun. Another shell entered the port side of the engine room and lifted chunks of machinery out through the skylight. The captain tried to communicate with his engineers, but none was left alive. The *Trewellard* began taking on water and settling by the stern.

Knowing how fast she could sink, Daneil gave the 'abandon ship' order. One of the lifeboats had been destroyed. The other three were successfully lowered, although the No 1 boat capsized, then righted itself. The No 2 boat with nine men and the No 3 with twelve aboard got away cleanly. The captain and three men made it into the remaining boat. Daneil turned back and looked at his ship. The raider for unknown reasons had stopped firing at her for a while. He told others to hold fast while he reboarded her and quickly searched for survivors. He found two severely injured men. The first was T Turley, the 'donkeyman' who operated the ship's auxiliary engine. His upper body and arms were scalded. Second Engineer W Gow had suffered extensive burns. With aid from one of the other men, he fitted the injured crewmen with flotation belts and hefted them into the lifeboat.

In capsizing, the No 1 boat had lost its oars and sails. The men pulled up floorboards and used them as paddles to get away from the starboard side of their ship, whose dead-weight cargo, like the *Maidan's*, was accelerating her submersion. The lifeboat's progress was sluggish, and the men were in danger of overturning and being sucked down with the ship. By then, the drift of the freighter had turned her starboard to the *Scheer*. The raider opened fire again, and the bridge burst into flames. The four healthy survivors in the lifeboat, including Captain Daneil, in the direct line of fire, dug the floorboards into the water as fast as the Keystone Kops in a Mack Sennett silent movie. About thirty shells penetrated the ship. The No 1 boat was about 150 yards off the stern of the Trewellard when the freighter's bow suddenly rose, and she plunged below the surface. She carried the bodies of fourteen crewmen with her. Turley and Gow did not last long. They were buried at sea off the lifeboat.[5]

About an hour into the scatter, with darkness setting in, the 8,100-ton tanker *San Demetrio*, bearing eastsoutheast and loaded with 11,200 tons of aviation fuel, faced a collision with an unidentified convoy ship. The helmsman took her hard to port and managed to slip by the other vessel. Now she was heading eastnortheast, her bows set square at the raider.

The *Admiral Scheer*, after her encounter with the *Trewellard*, had renewed her high-speed southerly search for more convoy ships. The wind was rising and the sea turning dirty. Air began strumming on the superstructure and around the lines. An upper observation post reported to the bridge: 'Shadow ahead. Second shadow beside first.'

The Germans identified the 'shadows' as a 10,000-ton freighter and a 14,000-ton tanker. The smaller vessel seemed to be the easier target, and the *Scheer's* medium guns opened fire. Krancke wanted to be sure the tanker did not get out of range, but the bigger ship turned tail at top speed and left a boiling wake behind. The captain was forced to play his hand. He switched the 5.9-inch guns to the tanker and followed up with the big guns. Krancke described the scene in his book *Pocket Battleship*:

> Seconds later a terrific mass of black smoke and a great sheet of flame leapt upward. Then spear after spear of flame shot three-hundred feet and more into the air...Flames were licking up the masts, running along the bridge and racing towards the ship's bows....Direct hits had been scored on oil tanks and they were exploding one after the other. Further direct hits were scored in the tanker's sides along the water line and everything went very swiftly. Rockets were shooting up from the bridge and bursting in the sky above the inferno...
>
> All those on board the *Scheer* who could watch the terrible work of destruction saw the tanker settling deeper and deeper into the water until the waves began to lap over both stern and bows. That target was settled and attention

was now turned to the...smaller ship...which was already burning amidships...Both big and medium guns now opened up on her, scoring hit after hit, and the *Scheer* sailed on leaving her burning furiously and heeling over rapidly.[6]

This lurid account of the clash with the *San Demetrio* is at odds with the British version. Krancke, with the disadvantage of limited visibility, could only grossly estimate the tonnage of his prey at nightfall. Also, every exploding shell or flaring tank of aeroplane fuel or burning section of superstructure appeared exaggerated in the darkness and the distance. Two convoy ships certainly were there, having just averted a collision. While the other ship's fate is something of a mystery, the *San Demetrio* took a beating, though according to her officers' statements it barely resembled Captain Krancke's perception.

In a report to the Shipping Casualties Section of the Trade Division in London fifteen days after the encounter with the *Scheer*, the *San Demetrio's* chief engineer Charles Pollard and second officer Arthur G Hawkins (neither identified with specific quotes) told their story:

We increased to full speed, about 13½ knots, and altered away [from the raider but] we were balked by other ships in the convoy.

I (probably Hawkins) went aft and opened fire with the 4.7-incher, but I only fired two shots because it was getting dark and the firing was giving away our position and the captain ordered me to cease. We prepared four smoke floats and dropped them over the side, and they worked very successfully.

We now changed our course to ENE (apparently due to the near collision) and when I went onto the bridge I could still see the raider who was now on our port quarter at a distance of about eight miles, and consequently just a blurred shape. However, he opened fire on us with a salvo which fell clear on our port side. The next salvo went right over our ship, but he registered a hit with the third shell which struck us on the bow about two feet above the water line. It was quite dark by this time.

Captain George Waite, convinced that his tanker was about to become a petrol-fuelled bomb, told the third officer to instruct the crew verbally to abandon her. As they lowered the boats, the shelling

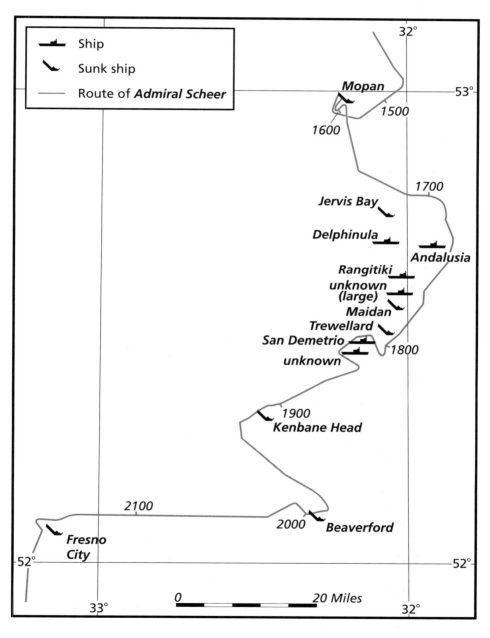

The battle during the afternoon and night of 5 November 1940, showing the *Scheer's* route and the ships that were sunk. *(Chris Robinson)*

grew heavier and splinters were everywhere, although, according to Hawkins, none of the shells hit the vessel during the abandon procedure. Three boats got away. The men in the No 1 boat, including Hawkins and Pollard, lost contact with the other two. According to the report, again probably in Hawkins's words: 'With the raider [now] at a distance of only five or six miles, he registered a direct hit on our ship with a really heavy salvo, and within 10 minutes of our abandoning her the *San Demetrio* was blazing furiously. Whilst in our boat, we almost collided with another vessel which loomed up in front of us. I don't know the name of the vessel, but it was the next ship to come under the raider's fire and [she] was seen blazing.'[7] (The *San Demetrio* ultimately was reboarded by the men in the Hawkins-Pollard lifeboat. Their saga is detailed in Chapter 17.)

The *Scheer* re-established her southwesterly track and continued hunting. There were ships to be sunk. Also, there were collisions to be avoided. For a while the Germans found nothing in the dark. By the same token, they were grateful that no convoy vessel blundered into them. With every minute spent combing the sea, the spread between convoy ships was growing. The bridge officers and the men at the lookout stations were alert, with senses vibrant and pupils open to the faint reflections from the night sky. At twenty-three knots, it was hard to perceive a dim shadow or a revealing sound with the rising chop of the sea surface slapping against their ship's hull and with the zinging and howling of the wind through the deck structures. If only they had the on-board skills and the parts to repair their radar!

One of the spotters barely made out a low-lying silhouette to one side. Krancke quickly brought the *Scheer's* port side around to confront the dark form. The bridge area became silent as the captain squinted through his glasses. He reckoned it was a freighter of about 7,000 tons. 'Searchlight ready?' he asked.

'Searchlight ready, sir.'

'Guns open fire as soon as [the target is illuminated],' he ordered.

'Very good, sir,' said Gunnery Officer Schumann, who figured the captain was using the searchlight to conserve on tracer shells.

The light was turned on, and its intense white beam lit up a freighter plugging along about two miles off the port beam. Krancke saw men on her bridge moving fast, some heading for the charthouse and others climbing down the ladders to the main deck.[8]

Captain Thomas F Milner, along with the other HX 84 masters, tried to anticipate the *Scheer's* moves. Like the Royal Navy planners who were now plotting out the search for the *Admiral Scheer*, he figured that after the attack on the convoy the German captain would take his ship home to Kiel or to a captured French Atlantic port, such as Brest. If Milner took his *Kenbane Head* west, he thought, it would be their best chance to get as far away from the *Scheer* as possible. His decision was based on no more than a roll of the dice. As it turned out, he was wrong. No convoy captain was inside Krancke's head; each had to make an immediate course decision and then leave the outcome to fate. The ships that went north escaped with no more than nicks and bruises from early in the battle. Milner and the captains who chose one of the other three directions placed their ships in jeopardy.

The German commander, whose pocket battleship could run at twice the speed of the fastest convoy vessels, at first tried to round them up the way a mounted cowhand would gather his herd. At first, he had driven the *Scheer* south, then looped east and south, then, because of the dark and his disabled radar, he swung to a southwesterly course, the beginning of his flight to avoid Royal Navy hunters. Everyone was playing with fate that night.

The *Kenbane Head's* officers and crew were feeling lucky. Far to the north they saw the burning *Jervis Bay*. They were stupefied by a huge explosion on the *Maidan*, followed by blackness and silence. Closer, a bit east of north, the *San Demetrio* was afire. Milner, his first mate Bill French, and three other men winced as the nearby *Trewellard*, beset by rapid-fire shell hits, broke into a series of fires and then flamed out as her bows rose and she sank. These sights gave the men of the *Kenbane Head* empathetic horrors. However, all of the unfortunate ships were to their north and east. They felt that they were out of harm's way. They did not expect the pocket battleship to come their way.

The 5,200-ton freighter, carrying a general cargo, suddenly was bathed in blinding white light. Before Milner and his men had a chance to react, 5.9-inch shells began hitting the ship. (Krancke saw a gun on the poop deck and, in his morbid fear of the *Scheer* taking any calibre of shell, he ordered a salvo from his big guns.) The cargo ship's steering gear was disabled immediately, her radio antennas destroyed, the gun blown away, and the magazine set afire. Several shells exploded in her engine room. Her funnel was blasted open. And big holes were torn along her hull above and below the water line. The starboard lifeboat was destroyed. (Krancke reported that an enemy shell exploded just off one side of the *Scheer*. Twenty or thirty yards closer, he said, and it would have hit the bridge. Reports from the *Kenbane Head* did not mention return fire.)

Milner brought his crew together at the bridge deck by the port lifeboat just as the final German salvo struck the ship. Several men were wounded. The lifeboat was lowered with all of the assembled crew aboard and immediately began to ship water through shrapnel holes. Those who could climbed back aboard the listing *Kenbane Head*, an arduous struggle with the ship tossing in the rising sea. Some of them heard a forlorn cry, 'Can I come down?' It was the lookout in the crow's nest; they had forgotten about him.

Apprentice Gerry Crangle raced below to his cabin and retrieved a photo of his girlfriend. Chief Steward Jimmy Dickey also managed to get to his room, for his overcoat. Bill McBride, an able seaman, found a life jacket for Apprentice Norman Walsh.

Under Milner's direction, the men pushed a raft over the side. They discovered, to their surprise, that the two jolly boats were undamaged. These small, unprovisioned boats, used primarily for recreation and each fitted with two sets of oars, were lowered and lashed to the raft. The men distributed themselves between the raft and the jollies and rowed their makeshift catamaran away from the ship. Many of them were lightly dressed, especially the engine-room and galley crews. As they pulled past the sinking lifeboat, they looked in and saw two dead stokers, clad in undershirts and trousers. They were a few hundred yards away when the *Kenbane Head* sank. Two of the forty-four-man crew were known dead and five were unaccounted for. The time was about 7:30 pm in the windy, frigid North Atlantic.

About eight hours later, with several of the men in severe shock and unconscious, the burning *San Demetrio* drifted down on them. She was listing and obviously unmanned. One of the shivering crew suggested that they board her. Though the prospect of heat was inviting, Milner vetoed the idea.[9]

The *Scheer's* 11-inch-gun crews took an on-station break, hoping for another victim. Inside the tight turret chambers the heat was stifling, and the men's faces were smoke-blackened. Sweat left dirty white patches and trails on their foreheads, cheeks, and necks, and down their backs. Some were resting against the walls of the chamber spaces and some were squatting. The big, gleaming breechblocks, each containing a shell, were closed and ready to fire. The next batch of shells were in the automatic lifts that had brought them up from their magazines. Empty brass casings from the expended ammunition rolled around and clanged together as the sea mounted. Instruments, controls, dials, levers, and other advanced gear contributed to the crowding of the chambers. The men did their jobs as if they were part of the apparatus. Indeed, they were assigned numbers in place of their names.

While the pocket battleship was strong enough to withstand the recoils of her big guns, she could not do so without pain. As Krancke saw it: 'the upper companionway on the starboard side looked almost as though it had a direct hit. Doors had been lifted off their hinges, flooring was torn up and broken, [and]...paint had flaked off bulkheads and was lying over the carpets.'

After a while, one of the lookouts spotted another dark shape. Alarms clanged throughout the ship, and gunners took their stations. The captain rang for full speed. Instead of a searchlight, he ordered incendiary shells, which lighted up the quarry when they hit it. He made out that she was a fairly large ship with a tarpaulin-covered deck cargo, possibly timber. He called for salvoes from the big guns.[10]

The 10,000-ton freighter—carrying a heavy load of maize, meats, cheeses, aluminium, copper, munitions, and chemicals in her holds and a load of timber on her deck—had been transmitting details of the battle. She was on a southerly escape course. Suddenly, out of the blackness, a bridge officer saw flashes, then fiery trails of incendiary shells coming straight in. In a few seconds the shells began hitting the ship. Fires broke out. Then she was ripped open by a salvo of 11-inch explosives. The captain of the doomed vessel sent out a message: 'it is our turn now. So long. The Captain and Crew of the SS Beaverford.'[11]

Krancke heard the Beaverford's final message as his big guns registered three hits and his medium artillery sixteen hits. He saw the cargo ship settle until water covered her decks. But that was as far as she submerged. Apparently the timber cargo was propping her up. Rather than waste any more of his dwindling supply of shells, he ordered a coup de grace: 'Torpedo tube No 8, fire.'

Nearby men felt a bit of a kickback as the torpedo left the ship and disappeared into the black water. The ride seemed to take forever, accustomed as the crew were to shells reaching their targets in seconds. Some of them began to think it was a miss. Then the torpedo struck. As viewed from the Scheer, there was a subsurface glow, followed by a huge internally lighted geyser. The silence was eerie. After a few seconds, the roar of the explosion rolled over the onlookers. The torpedo had hit the ship's forward section and the explosion raised her bow out of the water. No one knows what the captain and crew of the Beaverford were doing at that moment. All went down with the ship as she heeled over and plunged, torn bows first. The time was 8:30 pm.[12]

Krancke felt that he had completed the first phase of his mission to sink British merchantmen and disrupt operations of the Royal Navy. The attack on the convoy had lasted more than three hours, and the Scheer had used up a third of her heavy ammunition (220 shots) and half of her medium shells (550). The Royal Navy could be expected to have already mounted a massive search for her. Their ships probably were converging on the battle scene and moving to cut possible escape routes. Krancke's task now was to put as much due-west distance as possible between his ship and the British searchers.

At 9:17 pm, as the gun crews relaxed after their exhausting battle, the 'action stations' alarm jolted them back to their posts. The bridge lookout had sighted a ship of about 8,000 tons running just to starboard and parallel to the *Scheer*.

'At a range of less than 3,000 yards the guns opened up again,' Krancke later said. 'The big guns alone scored four direct hits.'[13]

Captain R Lawson of the *Fresno City*, a 5,000-ton freighter riding low under an 8,100-ton load of maize, brought her up to maximum speed as the convoy began scattering. He manoeuvred past the slower vessels ahead. After overtaking all but three or four of the others, he began altering his ship's course to starboard in 10-degree increments until she was heading back toward North America. Captain Lawrence of the *Briarwood* watched as 'the *Fresno City* passed us at fourteen knots with her crew waving to us and she steamed away to the westward.' The last ships she passed were the *Danae II* and the *Pacific Enterprise*. Then, Lawson reported: 'The *Beaverford*, bearing 110 degrees [eastsoutheast], was attacked and set on fire, distant about 10 miles...A few minutes before this attack took place, another vessel was attacked bearing 020 degrees. I altered my course at this time to 225 degrees with...engines working at utmost speed. The reflection of gunfire had been seen at intervals in the sky to the northward...At [9:40 pm]...without anything having been seen, suddenly a searchlight was directed upon my vessel by another ship close to the starboard quarter. Travelling at high speed, this vessel opened fire from about 200 feet.'

Lawson must have grossly underestimated the enemy's range, probably due to the blinding brilliance of the raider's searchlight. At two hundred feet, the *Scheer* would have caught splinters from her own exploding shells and she would have been a huge target for the merchantman's 4-inch weapon. Actually, the German guns were fired from nearly two miles in rapid succession rather than salvoes. Six shells penetrated the fore and aft engine rooms and four different holds. Fires broke out where the shells hit, the engines stopped, hatch covers were blown off, and the starboard wing of the bridge was demolished. With the alarm system disabled, Lawson instructed his first officer, First Mate S Payne, to muster all hands and prepare to abandon ship.

After waiting on the remaining section of bridge for five minutes, the captain descended and looked over the starboard side, where he saw a lifeboat that had been lowered to the water. It was empty. As he started forward to search for crew, the second mate, Mister Gleghorn, approached with eight men. He had been below escaping the shrapnel and had not heard about the muster. Lawson left them by the boat station. He found two severely wounded men, Able Seamen J J Mackie and N J Finnis. D R Smith was dead. Fourth Engineer J W Hopper and Junior Engineer W R Muir were on station in their wrecked engine room. The port lifeboat and the chief officer were missing.

Lawson and the engineers helped the injured men into the starboard boat and made them as comfortable as they could with blankets. Boarding was difficult due to the rising wind, snow, and swells. Thirteen seamen, including the captain, made it into the boat—apparently one man had been killed while waiting for Lawson's return from his search. They were on the windward side of the ship, and for a while it seemed that they could not put space between her and their boat. Finally, with the extreme effort of the crew of the racing shell, they pulled ahead of the drifting, burning freighter. There, they discovered Payne and twenty-two men in the port boat, which had an easier time of it on the sheltered side. The boats were tied together with a length of rope that soon parted, and they lost contact with each other in the dark and the increasing gale.

The *Fresno City*, still blazing, remained visible until she sank at 3:35 am.[14]

Krancke, now sure he had seen his last HX 84 ship, kept the *Admiral Scheer* on a westward bearing at full speed for a while and then swung her southward toward a rendezvous with her supply ship *Nordmark* near the Tropic of Cancer. It would take several days' sailing, if they managed to avoid British pursuit.[15]

14 Into the Icy Sea

MOST of the men who jumped into the sea that night could hardly breathe due to the cold shock. They were in subarctic water at a temperature of about 49 degrees Fahrenheit. The convoy had sailed through pack ice the day before. This and the worsening weather was the environment the remaining men on the *Jervis Bay* faced as they abandoned the burning, listing wreckage of their ship.

Canadian Everett Morrow, from Guelph, Ontario, was an able seaman whose regular duty was serving meals and bussing tables in the officers' mess. Immediately on hearing the 'action stations' alarm and shutting three watertight hatches, he helped put smoke floats over the side. Finally, he went to the outer decks to find wounded and injured men and take them down to the sickbay. He was away from the medical area when it was destroyed by a German shell.

Upon hearing Lieutenant Commander Morrison pass the 'abandon ship' order, which gave all hands leave to get off the ship any way they could, Morrow hurried to the No 1 lifeboat. It was badly holed and unserviceable. He found a cork float on the deck and slung it over one shoulder to supplement his life jacket. Then he checked the other lifeboats—all destroyed.

Someone yelled, 'Let's go and get those rafts over.'

Morrow joined about thirty men behind the funnel at the life-raft position. One of the two timber platforms was a full ten by fifteen feet, supported on six forty-gallon drums. It was held down by heavy sandbags intended to prevent it from drifting away should the ship be sinking. The other raft, originally of the same construction, was severely damaged and up-ended, with parts blown off, but it was capable of supporting several men.

As the *Admiral Scheer* continued pounding the *Jervis Bay* and new explosions wracked the guts of the stricken merchant cruiser, Morrow, Morrison, Tom Hanlon, and about a dozen others started to launch the shattered platform. Torn and dangling sections of superstructure were further shredded and blown into the surrounding water. The men tied a line to the raft and, with shell splinters cracking and clanging all around them, they dragged it to the port rail. During their struggles, several of them were struck and fell dead or wounded to the deck.

'I was very lucky in not getting hit,' Morrow later said. 'People alongside me got killed. It was devastating.'

The dead and wounded were pulled out of the way while the remaining sailors manhandled the half-raft overboard. In dropping down the hull, it smashed into the gangway platform and incurred more damage. When it finally hit the water, it was reduced in size to ten feet by six feet, with four, possibly five, drums missing. It started drifting about, never far from the ship. Some of the men managed to get down the rope directly onto the remaining planks. Others jumped into the freezing water, swam for it, and climbed aboard. Morrison held back, and Hanlon asked, 'Aren't you coming with us, sir?'

'No,' said the officer. 'I'll see what I can do to get some of the others off.' It was the last Hanlon saw of Morrison.[1]

As he was about to leave the ship, Hanlon came across a wounded Canadian crewman. He got on the rope first so that he could assist if the man's strength failed on the way down. They went down as far as they could, then dropped into the water. Hanlon helped the Canadian swim to the raft, which by then held about a dozen sailors, and they got onto it. Then a shout came from up on the deck: 'Wait for me. I can't swim.'

'Come down the rope,' Hanlon yelled, 'and we'll pick you up.'

'No, I'm not coming,' the man cried back. 'I tell you, I can't swim.'

The men on the raft were in no position to help their petrified shipmate. Morrow, without the patience to wait his turn on the rope and not prepared to bail out from the height of the boat deck, sprinted down to the main deck and took the still-formidable drop of twenty-five to thirty feet to the water. He plunged so deep he feared he'd never come up. Stroking and kicking with all his strength, he breached the surface, drew in some breaths, swam to the raft, and climbed on — one of the last men allowed aboard the truncated platform. It was overloaded, with seventeen survivors standing in water over their ankles. They looked as if they were on a sandbar just under the surface, but the sea floor was about 10,000 feet below. Others were swimming around the raft begging for a place. But the possessors felt that squeezing even one more rider into their space would swamp or overturn them and bring disaster to all.

There was a more imminent danger they faced. The raft was in a current flowing toward a hole in the hull. Though it was too big to pass through the opening, it could be held fast by the force of the water cascading into the ship. In that static situation, they could be hit or upended by German gunfire, or be blown away by an internal explosion, or be sucked down with the *Jervis Bay* when she sank, as inevitably she would. They agreed that the best thing they could do was to try and force their way out of the current and edge alongside the ship toward the bow. It was hard to make their maimed timber-and-barrel contraption move without proper oars. The men on the perimeter of the raft paddled frantically with salvaged pieces of floating wood, thrashed at the water with their arms, pushed against the side of the ship, did anything that gave them a bit of movement. They finally cleared the hull and then, exhausted, they paused as the sea continued building.[2]

The full-sized raft, which somehow escaped the bombardment with a few nicks, became the centre of attention of twenty-five or thirty men. After hefting the sandbags off the platform, they found that it was too heavy and awkward to carry or even drag. They managed to bring it upright on one of the shorter ends and then let it topple its fifteen-foot length onto the deck toward the gunwale. It took tremendous effort. They repeated the procedure until they put the raft over the starboard rail and into the water, steel drums down, timber deck up. As happened during the launch of the first raft, several of the labouring men were cut down or wounded by shrapnel.

In order to reach the platform, survivors had to leap the 40 feet from the boat deck into the black water or else, like Morrow, run through flying shrapnel to a lower deck for an easier drop. They had to make sure they came down near but not on top of the platform. Many crewmen left the ship that way. Others were afraid to jump. Ironically, a considerable number of the men, who chose the seafaring life, could not swim. Some of them had no intention of plunging into the Atlantic Ocean. In their desperation, the non-jumpers must not have retained the clarity of mind needed to understand what was in store for them if they went down with the ship. It was a kind of delusion that sometimes occurs under life-threatening duress. In any case, the raft was already near capacity.

Midshipman Butler, still on the *Jervis Bay*, came across the senior surviving officer, Commander Roe, on the port side of the boat deck. 'Shall I carry on, sir?' he asked. 'Go. Good luck,' said Roe, whose left trouser leg was bloody from an early salvo splinter. Butler stared at the officer for a few seconds, saluted, and moved off. He may have been the last man to see Roe alive.

The most expedient move for the confident midshipman, considering conditions on the ship, was to go off the starboard side near the stern. He climbed the rail, stood on the gunwale, made a standing broad jump into the deepening darkness, and hit the choppy surface rump first. After an arduous rising-and-falling swim half the length of the ship, he saw the intact raft and shouted above the noisy water. He was pulled out of the sea, one of the last survivors to board the platform. Butler caught his breath and pounded blood back into his freezing hands and feet. He looked around and estimated about forty men covered every square foot of space on the raft. It was so crowded that most of them were standing.[3]

Jack Barker had been left to himself at his anti-aircraft gun station on the boat deck when the rest of his crew, with nothing to shoot at, were taken away for fire fighting and debris-clearing. Alone and inexperienced, the nineteen-year-old from Harlesden, Middlesex, shuddered under the pounding his ship was taking. Though he would never forget Fegen's words of encouragement as the wounded captain passed his station, Barker was for the moment in a daze. His sense of reality had drifted off like a dandelion seed, and he found himself fantasising: *This can't be happening to me. It's not me going through this at all.*

Someone shook him: 'Come on, give us a hand and get this raft over.'

'Has "abandon ship" been given yet?' Barker asked.

'Don't stand there arguing. Come and get this raft over.'

That sharp response jarred him out of his reverie. Now he had something to do. He strained with the others and finally got the big raft into the water. The hard work and success of the effort brought back his adolescent aplomb. He found others who were still dazed and unable to jump. They, too, needed a firm shaking up. Sensitive to their feelings, having himself just emerged from a delusional mist, he managed to get some of them to go over the rail. When one of the cooks said he could not swim, Barker took off his own life jacket and put it on the man, who then jumped into the water.

The young gunner was a strong swimmer. He wisely removed his heavy boots and warm duffel coat (which could soak up water and drag him under), and clad only in trousers and his white football shirt, he went over the side. The air was cold, the water frigid. He overcame a momentary breathing paralysis and lit out for the raft with powerful strokes. Currents had pushed it against the ship. Leading Seamen James Wood and Tiddly Bonney and others on board managed to slide the raft along the hull and beyond the stern. By the time Barker arrived, the platform was jammed with men and surrounded with others about three deep. He figured that there were some forty men clustered around the perimeter. Those closest to the raft held onto the strapping and edges, while the others, Barker included, grasped the bodies or clothing of those in front of them. The encircling mass in the water looked like a clump of huge barnacles in the lurid, undulating light of the fires eating at the *Jervis Bay*.[4]

No one saw the portside jolly boat during the early part of the abandonment. It was tucked away on the main deck. The men scrambling up to the lifeboat and raft areas on the boat deck had forgotten about it. Fred Billinge and another gunner were down on the well deck collecting planks for a little raft they'd decided to lash together for themselves. However, they felt it was more urgent to find some wood and throw it overboard for a wounded cook to hold onto. The cook had been hit in the back by splinters as he climbed out of the forward magazine, after having carried out Lieutenant N E Wood's order to flood that compartment. They found a Jacob's ladder that they hung over the side to help the man down to the water. Just then they spotted the jolly boat. It had a hole in the stern, but it appeared seaworthy.

Petty Officer Charles Castle, who also had spied the 18-foot boat, got there first and organised some men to lower it over the side. They stopped its descent just below deck level and helped several wounded men into it. Then they let it down to the water. Castle, Titch Appleyard (who had led his ill-fated crew from the after-magazine to the deck), and several others went down the davit's rope falls. The little boat drifted a bit, and the last several men had to drop into the water. Appleyard, with two shrapnel wounds to his head, one of them above his right eye, tore his right hand in his slide down. He swam to the boat and climbed aboard.

Billinge had been among the first to spot the empty jolly boat. At a glance, he could see it filling with men. But his self-imposed priority was to aid the wounded cook. He shook his head and, with a touch of bitterness, thought, *There's been a proper rush for that.*

When he looked back, the cook was gone. He peered over the side and saw him standing on the rope-and-wood ladder halfway down the hull. He climbed down, stopped just above the man, and told him to drop into the water. The man refused.

'There's plenty of wood down there to hold on to,' he urged.

The man would not let go of the ladder. Angered by the cook's stubbornness and upset by the potential cost to himself, Billinge leaped past the immobile man into the water. His London Passenger Transport Board conductor's coat was immediately saturated and began dragging him under. He undid the buttons as fast as his cold, slippery fingers could manipulate them, and shook and pulled himself out of the heavy garment. His sea boots interfered with his swimming progress, and he took them off, too. Freezing now, he stroked as hard as he could and reached the overloaded boat. Billinge lifted himself halfway over a gunwale and lay there shivering and exhausted.

Wood, the *Jervis Bay*'s third officer, was in the boat, as were Lieutenant H G B Moss, Crackers Rushall, and Fred Gibbs, another London bus conductor. As senior officer, Wood took charge and had the men, two on each of the four oars, row away from the ship. The crowded dory rode low in the water, down almost to its gunwales. Every pull on the oars pressed the rowers' backs and elbows against the squeezed-in non-rowers. In spite of their discomfort, they were less wet and in a less precarious place than the men jammed on the rafts. According to Billinge's watch, which stopped after he hit the water, the time was about 6:30 pm[5]

The *Admiral Scheer* continued firing sporadically at the merchant cruiser, whose stern still produced misleading, gunfire-like flashes from exploding charges of cordite. It was about 7:00 pm, three-quarters of an hour after the 'abandon ship' order. On board the *Jervis Bay*, Sam Patience was still a bit woozy from having been blown down to the well deck. The shrapnel wounds in his right hip and leg and his head hurt, as did the burns on his left arm and hand. Suddenly, he was aware that he was the only man left near the P.2 gun station. He decided to move aft to see if any lifeboats or rafts were still there. But he could not find a way through the wall of fire spanning the wood deck and the superstructure.

How are you going to get out of this, Sam? he thought, weighing the daunting facts that German shells were exploding on and near the ship, splinters were zipping around him, the *Jervis Bay* was sinking, and he did not know how to swim. *Use your loaf,* he urged himself. He looked around and saw one other man, Bill Greenley, also a Scottish fisherman. They seemed to be the only ones alive forward of the bridge. 'I'm determined to get out of this,' he told the strangely placid Greenley. He went to the carpentry shop under the fo'c'sle and found a sack of wood shavings. He carried it back and told Greenley he was going over the side with it. As he lifted the sack across the railing, it split and the shavings fluttered in the wind down to the sea. Had Patience not been an optimistic, confident young man, the loss of the sack might have been a crushing blow.

No longer dazed, he scanned every surface that was visible to him. When his eyes lit on the well deck's after bulkhead, he could swear he saw a life buoy on it. How could others have missed it? He limped over to the hanging apparition and found out why it was still there. He could not pull it loose from the strong wood slats holding it in place. In a last go at it, the aspiring quartermaster grasped the casing, burnt hand and all, and with every ounce of strength in his legs, back, arms, and fingers he ripped it from its moorings. He lifted the red and white buoy away from the slats and found it sticky with fresh paint. It was a bit weird to him. The new paint seemed to embody some kind of significance, but he was too busy to give it much thought.

Greenley was waiting when he returned to the P.2 area. Patience said: 'Bill, come on, this is our last chance.'

'No,' Greenley said. 'I can't swim.'

'Neither can I. But I'm going over the side.'

'No, I'm not coming.'

Patience regarded his fellow fisherman with resignation and pity. Greenley was in one of those unreality spasms. There was no time to argue or to attempt to force him overboard. With the life buoy tucked under his right arm and about to jump, Patience noticed a line dangling into the water. Acting precipitately, he grabbed it in his burnt left hand and held the buoy under his right arm. As he began slipping down, he discovered that the 'rope' was a metal cable, possibly a paravane line. One hand was not enough to control his descent. In an instant, he opted to tighten his squeeze on the crucial life buoy. Before he understood what was happening, his left-handed slide resulted in flesh being torn away down to the bone. Entering the water about 30 feet below, he managed to struggle to the surface and pull the life buoy around his chest and under his arms. He nudged off the new shoes he had been breaking in at the *Jervis Bay's* helm.

'I thought I was good enough and strong enough with a life buoy to last until the morning,' he later said.

As he stroked with his right arm, keeping his severely damaged left hand above the added agony that salt water would produce, Patience heard splinters punching into the sea. They were from the final salvoes the *Scheer* fired at the *Jervis Bay*. As he looked back and saw the boat deck totally ablaze, he thought he saw some movement on the settling aft part of the ship. The superstructure no longer was recognisable as a major component of a large ship. It was dangling down the port side, looking as if it were a huge erector set kicked over by a destructive child. The hull was ripped open from stem to stern. Many of the buoyant barrels were cascading out of torn holds or popping up from spaces opened below the surface.

From the time Patience told himself to use his 'loaf' until he began his one-armed swim into the darkness, less than ten minutes had passed. The lone sailor in the freezing sea saw his ship bow up, listing to port, sliding under. He thought about Greenley, afraid to enter the ocean. He imagined him locking himself in a cabin for the safety of the air bubble. As the ship stood on her stern, he envisioned his shipmate tumbling down the cabin deck to the aft wall. The Greenley he saw was bruised and scared, but still feeling a modicum of safety, when suddenly the sea burst through the locked hatches. Patience felt the panic, the thrashing, lung-burning, choking, black agony of the trapped seaman drowning. The horrifying fantasy occupied Patience's mind for a few seconds. Then he fastened his attention on one-armed swimming into the black nowhere.[6]

P.3 gunner Tom Davison had spent his adult life at sea, and this was the first time he had had to abandon a ship. He was twenty-seven, a wiry five foot eight, and balding. Typical of men of Kent, he had high cheekbones and a firm chin. Still barefoot, after having run straight out of a bathtub to his aft action station, he made his way up the port side of the boat deck looking for a lifeboat, which he preferred, or a raft, if necessary. As he approached the canteen, a small voice called, 'Davo, will you help me?'

It was Nobby Clark, a young, slight, gentle steward. Davison, whose character and physicality were the reverse of Clark's, did not know him well, but he had talked with him now and then, and regarded him as a nice chap. The man's leg was torn open, and he could not walk.

'You'll look after me,' said Clark, 'won't you, Davo?'

'Of course, I'll look after you, Nobby.'

Though he gave Clark some faith to hold onto, Davison did not deceive himself. The only hope for the immobile steward lay through the same forest of flames that had confined Sam Patience to the forward part of the ship. Since the boat deck was forward of him, Davison reckoned that he had to find a way through the fires. 'You hang on here,' he told Clark. 'I'm going forward. We might be able to get some boats away.'

He got on his hands and knees and managed to avoid the flames and the hot air that threatened to scorch his lungs. The acrid smell of burning paint made him gag and caused his eyes to tear. When he had passed through the blazing remains of the superstructure, he stood up. The intense heat of the fires inside the ship rose through the decking. Davison scooted around until he found a place where he could keep his feet from roasting. Two young naval reservists, Bob Liddle and Maurice Farthing, were in the same area. Liddle's eyes revealed his dread: 'I can't swim, Davo. See to us all right, will you?'

Davison seemed to be attracting lambs. 'I can't put my arms around the pair of you in the water,' he said. 'But, I'll tell you what: you keep close to me and we'll see what we can do.'

As they scrabbled forward, the heat intensified. Davison spied the jolly boat surrounded by men who were lowering it. 'We'll try to get you in that,' he told the two dependent lads. But he could see that too many men already had laid claim to a place in it, and he said: 'Come on, you follow me. We'll get on the deck above, and there may be a chance to slide down the falls and get into the boat that way.' He climbed to what remained of the bridge deck where the jolly boat davits were. He grasped one of the twine falls and turned back to Liddle and Farthing. They were not there. He looked over the rail to the main deck and saw neither of them. The boat was gone, too. He took the rope again and leaned over the side of the ship. There it was, in the water and filled with men. The two young men must be in it, he thought. They were not among the survivors.

Then he remembered—what about Nobby Clark? The wounded cook had slipped from Davison's mind while he was trying to help Liddle and Farthing. He had given Nobby his promise. The little man was depending on him, but they were separated by the fires that continued to burn across the ship's beam. Davison felt a wave of anguish. He hopscotched barefoot over the deck, doing his best to avoid the hot spots. This time, however, he could not find a path through the flames. He flagellated himself: *I've let him down. I forgot about him.*

Davison remained obsessed for the rest of the war and beyond with the question: What was Nobby thinking of me when he died?

The remorse he suffered did not prevent the selfless old hand finally from taking steps to save himself. About the same time that Sam Patience looked around and saw only Bill Greenley in the forward area, Davison, who saw neither of them, lowered himself over the side and slid into the sea. Wearing only trousers and a jersey, and no shoes, he sucked in air and gagged on it as icy water rose up his torso. As happened to many other men, he at first could not move his diaphragm. He began clawing at the hull. Just as quickly, he squelched the climbing instinct and began applying his experience and intelligence. Realising that he could never make it up the ship's side and that the *Jervis Bay* was going to sink, he started swimming away from her. The effort generated the breathing reflex and body heat and kept his arms and legs from numbing.[7]

Time was running out for the men on the after part of the *Jervis Bay*. Her stern had settled so deeply that only the poop deck remained above the surface. As Patience had briefly seen after he swam away from the ship, several men were in that small space. One of them was the fifty-nine-year-old paymaster, Lieutenant Commander Ernest W White, who clutched a metal box containing the ship's papers. Taking their only viable alternative, they entered the water. White never got to a raft or the jolly boat. The fate of the others, all unidentified, is not known.

Radio Officer Richard Shackleton and Chief Gunner Edward R Stannard were on a dry part of the after well deck, which rose as the stern sank. The rest of the ship forward of them was a bonfire in the sky. As they watched White and the other men leave the poop and slip into the sea, Stannard said: 'We'll have to go over the side.'

'I'm going to stay on the ship,' Shackleton said. He explained that he was not much of a swimmer. Besides, he thought the buoyancy barrels would keep the ship afloat until help came. Before long, the hull's list increased to about 40 degrees. It became more and more difficult to hold on. Their part of the deck was almost awash.

Stannard, an excellent swimmer, had stuck with Shackleton as long as he could. He was not about to go down with the ship. In a commanding voice, he said: 'Come on, let's get into the water.' The radio officer realised his best bet was to be with the gunner. He peeled his heavy pea jacket, pulled off his shoes, and with his life belt secure, he followed Stannard into the sea. They immediately felt the awful contrast of the cold water on their bodies and the heat of the fires on their faces. By then, many of the sealed barrels had left the hull. The loss of buoyancy accelerated the sinking. As the burning forward section reared up, the poop slipped under, followed by the well-deck position they had just stepped off. They swam away and reached no farther than twenty yards when Shackleton felt the water open under him. He began spiralling down, and the sea filled in over him as suction from the descending *Jervis Bay* drew him irresistibly. His lungs throbbed and stung and demanded air. He kicked and thrashed in a blind panic, when suddenly he was borne to the surface by an upwelling.

Shackleton gasped repeatedly, then became aware that the sea in front of him appeared an eerie red. His first thought was that a lack of oxygen must have affected his vision. He heard an ear-splitting hiss and saw steam clouds rising above the water. Blackness was everywhere else. Then he knew his ship was beneath the water with internal fires still raging: what he saw were the glowing hull plates.

He turned away, and there was Stannard in front of him. As they gratefully acknowledged their escape, both were drawn under again. The pull was not as strong on Shackleton as it had been in the first gyre. Buoyed by his inflated belt, he more rapidly resurfaced. He looked around for the gunner, but Stannard could only have been swirling down with the ship.

Shackleton was covered with fuel oil. Some of it got into his mouth and sickened him. He managed to swim for a few minutes. Then he stopped to conserve energy. He shouted several times but heard no response. If there were any human responses, they'd have been washed out by the noise of the building wind and the roughening chop of the water. The radio officer was alone in blackness in the middle of the wintry North Atlantic, with a gale beginning to ride in and nothing but a life belt between him and the bottom. He alternately cringed in terror, retched from the ingested oil, and basked in a fatalistic serenity. Though it did not occur to him, the positive thing in his predicament was that the oil coating his body insulated him against the frigid water.

The time was about 8:00 pm, two hours and forty-five minutes since the *Admiral Scheer* opened fire on the *Jervis Bay*.[8]

Other men in the water were precariously supported by makeshift floats and pieces of wood. Two of them had lugged Tom Hanlon's big wire-and-wood cage to an outer deck, released his six Bermuda parakeets, and gone overboard with it. It was keeping them afloat for the time being. The small tropical birds stood as little chance of finding their way home as did the men who had set them free. Two other sailors, one of them Master-at-Arms James Hardy Kershaw, drifted up to the large raft on a locker they had thrown off the deck. They were invited to join the crowd.

'No,' Kershaw said. 'I'll take my chance.'

None of the four men turned up among the survivors.[9]

For one of the *Jervis Bay* crew, a deep foreboding started as the convoy left Halifax. It heightened with the approach of 5 November and became almost unbearable as the day lengthened and the *Admiral Scheer* appeared on the northern horizon. He was the stolid, metropolitan ex-policeman who had been warned by a fortune-teller during her arrest that he would never see his twenty-eighth birthday. That day was seven hours away. No records have been found that identify the man. Five twenty-seven-year-olds died in the action, but only one of them was from a metropolitan area: John Stanislaus Jeffcott of Lambeth, London. He was listed, like most of the other casualties, as 'Lost at Sea'; it is not known how he died or whether he was on or off the ship at the time. One can only imagine the intensity of the fear that must have burned through his veins in those last hours.[10]

15 We Go Back

SAM Patience used his right arm to stroke as hard as he could, and he strained to keep his raw left hand out of the salt water. He had put about 200 yards between himself and the *Jervis Bay* when he saw her fiery body disappear into the sea. The sight broke his heart. The hiss and the sudden blackout felt like a world ending. But, he reminded himself, he was lucky to be alive and supported by a life buoy. Surely, he would be picked up. He almost continuously kicked his legs and pulled water with his right arm—keeping the numbness at bay, his head above the surface, and his mind awake—and moved himself slowly through the night. At first, he produced so much internal heat that he didn't notice the cold. As time and his exertions advanced, so did fatigue. He began to realise that 'it was so cold, it was bitter bloody cold.' Nevertheless, the self-possessed young able seaman was sure he could hold out into the morning.

As the waves grew rougher and he caught occasional breakers in his face, Patience became concerned that his visibility to any rescuers was diminishing. It was up to him to be vigilant, to spot a raft or the jolly boat or a ship, and to attract their attention. To the southeast he saw gunfire flashes followed by a few sudden brightenings as convoy ships were hit by the German raider. *At least,* he thought, *they're not getting a lot of our ships.*[1]

The men jammed in the jolly boat, now weighted down almost to its gunwales, sadly watched their ship sink. Lieutenant Wood tried to cheer them up as they nestled under some blankets stored in the little recreation craft. One of the men passed out cigarettes he had somehow salvaged. The smokers shielded the glowing ends with their hands, making sure they would not be spotted by an enemy ship. Wood encouraged them to sing popular ditties. It kept them going, even after some of their shipmates died of wounds or hypothermia and were put over the side. Then he began clicking out S O S messages with his torch every few minutes.

Suddenly, a hand reached out of the water and clamped onto a gunwale. A face then appeared alongside. It was the second time that day that Patience seemed to materialise out of nowhere (the first when he was blown off his P.1 gun station and dropped unconscious in front of the P.2 crew 15 feet below). God, how could they squeeze one more body aboard?

'Let's get in the boat,' the swimmer said to himself aloud.

Somebody in the boat said, 'We're full up.'

'Chuck that life buoy over here,' another voice said.

'I'm not chuckin' no life buoy,' Patience insisted.

No way was he going to surrender the float that had kept him alive, alone, in the subarctic sea in the mounting gale. The tough North Sea fisherman tried to mount the boat's low-riding gunwale, but his strength failed and he slipped back. Some hands finally reached over and dragged him and his life buoy into the boat. Patience collapsed into a tiny space on the bottom, barely aware of where he was. After some time, he recovered enough to realise he had deluded himself that he could endure through the night. The fates that had helped him through earlier naval actions had come to his aid again and carried him into the jolly boat's path.

Patience looked at the barely perceptible faces around him and did not know any of them. Having joined the *Jervis Bay* the night before she sailed, he had had little time to get acquainted with the crew. Though uncomfortable in being a bit of an outsider, he assumed he could depend on them in a pickle. As the overloaded dory increasingly shipped water, more men took to scooping it out by cupped handfuls. Patience was excused from bailing duty because of his torn hand. He was grateful to be with the solicitous Lieutenant Wood and the eighteen other survivors as they rode the slopes of the waves and came close to swamping at times.[2]

Captain Sven David Olander of the Swedish freighter *Stureholm* knew the convoy rules. One rule required that if any ship were sunk by enemy action, no other ship might stop to pick up survivors. To do so would place the would-be rescuer in jeopardy. Olander disobeyed the no-rescue rule.

The *Stureholm* was a 4,600-ton, diesel-powered ship that left Boston carrying more than 4,000 tons of steel plate and about 2,700 tons of scrap iron. If she were opened up by shellfire, the deadweight cargo would drag her under in minutes. On seeing the commodore's scatter signal, Olander immediately took the ship on a west-by-northwest bearing. And, like most of the other convoy captains, he stayed behind smoke and kept her stern to the flashes from the *Admiral Scheer*'s armament. At the same time he followed the progress of the *Jervis Bay*'s action against the German raider.

The roly-poly Swede was deeply affected by what he saw. He later said: 'All my life I will remember those brave men on the *Jervis Bay*.' He felt that his men could not simply flee and leave their defenders to their fate. He pondered the situation for a while. Then he called the crew together and put a proposal to them. Consultation was a custom (going back to the Laws of Oleron in

1400) among merchant seamen when a captain wanted to depart from normal practice. It was to be, in effect, a binding poll. Olander made an emotional presentation: 'You saw what the *Jervis Bay* has done to save us all. She was right in the guns of the enemy. She did not have a chance and we all knew it. But, she rode like a hero and stayed to the last to give us a chance to run for it. Now, I would like to go back and see if there's anyone still in the water. I shan't do it without your agreement. Those who agree put up their hands.'

Most of the crew were from Sweden, a neutral in the war—though many Swedes sympathised with Germany. They had good reasons to keep moving away from the scene, not the least of which was that the German raider was still sinking convoy ships. They could see the flashes and explosions in the night sky. As the men—nineteen Swedes, six Danes, two Norwegians, one Finn, one Dutchman, and one Scotsman—weighed the alternatives, Captain Olander stood on the bridge deck, bulging in his sheepskin coat, his round, pink, usually good-humoured face tense and grim. Open hands began rising. When the votes were in, an agreement to search for *Jervis Bay* survivors was nearly unanimous. Olander grinned. 'We go back.'[3]

Tom Davison swam through debris, none of it substantial enough to climb onto and get out of the subarctic water. He had to continue searching for help. And he needed to swim in order to keep his shrinking store of energy flowing. Time passed and fatigue began to overwhelm him. The desire to sleep pressed on his brain. Then, in the darkness, he came upon the undamaged raft and grasped its edge. It was packed like a Tokyo subway car. Most of the men were standing. The more badly hurt were allowed to sit or sprawl among the grove of legs.

A seaman named Ginger leaned over and said: 'Don't come on here, Davo. There's not enough room for us.' Knowing he would not be allowed to climb aboard and too tired to fight, Davison said: 'I'll just hang on a minute. I only want to get my wind back. I'll look for something else.' Anyway, it would do no good to just hold onto the raft. The freezing water would put an end to him faster than if he were swimming in it.

Ginger took Davison's hand and gave it a farewell shake. 'I'll be seeing you, Davo.'

'Yes, I'll be seeing you, Ginger.'

The exchange between them was hardly noticed by the other men on the raft. Some of them were raucous and singing. All were focused on their own plights. Ginger did not survive the night.

Davison, without the support of a life belt and having no clue to which way he should go, swam off. His greatest strength during the ordeal was his determination to stay alive. As he swam, an image of his hometown, West Hougham, slipped into his mind. The natives of the tiny West Kent village had a fantasy that none of them would die before their eightieth birthday. They were proud of their legendary long life. The twenty-seven-year-old Davison resolved not to disappoint them.

After a while, a faint, recurring sound brushed at his eardrums. But the wind noise, the rain and sleet, and the swash of the choppy rollers interfered as he tried to tune in to whatever it was. The night was too dark to see anything beyond a few yards, even as he rose to the wave crests. As his strength waned, he stopped swimming to rest momentarily and listen. Then, definite sounds, not of the sea, came to him. He moved toward them, rested, listened, and moved again. Filtering through the natural static around him, the sounds grew louder, then resolved into talking, shouting, and singing. A dreadful question pulsed through his body: Was it the same raft that had denied him boarding rights a quarter of an hour before? Davison suppressed his unhappy speculation and splashed painfully toward his only chance. It was the other raft.

What he dimly saw was not encouraging. The men, now fourteen of them, were standing upright in water that had risen almost to their knees. The platform, only 40 percent of its original size and supported by the single remaining watertight drum, rode tilted beneath the surface. Most of it was not visible. Davison swam over to it, took a space left by the loss of one of the original occupants, and stood up with the rest of the survivors.

Their prospects were dismal. Their feet and legs were freezing. The waves, the frigid wind, and the driving mix of sleet, snow, and rain exacerbated their misery. Most of the men had left their pea jackets behind in responding to the 'action stations' order or had shed them in abandoning the ship. They shivered and clung to each other, those in the centre of the huddle receiving the most benefit from the insulation other bodies provided. They took turns massaging each other's arms and backs. What kept them going was an amalgam of gall, spirit, and almost foolhardy optimism. They joked and shouted and sang their defiance of the North Atlantic Ocean and Hitler. They belted out one of beleaguered Britain's top songs of the day, 'We'll Hang Out Our Washing on the Siegfried Line,' and the old standby 'Roll Out the Barrel.' Without their bravado raucousness to catch his attention, Davison would still have been in the ocean.

In swimming up to the raft, he saw a faint light coming from under the water. It was a torch that belonged to Tom Hanlon, who had tossed it to the bottom of the raft because a defective switch prevented him from turning it off. He didn't want it to be visible to the enemy. Davison, in a strenuous effort to bend down without knocking anyone or himself off the float, picked it up and somehow switched it off. He tucked it behind his trouser belt.

One man pulled cigarettes out of his shirt pocket. The packaging must have been watertight, for the contents were fresh and fragrant. He handed them around. Hanlon passed around a lighter that, in another small miracle, had survived the immersion test. The treat was an ephemeral, uplifting reminder of normal life.

A while after Davison joined them, one of the men slowly sat down in water up to his waist. His head sank to his chest. Another man could not rouse him. He had given up, lost consciousness, and died. A second man slumped the same way. He was big and brawny, a fitness devotee. Like most of the men, he had no peacoat. He was not a lifelong seaman, and, as impressive as his body was, he lacked the toughness to resist the rigors of the northern sea. Another man went down. The three of them were put off the raft. The remaining occupants gained enough space to relieve the crowding a bit, but they dared not sit. That would submerge their bodies deeper into the subarctic water and drastically reduce their endurance. Standing on the underwater platform continually fighting off waves was as precarious as it was exhausting and painful. It was their only survival option.

Seeing men die at sea was a new experience for Davison. He had thought the final minutes would be horrible, a gasping, choking struggle. Here in the freezing North Atlantic, however, they passed through the initial pain of hypothermia and then sank peacefully into oblivion. The realisation that he could simply go to sleep was comforting. It was the siren song that he and the other men heard as they approached their limits.

Suddenly, there was a light above the water. Davison pulled the torch from his waistband and flashed it. The men shouted and waved their arms. But the light disappeared…and much of their hope with it.

The cold anaesthesia intensified in their legs and crept higher into their bodies, and the desire to sleep grew overwhelming. Yet they were not ready to succumb to the sea. Those who were able sang and shouted and jostled their drowsy neighbours into wakefulness. The barefooted Davison prayed silently for them all.[4]

When Midshipman Butler boarded the intact raft, he discovered that it held three or four other, higher-ranking officers, all of them specialists, including Lieutenant Robertson of the engineering branch. As the only survivor among the *Jervis Bay*'s executive officers, the young midshipman took command. He was hardly more than an adolescent. His sea time was limited. But almost at once he proved his competence. Several men suggested that they paddle back to the ship and see if they could find a sound lifeboat. It seemed a good idea, except the *Jervis Bay* was still under fire, and now there were thirty to forty men clustered around the raft. After consulting with the other officers, the midshipman turned down the proposal. Then, with surprising authority, he said: 'If anyone wants to have a go at it, they can try and swim back to the ship.'

He ordered the men to get the raft away from the battered merchant cruiser as fast as they could. Oil was spreading over the sea surface and could be ignited by fiery materials blowing off the superstructure or the searing blasts of enemy near misses. Men at the six steel-drum locations, which had no handholds for those in the water, used lengths of wood that had come off the ship to paddle as hard as they could. One of the men, apparently in a battle-induced fantasy, wildly swung his wood up instead of into the sea. A sub-lieutenant, the only survivor of the paymaster's office, placed his hand on the air-paddler's shoulder and said: 'Dip the bloody thing in the water occasionally, old man.'

A struggle with the makeshift paddles moved them a few hundred yards away from immediate danger. Then they gave their arms and backs a rest. All around them was darkness except for their burning, exploding ship. As they watched her being consumed by flames and starting to list and settle by the stern, a professional boxer and a muscular food-supply businessman slid off the raft and disappeared. A sorely wounded lad sitting next to Robertson started tilting. The lieutenant kept pulling him upright until he realised the young man was dead. His body was put into the sea. As the dying and dead left the raft, generally their spaces were taken by the strongest men still hanging onto it. When someone in the water revealed he was injured or badly wounded by shrapnel, others shouted something like, make a bit of room for a bloke that's been wounded. In some cases, the men on the platform managed to squeeze them aboard.

The *Jervis Bay* finally sank and left them in a violent, featureless, depressing void.

The frigid ocean was also taking a toll of the waterlogged men hanging on to the edges of the raft. It sucked away their body heat, numbing their legs, then their torsos. Several of them swam away looking for any flotsam they could climb onto and get out of the water. Flotation barrels that had escaped through holes in the ship's hull attracted a few swimmers, but the damned things were as unstable in the water as they were unsinkable. Even desperate men knew there was no way of mounting them. Their search for the support of planks, hatch covers, and other floating debris failed. The cold soon paralysed and mercifully sedated them. They drifted and died quickly and, many of them, peacefully.

Most of the remaining crewmen around the raft also lost their will to stay awake. Their number thinned out until all were gone. A few of the toughest ones had climbed aboard as openings occurred. Jack Barker, having regained the invincibility of youth, was one of them.

The weight of the survivors eventually submerged the six supporting drums and forced the timber platform so low that its topside rode a few inches above the surface. Like the men on the damaged raft, most of them stood upright. Some of the wounded and injured were allowed to get off their feet and worm into interstitial spaces between legs.

Though the raft was packed with men, they felt a kind of group aloneness. It took Butler's confidence and leadership and the forceful personality of Leading Seaman James Wood, called Slinger by the crew, to lift them out of their doldrums.

The thirty-year-old Wood, from Southport, Lancaster, was a powerful man, an experienced sailor. His jutting jaw imparted a toughness that drew respect from the crew. Yet he usually masked his natural authority with an amiable smile. He organised the paddlers. He managed to move among the tightly packed survivors, comforting and soothing the wounded. He cheered them up and encouraged them. He insisted that the men sing, and he led them bawling into the storm and the waves such inspirational numbers as 'There'll Always Be an England' and the ubiquitous 'Roll Out the Barrel.'

As time wore on, the raft lost more buoyancy and listed until part of it submerged. Desperation again began to tell on Barker, as it had when he was left alone at his station on the ship. He lapsed into a dream world and sat down in water up to his chest. In his thin rugby shirt, he studied the phosphorescent swirls running over his arms and legs. He tried to lift the green glow with his hands, thinking it would warm him. The deep cold in his body changed into a feeling of comfort and drowsiness. Every time he was about to drift off, Wood or someone else shouted something like, 'Come on. One, two, three. Hurrah.' They got Barker and others nearing unconsciousness to rouse themselves and join in shouting and singing.

Then, out of the night, a swimmer appeared alongside the raft. He was covered with oil, black and unrecognisable. They knew he was one of their shipmates. But who? They dragged him onto an above-water section of the platform and let him recover somewhat from his ordeal. It turned out to be Richard Shackleton, who had been in the water, supported by his life belt, for about five hours. His legs were numb, and he could not feel his feet. He had been kept alive by the coating of oil on his body and clothes.[5]

It was about 11:00 pm when an alert young Scotsman in the tossing bows of the jolly boat sang out: 'I can see a light coming.'

The inevitable response came from a man squinting into the darkness: 'You're seeing things. There aren't any lights.'

Petty Officer Castle thought he saw a flashing blue light. He turned to Lieutenant Wood: 'Do you think it's a light, or am I seeing things?'

'Yes, I think it is.'

Then they saw a big shape, blacker than the night. It moved closer, slowly. It was a ship. Guttural voices wafted over the water toward them.

'She's a prison ship,' one of them said, in a voice charged with certainty.

'I'm not going to be taken prisoner,' a second man chimed in.

Others agreed, but nobody suggested a course of action.

The jolly boat was taking a lot of water, and the black ship was upon them. The voices coming down to them were foreign, but now they did not seem German. The men paddled around the stern of the ship, and they could hardly believe what they heard: 'Aye, ye're all right now, boys.' The burr came from the Scots greaser on the *Stureholm*. The response from the jolly boat was uproarious.

Jacob's ladders dropped down the side of the Swedish ship. About half of the men managed to climb aboard. Others could not muster the strength to get up the ladders. Several muscular *Stureholm* crewmen, wearing pirate stocking caps, helped the weakened and wounded sailors to the deck, carrying some of them up the ladders.

The twenty *Jervis Bay* survivors were taken to the ship's saloon. Those with waterlogged clothes were stripped and rubbed down with big, rough towels until their circulation returned to a more normal level. The blood pressing through their numbed legs at first stung like bee venom. Dry clothing was provided. All were doused with black coffee and spirits. Since the *Stureholm* sailed without a doctor, her second mate fetched first-aid kits from the ship's dispensary and treated the wounded as best he could. Then, in a grand gesture, the Swedish officers turned over their comfortable quarters to the most severely disabled men.

The seas worsened, and waves rose to ten to twelve feet, and the big raft, with its burden of more than forty men, was too heavy to ride over the crests. It rocked ponderously and listed up to 45 degrees. Water rolled over it, and the standing men grasped each other and parts of the raft to keep from toppling or washing overboard. Some of them were torn away from their moorings. Most managed to swim back and reboard.

On their half-submerged raft in a rough, freezing ocean in the dead of a northern November night with a rising gale tearing at them, the men justifiably could have given up their struggle to stay alive. A few of them did. With cold paralysis clamping ever more tightly on their bodies and minds, they let go and slipped into the sea. The rest of the miserable survivors, led by the self-assured, nineteen-year-old Butler, hung on. They knew the convoy ships had scattered and hoped somebody would find them in this terrible ocean. Forty-four-year-old Leading Seaman Tiddly Bonney, who had begun serving in the Royal Navy before Butler was born, later said: 'You'd think he was a seasoned naval officer instead of just a young boy.'

Prodded by the indomitable Leading Seaman Wood, the men continued shouting and singing into the night. For the time being, the raft was their world. They were all shipmates, they would keep up their spirits and their resolve, they would help each other, they would stay alive.

The struggle went on for hours. At about 3:30 am, some eight and a half hours after the raft was dropped off the *Jervis Bay*, a young engineering officer took Bonney's arm: 'You've seen more shipping than I have. Is that a ship?'

Bonney sighted along the man's pointing finger and then said: 'The wish is the father to the thought…but I believe it is.'

Butler, who had been torching S O S signals intermittently in all directions, aimed a continuous set of them at the black shape. After a while, a boat emerged from the darkness. A voice called out: 'How many of you iss dere?'

Like the jolly-boat survivors, the men at first mistook the guttural accent for German. They braced themselves for the voice to reveal the speaker's nationality. When the boat nudged up to the raft, to their great relief they saw stocking caps on some of the oarsmen. Whoever the rescuers were, they were not Germans, and, in fact, they were in the *Jervis Bay's* jolly boat, which the *Stureholm* crew thought best to use in their search for survivors. A dozen of those with the worst wounds and exposure were transferred to the little boat and were rowed back to the Swedish freighter.

By then the weather had worsened to a perilous level, and Captain Olander ordered the jolly boat removed from further rescue operations. Instead, he estimated the flow of the sea and manoeuvred his ship to a position that he hoped would intersect the drift of the raft. Some fifteen minutes later the partly submerged platform with drenched, freezing riders lurched against the *Stureholm's* hull.

The Swedes directed a floodlight down at the wildly tossing raft, which slammed against the ship with almost every wave. They dropped a Jacob's ladder. Under Butler's discipline, the men transferred one at a time to the ladder as the sea kept tossing the raft halfway up and down the ship's side. Anyone who lost his grasp or his footing and fell between the heavy timbers and the ship could not expect any help. Amazingly, these numbed, exhausted men reached the *Stureholm's* deck without a misstep or a casualty.

Not until the raft's thirty-six survivors were in the freighter's saloon, being treated for wounds, injuries, and exposure, did they understand all that Slinger Wood had done. They had been grateful for his leadership in moving their big raft away from the sinking *Jervis Bay*, in aiding the wounded and injured, and in rallying the men into clamorous singing-yelling performances that kept them awake and alive. It was only after seeing serious wounds to both of his thighs that they fully appreciated his selfless courage during their ordeal, and they were tremendously stirred by it. The only hint anyone on the raft had of Wood's distress was his offhand comment

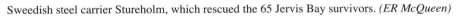

Sweedish steel carrier Stureholm, which rescued the 65 Jervis Bay survivors. *(ER McQueen)*

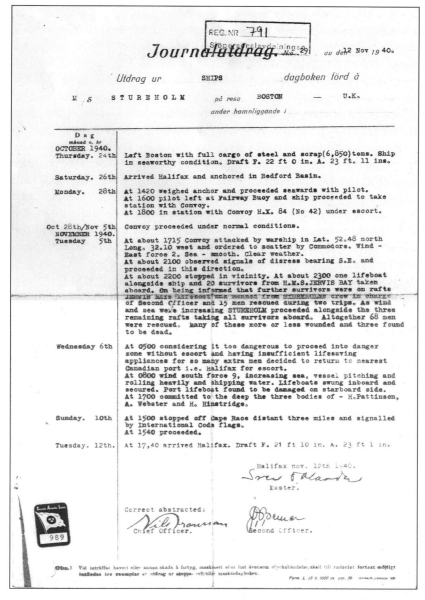

Copy of the *Stureholm* logbook entry covering the *Jervis Bay* survivors rescue operation. *(Chris Davison)*

to Tiddly Bonney that his legs were cramped.

Captain Olander felt almost fulfilled after rescuing the survivors from the *Jervis Bay's* jolly boat and big raft. There was one more raft to go.[6]

It was about ten hours since Commander Roe had ordered the merchant cruiser's crew to abandon the ship. Of the three groups of survivors, those on the remnant of the second raft were the most miserable and imperilled (except, of course, for the tangle of men in the frigid water around the large raft who had already given up the struggle). And they had to hold on longer than the others. The splintered platform, tilted on its only steel drum, had so settled that the standing men were visible only above their knees. Waves rose up their chests and sometimes over their heads. By some wondrous intervention, most of the men and the raft stuck together like a single organism. Some of them sloughed off the tightly knit mass and were swept away. Two or three managed to swim back to the raft and refastened themselves to their mates. Tom Hanlon unravelled the long bandage around his head and tied one end to his wrist and the other to an underwater timber. They were a heartrending, magnificently impossible congregation.

Danny Bain, who had received severe burns in trying to save a flaming shipmate and was himself saved by Fred Billinge, was in the centre of the small tossing cluster, propped up by the men around him. Since Billinge had escaped to the jolly boat, none of the men on the half-raft knew about Bain's condition, except for burns on his face. It seemed to them, however, that the young fisherman was not able to help himself. They massaged his arms and shoulders to keep him awake. They did not know they were rubbing off his burnt skin down to raw muscle. Bain did not complain. He probably was anaesthetised in some way after more than ten hours of excruciating pain. His spirit was his strength; he knew he was going to be rescued.

At 4:40 am, the *Stureholm* spotted the torch beam Davison swept in a cone through the gale and found them. The crew were unable to see the submerged raft, and it looked as if the last twelve survivors were planted in lumpy water. The men were brought on board to the comfort of Swedish care and hospitality. All told, the self-obligated, courageous, independent-minded Olander and his crew pulled 68 of the *Jervis Bay's* 265 men out of the sea. Three of them were dead and were committed to the deep that night.

Again, Olander called for a consultation with the officers and crew of the freighter. He felt that it would be safer to alter course and return to Halifax. The men agreed, and they arrived back at their port of embarkation on 12 November. Most of the survivors were transferred to HMS *Cormorin*, another armed merchant cruiser, and nine of the wounded and injured men were taken to a local hospital. Some of them were still laid up when the *Stureholm* set sail on her next and final adventure.[7]

HMS *Jervis Bay* survivors aboard MV *Stureholm. (E R McQueen)*

HMS *Jervis Bay* survivors aboard MV *Stureholm. (E R McQueen)*

HMS *Jervis Bay* survivors aboard MV *Stureholm*. At the back far right is William McQueen wearing a cap. *(E R McQueen)*

Survivors at the Ajax club in Halifax Nova Scotia. The *Stureholm's* Captain Olander is at the centre with William McQueen second from the left at the rear. *(E R McQueen)*

16 Search and Getaway

AS the *Admiral Scheer* pounded due south through heavy seas that held her speed down to fifteen knots, the Royal Navy was already out hunting for her. Eight minutes after the Admiralty received the *Rangitiki's* signal that convoy HX 84 was being approached by a *Graf Spee*–class ship, a signalman entered the wardroom of the destroyer HMS *Eskimo* as her officers were finishing dinner just after 8:00 pm and handed Commander Micklethwait (first name missing) a copy of the message. Micklethwait repeated the news to his staff and said: 'Two to one we will slip [get under way] by midnight.'

At 8:13 the battle cruisers HMS *Hood* and *Repulse* were ordered to raise steam immediately. Three light cruisers and six destroyers received the same orders minutes later. After an inexplicable, twenty-five-minute delay in transmission, the Admiralty received the *Jervis Bay's* signal 'To: Any British Man of War...' on the 500-kilocycle distress frequency at 8:31.

One hour and nine minutes later, a disheartening, uncompleted message from the convoy ship *Sovac* radiated into Admiralty antennas: 'Raider apparently *Graf Spee* Class, attacking ships one by one leisurely about...'

Without being given the time to top off their bunkers, the eleven warships, among them the *Eskimo*, which was held up for a half-hour by a jammed exit gate, cleared Scapa Flow by midnight. An impressed American naval observer aboard the *Eskimo* noted that Micklethwait won his bet that had no takers.

The vessels manoeuvred into their customary anti–U-boat formation. Destroyers spread out ahead of and alongside the battle cruisers, with cruisers strung out behind in single file. After a two-and-a-half-hour wait they received operational instructions. The *Hood*, the cruisers *Phoebe* and *Naiad*, and three destroyers were ordered to patrol the Bay of Biscay approaches to German-occupied French Atlantic ports. The *Repulse*, the cruiser *Bonaventure*, and the other three destroyers were dispatched to the area of the attack to look for survivors and sink the *Scheer* if they found her.[1]

Indeed, Krancke would have courted disaster had he cruised around the vicinity waiting for another Halifax convoy or had he attempted to run a Royal Navy gauntlet toward a French Atlantic or home port. A westward heading into the American-declared neutral zone—thereby challenging the US Navy—also would have been perilous. The only escape route not infested with enemy warships was to the south. In any case, the *Scheer* was scheduled to rendezvous with her resupply ship *Nordmark* in mid-ocean below the Tropic of Cancer.

During the flight south, Krancke and some of his officers mulled over the reports of the battle observers and compared them with their own perceptions of the attack on the British convoy. They took pains to be meticulous and as objective as possible in their count. Only ships that were seen to sink or were burning and appeared to be so severely damaged that they could be written off were included in the tally. But their observations had been hampered by the night, the smoke screens, and the confusion of concentrating on the escort before turning to the other thirty-seven scattering ships. In their radioed report to Berlin, they identified nine ships (86,000 tons) sunk and five damaged.

The Nazi propaganda machine immediately claimed the *Scheer* had destroyed an entire British convoy. Waiting over a week for the last of the surviving HX 84 ships to reach port, the Admiralty released its final score: five cargo ships, the *Jervis Bay*, and the independent *Mopan* sunk (48,000 tons altogether) and the tanker *San Demetrio* damaged.

The *Scheer* did not get away unscathed. Recoils and blasts from the 11-inch guns caused some serious damage and put as many as thirty crew members into the sickbay with broken bones and other injuries.

The exposed 'parrot' on its catapult was incapacitated. Its rudder and ailerons were destroyed, ribs broken, and surfaces buckled. Normally, a seaplane in such condition would be hoisted off its perch and dumped into the sea. But a replacement on the scheduled cruise was out of the question. Lieutenant Pietsch received permission to try and return it to flight health with assistance from ship's mechanics, carpenters, and others.

Other minor damage, such as torn-away hatch covers and flaked paint, was quickly repaired. Electronics specialists worked over the disabled radar. A replacement crystal was not to be received until months later.[2]

After sending the *Hood* and the *Repulse* on their futile ways, Admiral Sir John Tovey, commander in chief of the Home Fleet, assigned the battleships *Rodney* (his only fully fuelled capital ship) and *Nelson* (his flagship), the cruiser *Southampton*, and six destroyers to the area between the Faro Islands and Iceland to intercept any attempt by the raider to return to Germany. They left Scapa at dawn on 6 November. At the admiral's request, several patrol planes were made available to extend the area of the searches around Iceland and the Bay of Biscay approaches to the French ports. Canada joined the task groups, contributing four destroyers and three reconnaissance planes. Later that day, Tovey was puzzled by an Admiralty order removing the *Rodney* from her foxhound mission and reassigning her as escort to an eastbound Halifax convoy.

Shortly before the *Nelson* sailed, Winston Churchill, who thoroughly enjoyed the unsolicited role of naval operations adviser, contacted the commander in chief. According to Tovey's war diary: 'Prime Minister has telephoned to say that as we consider it possible that the *Scheer*...may return to Brest, St Nazaire or Le Verdun [sic], it is essential to keep a close watch on those places for the earliest time at which she may arrive there and that arrangements must be made to bomb her intensively should she be located.'

The admiral did not reveal his response to Churchill or the effect of the advice on his temper. Another message he recorded in his war diary came from the Air chief of staff: 'We are taking all action necessary to locate and bomb *Admiral Scheer*. Coastal Command are arranging the necessary reconnaissance and have a striking force of three squadrons...standing by to attack. Bomber Command are also on top line to bomb the ship when located. Provided *Admiral Scheer* comes within our orbit I think you will find us prepared.'

The British would have slaughtered the pocket battleship...if only she had blundered into one of their ambushes.[3]

The first night of the search, as the naval forces headed for their assigned areas, a message from the Admiralty notified Tovey that the *Scheer* was about 150 miles northwest of the position where the convoy was attacked. It indicated that, while the bearing was not too reliable, the raider definitely was moving northward. The admiral was in a predicament: Churchill had suggested the pocket battleship was approaching the French coast, and the Admiralty had placed her on a tack to Germany or Norway. She also could be (in fact, was) running south, in which case his ships, having had little or no time to fuel, would be sorely limited in range and unable to pursue her.

The next day, the commander in chief scheduled the battle cruisers and their screens back to Scapa Flow on 11 November to fill their bunkers. The Royal Navy had been so unprepared for the demanding search that the fuel situation gave the German raider time to cover nearly 3,000 miles before those ships were ready to renew the hunt.[4]

On 10 November Captain Krancke gathered his crew on deck in dress uniform. The German flag was brought down to half-mast in a formal commemoration of the two shipmates who had lost their lives in the polar hurricane during the raider's breakout through the Denmark Strait. Krancke eulogised them, and the band played 'Ich hat' ein Kamerad.' The officers and men stood bareheaded for a while. Then they settled back into their work clothes and regular duties, and sailed on to their resupply rendezvous.[5]

On the way home, the *Repulse* task group swept the storm-ridden battle zone, then rode the northeastward current, but found no survivors, no debris, and no *Admiral Scheer*. Enduring four days of rough seas, they arrived back at Scapa on schedule, just ahead of the *Hood* and her screen, which, of course, did not find the raider in the Bay of Biscay approaches.

With the wide-scale search temporarily hobbled as a result of the fuel problem, and with the *Scheer* supposedly in the Iceland-Faros area, only the *Nelson* continued patrolling the northern ocean with her cruiser and six destroyers. She was replaced about 13 November by the *Repulse*, whose bunkers were now topped off.

As the Home Fleet engaged in the intermittent search patterns, perceptions of the *Scheer*'s position shifted. Movements of several convoys were altered. The eastbound SC 10 (out of Sydney, Nova Scotia), about a hundred miles away when the raider attacked the *Jervis Bay* convoy, was directed to 'steer to the southward.' Thirteen minutes later the order was cancelled. Convoys BHX 86 and HX 86 were ordered back to, respectively, Bermuda and Halifax. SC 11, OB 240 (outward-bound from Britain), and other convoys were held in their ports pending further instructions. Still other convoys were sent back to Gibraltar. All independent sailings were suspended between Britain and North America and all eastern Atlantic ports south to Freetown. This last restriction was lifted in less than twenty-four hours.

HX 85, escorted by the AMC *Voltaire*, whose captain was Fegen's former executive officer J A P Blackburn, received a midnight instruction to return to Halifax. Then, because of overcrowding at that port, HX 85 was re-routed to Sydney; then to St. John's, Newfoundland; then to anchorages at Trinity and Bell Isle (also in Newfoundland); and finally back to Sydney. The fifty ships of the convoy and their original escort regrouped and sailed on 10 November. Meanwhile, the *Voltaire* escorted HX 86 until she handed them over to the heavyweight *Rodney* near the Western Approaches on 21 November. On her way back to Halifax, Blackburn took her to the site of the *Jervis Bay* sinking. He brought the ship to a dead slow and ordered a rifle volley salute to his former ship and shipmates resting on the bed of the sea.

These and the other reactions to the *Admiral Scheer*'s attack on HX 84 resulted in harbour congestion, chaos, and delays of up to two weeks in delivery of cargoes carried along the vital North Atlantic convoy routes. In this 'uniquely perilous time,' every shipload was

At the end of 1940, Captain JAP Blackburn and crew of the armed merchant cruiser HMS *Voltaire* held a memorial service at the site of the sinking of HMS *Jervis Bay*.
(Courtesy of #53 Jervis Bay Branch, Royal Canadian Legion, Saint John, New Brunswick)

critical. The normal convoy cycle was not resumed in the North Atlantic until HX 89 sailed on 17 November. According to naval historian Captain S W Roskill: 'The loss of imports caused by the pocket battleship's sudden appearance on our principal convoy route was, therefore, far greater than the cargoes actually sunk by her.'[6]

On the other side of the ocean, off the northwestern coast of Africa, convoy SLF 53, with ships from the South Pacific and Indian Oceans and various ports in southern and western Africa, was instructed on 6 November to proceed to a position between the Azores and Madeira Island. HG 46, originating in Gibraltar and carrying North African, eastern Mediterranean, and trans-Suez cargoes, received the same orders. Instead of taking the usual HG route to the west and then north to Britain, the convoy continued westward until it rendezvoused with SLF 53. The battle cruiser *Renown* and three destroyers joined the merged super-convoy and started shepherding the ships home at HG 46's seven-knot limit. On 6 November, the heavy cruiser *Australia*, with a newly repaired turbine, took over the *Renown's* escort role.

Not realising that the battle cruiser, one of only three Royal Navy ships able to outrun and outgun the *Scheer*, was in a prime position to hunt her, the commander in the region sent her to a Mediterranean operation against the Italian fleet.

On 17 November Admiral Tovey recorded in his war diary: 'Reports received point to *Admiral Scheer* being near the Azores.' He ordered the *Renown*, the aircraft carrier *Ark Royal*, and a destroyer screen 'to proceed to Gibraltar at maximum speed, and after fuelling, to proceed towards the Azores.' A full gale held them down to nine knots. It mattered little, however, for five days earlier the *Scheer* had reached her resupply station at Point Green, about 1,300 miles southwest of the Azores.[7]

On the way to rendezvous with the tanker/freighter *Nordmark*, Captain Krancke gathered the crew and laid out his short-term plans to resupply the *Scheer* and then set out for the next area of operations. He felt that letting his men know his thoughts and decisions engendered loyalty and co-operation—for that time, an unusually sensitive naval command style. The captain also read out a message of congratulations to the ship's company from the commander in chief, Grand Admiral Erich Raeder.

Then Krancke reviewed what had happened on 5 November. The men were pleased with what they considered a successful convoy attack. But they were not elated. In general, they empathised with the crews of the sunken ships: 'Poor devils.' The British sailors seemed almost to be their shipmates, but they were the enemy. None of them wanted to see 'brothers' go down with their ships or fight for survival in a cold, violent sea. It could just as easily have been themselves.

One thing the captain had not revealed to his officers or men—he never explained why he withheld the information—was that he had received instructions to meet the tanker *Eurofeld* at Point Green on 12 November and help repair her damaged engines. Her top speed had been reduced to five knots early in the war, and she could not get through the Royal Navy to a dry dock. She had been used sparingly to refuel German armed merchant raiders, the last of them the *Widder* in early October. Since then the crippled *Eurofeld* had hung around the rendezvous point waiting for whoever might show up.

When the tanker's unfamiliar masts appeared over the horizon, the men on the *Scheer* were surprised that alarms did not sound. They did not understand Krancke's reaction; he was seen on the bridge lounging in a deck chair and smoking one of his black cigars. When the almost motionless old ship, riding half-empty and high, finally hove up before them, the fastidious crew of the *Scheer* could hardly believe their eyes. The *Eurofeld's* visible hull was smeary red all over from weather-beaten rust and blotched with huge clusters of barnacles. The ugliest ship they had ever seen.

Krancke sent some engineers over who quickly patched the *Eurofeld's* broken-down power plants.

The Germans, whose small navy made a strategic point of avoiding contact with the Royal Navy, had developed intricate mid-ocean resupply and scheduling techniques. The *Eurofeld* quickly departed on a short run to refuel the *Thor*, another converted merchant raider in the South Atlantic. She was expected back at Point Green on 17 November to be reloaded by the *Nordmark*, which was slated to arrive the same day. The *Scheer* spent those blank days cruising back and forth waiting for her resupplier to show up.

The *Eurofeld* returned to Point Green at dawn on 16 November. Just after noon, the 23,000-ton *Nordmark*, manned by friends who had trained with the *Scheer* crew, steamed into the gathering. Krancke called out the ship's band to add to the cheer of the occasion. The bandleader mischievously considered striking up 'The Star Spangled Banner' in recognition of the *Nordmark's* masquerade as an American merchantman with the name 'Prairie' on her bows and a big US flag painted beneath. But, as he later told the captain, he thought better of it.

The rejuvenated *Eurofeld* had her cargo areas filled by the big tanker and immediately sailed off in streaky red glory with her barnacles trailing side wakes.

Refuelling the pocket battleship was going to be a bit tricky with swells so heavy that at times the two vessels were not visible to each other. The *Nordmark* moved slowly ahead, and the *Scheer* fell about three hundred yards behind her. The tanker dropped a thin line off her stern that was kept afloat by a balloon at its end. It was captured and lifted onto the bow of the *Scheer*, followed by a thicker line, then by a strong rope that in turn was attached to a heavy towing hawser. Under the urging of the first officer and a rhythmic whistle from the bo'sun's pipe, a muscle-bound crew lugged the hawser aboard and made it fast to the tow stanchion. Then, using two lines that came up with the hawser, they lifted two diesel-oil pipelines from the tanker and connected them to the fuel intakes.

The *Nordmark* took the *Scheer* under a slow tow to keep the ships from drifting apart and rupturing the slack fuel lines. She started her pumps and began the diesel refuelling. During the several hours it took to top off the bunkers and for the next two days, every available boat was used in the heavy sea to fully replenish the raider with ammunition and other stores. One 11-inch shell was damaged, one keg of beer was dropped three decks and destroyed, and no crew injuries occurred. The hazardous operation was a remarkable success.[8]

The Admiralty had kept several British and Canadian destroyers, including ex-American four-stackers, and some cruisers searching for survivors without success long after the *Stureholm* had returned to Halifax with the 65 *Jervis Bay* men she had picked up, and after two independent ships, the *Gloucester City* and the *Mount Taygetus*, had delivered the convoy's 166 other survivors to Canadian ports.

All told, the attack on convoy HX 84 brought five hastily assembled and widely dispersed Royal Navy task groups—totalling two battleships, three battle cruisers, an aircraft carrier, five cruisers, and fifteen destroyers—into the hunt for the *Admiral Scheer*. The search kept the Royal Navy scurrying for two frustrating weeks before it was called off. Provoking the British to pull this many ships out of normal naval operations was one of Krancke's major objectives. He intended to draw the British into disruptive searches throughout the raider's extended cruise in the southern oceans.

On 20 November, about the same time the search ended, the *Scheer* sailed from Point Green toward her next operational destination along the Antilles-to-Azores shipping lanes.[9]

17 The *San Demetrio* Saga

THE oil port of Aruba lay sweltering in the mid-October Caribbean sun 12 degrees above the equator. Tied against one of the quays, the 8,073-ton tanker *San Demetrio* stood ready to receive her cargo. Hoses stretched along the concrete like snakes soaking up the heat of the day. They writhed briefly as the pumps started and then snapped rigid with the flow of aviation fuel. When eight of the nine tanks had been filled with 11,200 tons of sorely needed petrol for the Royal Air Force, the hoses were detached, and the captain immediately called for a tug. After a nudge to open water, the awkward vessel got under way, slipped northward through the West Indies, and ran up the US and Canadian coasts to Halifax, where convoy HX 84 was assembling.

The *San Demetrio's* master, George Waite, held the Order of the British Empire for his enterprise in an action involving another tanker, the *San Alberto*. In late December 1939 that ship was broken in two by a German torpedo. Her after section remained afloat. Waite and some other officers and crew in a lifeboat reboarded it. They found the main engine intact, ran it in reverse, and, with the propeller pulling her like an aeroplane, undamaged stern first, they set sail for Britain. The ship, however, could not maintain a straight course. Flared plates on the sheared-off end of the hull acted as fixed rudders and kept her turning in a great circle. For two days, they tried to offset the go-around with the *San Alberto's* true rudder (now preceding instead of following the ship). Waite and his men finally gave up and were taken aboard a destroyer, which sank the navigation menace with gunfire. Though the captain himself was to be involved only in the first stage of the coming *San Demetrio* adventure, it was a strikingly similar exploit.

Versions of the *Admiral Scheer's* attack on the *San Demetrio* (those of Second Officer Arthur Hawkins in chapter 13, above, and Captain Waite's, given here) differ somewhat. According to Waite, a decisive commander, upon seeing the 'convoy scatter' signal, he called for full speed, ordered the gun crew to fire, and had the lifeboats swung over the sides ready for loading and lowering. The crew pulled on their life jackets. Hawkins went aft to the 4.7-inch gun and lobbed two shells toward the pocket battleship.

'For God's sake,' the suddenly circumspect Waite bellowed, 'stop firing. It'll only get her back up.'

The tanker was heading away from the *Scheer*, but toward other ships then under fire. The captain discussed the situation with other bridge officers; all agreed the *San Demetrio* probably was the next target and they should at once alter direction.

Waite ordered, 'Hard-a-starboard.'

At the same moment, a nearby ship veered to the port. The two were on a collision course. Waite quickly tightened his turn and narrowly averted a disaster. But, by then, the tanker had completed a U-turn and was heading straight at the closing raider. The other ship in that wild avoidance manoeuvre (probably the *Kenbane Head*) was immediately shelled. As her bow rose out of the sea, men on the tanker's deck heard screams and saw bodies falling into the water.

The *Scheer*'s next salvo straddled the *San Demetrio*, silhouetted against the fading orange of the last minutes of twilight. Waite at once issued a prearranged order, 'Finished with engines,' which meant 'stop the engines and abandon the ship.' He was not going to allow his crew to be incinerated by thousands of tons of flashing aviation fuel. His next command—perhaps based on his *San Alberto* experience— was to drop Jacob's ladders over the sides for a possible return. As the crew began lowering the three available lifeboats, another flight of shells left the raider's guns. Two boats were in the water, and the last one, holding Waite and three men, was still inching downward when the projectiles struck the starboard amidships and near the No 5 cargo tank just aft of the bridge. Fires broke out at once. The only gunfire casualties were two young radio operators, still tapping out attack reports, and another crewman blown off the ship. Why they did not leave the ship with the rest of the crew is not known.[1]

Chief Engineer Charles Pollard climbed into his lifeboat on the starboard side with eight other men. They were the first afloat. As they were about to unhook the falls and push off from the ship, they heard a shout: 'Hold on!' Seven other men clustered at the davits shimmied down the falls and joined them. This was not an easy exercise. In helping the descending men into the tossing boat, Pollard, a tough, fifty-ish veteran merchant seaman, disabled his right hand by inadvertently jamming it between one of the tight lines and the hull. Storekeeper John Davies, about Pollard's age, and John Boyle, a twenty-five-year-old greaser, fell hard into the boat and suffered broken ribs. No one suspected that Boyle was bleeding internally from his injury.

The shell fire—both 11-inch and medium-calibre—grew heavier. Shrapnel pelted the tanker and the water around the lifeboat, all of it coming from near misses. For a time, the Germans seemed to have taken a holiday from their normally superb gunnery. Even the splinters avoided human targets. In these crucial minutes, Hawkins, the highest ranking line officer in the boat, assumed command

(Pollard, higher in rank, was an engineering officer). He called on the men at the oars to strain: 'Put your backs into it, boys. Let's get to the windward of her. If she blows up, we don't stand a chance.'

About ten minutes of hard rowing moved the lifeboat out of the danger zone. Then the *Scheer's* gunners re-established the range and hit the *San Demetrio* repeatedly. Fires burst out amidships and at the poop. On the *Scheer* Captain Krancke, sure the blazing tanker would sink, ordered a cease-fire and went after other ships. By then, darkness was spreading, the gale started blowing in, the sea rose, and the sixteen survivors were soaked and freezing. Contact with twenty-three shipmates in the other two lifeboats was lost.

Because the storm escalated during the night, the men had no time to relax. Rough-crested waves broke over the prow and kept the men wet, cold, and miserable. Bailing was a constant demand. They kept the boat into the wind and the sea by putting out a sea anchor and rowing without let-up. Boyle, who kept the pain from his injury to himself, was one of the labouring oarsmen.[2]

When daylight came, the storm was in full force and the cold, drenched, exhausted men were still rowing. Hawkins broke out the first allotment of biscuits and a dipper of water for each man. Oswald Preston looked at the handout and loudly declared: 'How are we gonna eat biscuits? We left our dentures on board.'

Preston, who had signed on as an able seaman just before the trip, was called 'The Yank' by his new shipmates. No one remembered how the nickname got attached to him. He was Canadian-born and had a reckless and non-co-operative demeanour, perhaps an American stereotype to the British merchant seamen. His keen, freckled face projected wit. The Yank was known as a slacker, avoiding most duties while they were in convoy and behaving as if he were on a pleasure cruise. When he got into the lifeboat, his slothful manner turned 180°. He worked like a demon, volunteered for tasks that daunted others, and he raised the men's spirits with his boisterous humour. Hawkins said that 'his cheerfulness was catching.'

Early in the light of morning, they sighted a ship. The men shouted and redoubled their pull on the oars and set off flares, but she soon vanished. The disappointment alone almost drained their flagging store of energy. To help restore their spirits, the Yank claimed she was a German merchant cruiser and they were lucky she didn't spot them.

In the afternoon, another ship appeared. Again, they stepped up the pace of their rowing. Drawing closer, they could see she was drifting and smoking from internal fires, apparently abandoned. Her lines seemed familiar. Then the bo'sun, Fletcher (given name unknown), noticed that her masts and funnel were almost completely painted vermilion. He turned to the Yank and grinned: '*San Demetrio*. You never finished chipping and painting the funnel.'

Preston stared, mouth open but unnaturally silent for a stretch, until he mumbled: 'I'll be goddamned.'

The wind and the currents were pushing her toward them. As the distance between them diminished, it became evident that the water around her was blanketed with aviation fuel. The sea was still rough, and they thought better of approaching her too closely. Should the lifeboat scrape against the *San Demetrio's* side and strike sparks, the fuel around them could ignite and the whole tanker could blow. Hawkins ordered the men to row around the stern and stay on the ship's weather side, lest the wind push her down on them in the coming darkness.

They rigged a canvas shelter over the bows of the boat and prepared to pass the night. Hawkins rationed out more biscuits and water, and a bit of bully beef. They took turns rowing, bailing, fighting off the freezing rain and sleet and seasickness, resting, huddling under blankets, and keeping watch (though their ship was not visible through the violent black air and sea around them). Some of the men discussed their options: Should they board a helpless, burning vessel with a good chance of flashing into a holocaust? Or stay in a flimsy boat in a storm in the middle of the freezing North Atlantic?

Suddenly, an opening in the scudding clouds revealed a light. Someone shouted: 'A plane! A plane!'

Another voice called, 'Get the flares out!'

From the stern, Apprentice John Lewis Jones, a born seaman, ruefully dashed their hope in a soft Welsh inflection: 'That's no plane. That's bloody Jupiter.' His reckoning was soon confirmed by other experienced navigators.[3]

At about 3:00 am, they saw a terrific burst of flame. It came from the aft part of the ship, and in the ensuing eerie glow they saw her head begin to settle. Then the light faded, and the *San Demetrio* disappeared again. The men got through the rest of the blustery, frosty night buoyed by a ridiculous argument over where the governor-general of Canada had been educated.

The second dawn rose with their boat still tossing over a high, running, empty sea. Some men thought the early morning explosion might have sunk the ship. Nevertheless, most of them were upset that they had not reboarded her. In spite of the danger from her volatile cargo, she was their ship. She could protect them from the storm. She had sought them out in the storm and found them, even after they had abandoned her. Maybe she was still afloat. They would not fail her if she found them again. As these metaphysical thoughts played on, one of the men almost whispered that he thought he saw her.

Indeed, there was smoke in the distance. Through the night, the wind had pushed at the tanker's port side, which behaved as a huge sail and moved her far ahead of the lifeboat. Now, somehow, she revealed herself.

'Bend your backs, boys,' Hawkins again told his fatigued men. They moved just close enough to resolve the vision into a long, low silhouette with three humps in the right places—fo'c'sle, bridge, and poop—and smoke rising from deep fires eating away at her stern and amidships. No doubt, it was the *San Demetrio*. But their progress was painfully slow, until fate came to their rescue and inserted a lull in the storm. For the first time, the wind fell off enough to risk hoisting the sail.

'Who knows sailing?' Hawkins asked. Fortune again was kind in placing Colum McNeil among them. A smiling, moon-faced, sandy-haired, twenty-six-year-old fisherman from the Hebrides, McNeil was a master at sailing small craft. Under his skilled hand, the lug and jib sails caught air, and the awkward lifeboat closed the mother ship swiftly. Just before noon, the sixteen crewmen passed the tanker astern and swung around to her lee, where they were protected from the rebuilding wind and sea.

They drew along the after starboard side under one of the Jacob's ladders Captain Waite had made sure would be there if needed. Blankets were draped over the gunwale to prevent the boat's steel side from striking sparks off the hull and igniting the petrol surrounding the ship. The drenched, seasick men climbed single-file up the unsteady rope-and-wood-slat ladder. For the injured, the twenty-four-foot ascent was another test of their grit. Pollard provided some needed laughs when, halfway up, he slipped on a wet slat and split his trousers. His embarrassment lasted only until he pulled on a boiler suit he found in a hasty search of the cabins.

After the men settled in on the *San Demetrio's* boat deck, Hawkins quickly considered his position. As acting captain, his responsibility was the lives of his crew, the safety of the ship, and delivery of her vital cargo. It was a terrible burden for an untested man in his mid-twenties. Hawkins recognised all of this, but he was thrust into the situation and he embodied the confidence of youth. He turned his attention to his crew. It was obvious to him that they were not in tiptop condition after their experience in the lifeboat. Boyle and Davies were in severe pain from their broken ribs. No one yet knew that Boyle had suffered much worse than cracked bones. Jones's lips were swollen and blistered. Third Engineer George Willey's feet were blackened from exposure. And Pollard's right hand remained crippled.

First, a tot of rum that survived in the second engineer's cabin was passed around for sixteen sips. And Pollard, who came across a mug of tea, topped with cinders and reeking of cordite fumes, was so thirsty that he downed it in a few gulps. Then, the acting captain mapped out a procedure with Pollard's assistance.[4]

Hawkins then ordered the entire crew to lift the lifeboat onto the ship, in case they had to abandon her again. It was banging against the tanker's rudder, threatening to damage the steering mechanism and itself. The Yank volunteered to drop down to the boat attached to a lifeline. They worked it along the starboard side, again careful to prevent sparking, until it inched directly under the undamaged after-davits. He bailed out some water, then manhandled it to a position under the falls, which he hitched to its lift fittings. The men heaved on the ropes and inched the boat up the ship's side. After rising about 6 feet, its waterlogged weight defeated their effort. They found no way of tipping the water out of it. They left the boat dangling and unsecured, and the Yank scrambled up his lifeline to the deck.

With the suspended lifeboat dashing against the rocking hull, the men turned to assessing the *San Demetrio's* damage and determining what measures were needed to bring her back to some kind of operating status. Hawkins organised them into fire and repair teams.

The whole amidships, including the wreckage of the bridge, was smouldering and began shooting flames here and there above the Nos 5, 6, and 7 tanks. Much of the twisted steelwork and the steel of the deck were glowing red or white. The fire-fighters began snuffing out the embers in what was left of the wooden fittings and decking with buckets of water pulled up from the sea. The main-deck plating, over the cargo tanks, was buckled by fires. No shells had penetrated to the cargo and exploded, though several tanks were pierced by splinters. The crew considered it a miracle that the volatile fuel in the tanks failed to ignite. Had they reboarded the ship fifteen minutes later, McNeil reckoned, the No 7 tank would have flashed and that would have been the end for them. Pollard suspected the heat of the fires created pressure in the tanks that kept the flames away from the cargo.

When the ship rode over waves, the sloshing liquid in some tanks squirted up through shrapnel holes onto sections of deck that were hot enough to vaporise it. One spark to a dense cloud of aviation fuel and 11,000 tons of it could blow them sky high.

All crew accommodations except the starboard aft room were

gutted by still burning fires, which the men doused with six extinguishers. Adjacent to this area, the large, steel-clad meat-storage refrigerator presented a major problem. Its twelve inches of cork insulation was burning and chucking out glowing clinkers. Since the extinguishers could not reach all the smouldering cork, some men began chopping away at the insulation, which included concrete. Progress was slow.

Hawkins found cans of white paint in an undamaged store below. He gave them to some deck hands and had them brush 'HELP' and 'SOS' in huge letters across the bridge, on forward bulkheads, across the aft end of the poop, and on a board hung over the side. After a while, one of the painters on the starboard side heard a clatter and a splash, and he called out that the lifeboat was gone. Heavy seas had strained the twine falls to parting, and the boat had dropped to the water. Several men on the deck sadly watched as it drifted out of sight. 'There goes our last resort,' one of them mumbled.

Four repair-team men entered the engine room. 'Gee, what a hell of a mess,' said Pollard. About four feet of water covered the deck up to the crew's working platforms. Everything was wet...but the diesels, the fuel units, and the lubricating and cooling systems were undamaged. After deciding the engine room was in surprisingly good condition, Pollard, along with Willey, Boyle, and Davies, looked at the electrical generator that fed the degaussing coils. It had been dismantled for overhaul, just before the German attack began. All its parts were undamaged. The men quickly reassembled the machine and, with degaussing/magnetic-mine protection far down the list of priorities, they connected it to a boiler fuel unit. When current did not flow, they discovered that cables were damaged. Willey cut and spliced them, restarted the generator, and one of the boilers immediately came to life. Steam quickly rose to eighty pounds and was fed to the aft ballast pump, which someone had connected to fire hoses. After the more serious fires were contained—except for the one eating away at the refrigerator insulation—the pump was used alternately to bail out the engine room and to feed the hoses when they were needed.

The men in the meat-storage room kept chipping and hacking away at the cooler's thick layer of cork and concrete between the inner and steel outer walls. Whenever wind entered the room through holes in the poop, fires flared up and threatened to ignite petrol sloshing about on the decks above. It took until daylight, and a pile of broken cork on the deck, to penetrate the insulation with a hose and soak it thoroughly. One of the fire-fighters entered the refrigerator and discovered a 'roasted' joint of beef and four cases of eggs that

The *San Demetrio* showing damage on the port side of the poop, the Chief Engineer's cabin above and refrigerator room below. *(Imperial War Museum)*

had been baked in the heat of the burning cork. Both were edible, though some of the beef was tainted with extinguisher chemicals and sickened a few men. The rest of the fatigued crew was called in, and they enjoyed their first semblance of a meal in more than two days.

Pumping continued in the engine room, and before dawn it was dried out.[5]

Morning came, 8 November, and its first hours were critical. All parts of the propulsion system seemed ready to start up. But if the tanker got under way, would her torn bows stand the pounding they would have to take? The radio equipment was destroyed, along with the two young men who operated it. The binnacle was missing, the wheelhouse was beyond repair, and communication was lost between the damaged auxiliary steering controls and the engine room.

The binnacle was found with its seemingly undamaged compass three decks below the wrecked bridge. It was carried up to the after steering position and set in place. The men noticed an ominous bubble in the compass fluid, but for the moment they shrugged it off.

The little auxiliary steering wheel was left with four fire-eaten spokes and a small remaining arc of blackened rim. Its pedestal was ready to drop through the burned deck boards. The repair team cut some heavy planks and jammed them in place to shore up the mount.

Pollard developed an ingenious makeshift signalling system for communications from the substitute bridge to the engine room. He installed three lamps on the starboard side high above the engines, where the engineering officer on duty could easily see them. When the forward lamp lighted, it indicated 'ahead.' Controlled flickering meant either 'increase speed' or 'decrease speed.' The centre light was the 'stop engines' order and the after light called for 'astern.' To draw attention to the signals, a deck hand banged on the skylight above the engine room.

By 2:00 pm, most fires were doused and the essential repairs completed. Hawkins ordered a start-up, and Pollard tested the diesels ahead and in reverse. They turned over and transmitted rotational power to the propeller as easily as if they had just emerged from a shipyard overhaul. The confident young acting captain ordered 'ahead' at 120 revolutions, bringing the ship to twelve knots. Then he realised that top speed against the heavy seas would invite further damage to the bows, and he signalled a drop to nine knots. Hawkins next put the tanker through an S-shaped test run. The fragile auxiliary wheel held intact as it controlled the steam-driven steering engine, which in turn operated the rudder. So far, all systems were working. They were ready to head for home, and the acting captain set a course of 125 degrees (ESE).[6]

As the *San Demetrio* roughed it through the northeasterly gale, navigation became a major challenge for Hawkins. He set up alternating two-hour watches with the apprentice Jones, whose knowledge of the stars he valued. That night, with stars intermittently

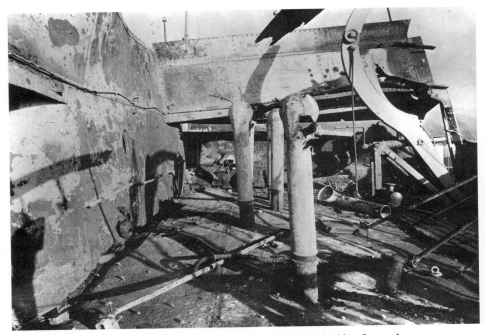

More *San Demetrio* damage on the starboard upper bridge deck looking forward.
(Imperial War Museum)

visible, the first check of some of their positions revealed that the ship was moving due south, while the compass still showed the original ESE heading. When the stars next showed through the clouds, Hawkins brought the ship around to due east (90 degrees), but the needle remained stuck on 125. They might as well have left the compass and its binnacle where they had fallen on the well deck. The men improvised a way of maintaining a more or less reliable heading. They used the positions of the stars, when the right ones were visible, and sightings on the rising and setting sun. These sketchy fixes were supplemented by keeping their wake straight as far back as they could see on the turbulent surface and by including in their reckoning the known direction of the prevailing wind. Navigation was made all the more difficult by the lack of a timepiece: the ship's chronometer was out of commission, and the men's wristwatches all were gagged with water. Latitude and longitude were impossible to compute accurately without the correct time, and vice versa.

The skeleton crew nursed the sorely wounded ship along, as she plunged and heaved in the storm and took heavy water over the well decks. They kept operations as routine as possible under exceedingly abnormal conditions. What rest they snatched was little more than a catnap here and a mug of tea there. The sixteen sailors were down close to the minimum number needed to keep the *San Demetrio* on course. If as few as two of them became disabled, she could turn into a wallowing derelict.

With virtually every pitch, yaw, and roll of the vessel, petrol spouted out of breaches in the tank tops and spilled down some companionways. It remained a flash peril. During a lull in the storm, Hawkins put four men on a detail plugging the holes. The pegs they used were fashioned from cotton wrapped around cores of softwood they had shaped to fit the openings. The Yank continued proving his worth by working cheerfully in the most difficult locations, sometimes up to his neck in water. Replacement of popped plugs was to be a demand all the way home.

Everyone was careful to keep flames, sparks, anything that could ignite petrol fumes suppressed. When Hawkins smelled food cooking, he jerked to attention. *Good God, he thought, who could be stupid enough to light a fire on this explosive bucket?*

He hurried after his nose down to the engine room and found Pollard hunched over two steaming pots. The chief engineer turned to Hawkins with a smile and said the men could use some hot food so he thought he'd take a turn as chief steward.

He explained he used to clean his greasy boiler suits in a pail of suds heated and swished by steam out of a boiler drain pipe. It occurred to him that he might try the same technique, less the soap, to boil the raw potatoes and onions that had been found in the undamaged mess store along with two tanks of drinking water.

Hawkins was relieved, and not a little impressed with the engineer's innovation. Pollard's fare, especially some onions he roasted on a boiler cover, warmed the crew's guts and lifted their spirits.

In spite of the treat, the men were in wretched condition. Most of them were almost continuously seasick and affected by some degree of exposure. All medical stores were destroyed. By Saturday, 9 November, Boyle could no longer do useful work. He was in deep pain from the fractured ribs; and the unrecognised internal haemorrhaging left him weakened and chilled to the bone. Pollard settled him in the least damaged cabin and made him as comfortable as he could. The chief engineer patched some pipes and fed steam into the cabin radiator.

'How do you feel now, sonny?' he asked Boyle.

'Not too bad. My stomach hurts.'

Davies also was hurting from his two broken ribs.

'You've got growing pains,' Pollard told him.

Davies could not laugh, but he managed a smile and carried on.

Willey's blackened feet felt nothing but the buzzing pain of numbness. Standing on them was almost unbearable. Jack Halloran, the second steward, also was severely afflicted with exposure. Yet all the men, except the prostrate Boyle, carried out their duties. They needed no urging.

One of the fingers on Pollard's injured right hand swelled until it looked as if it would burst. The Yank, who took over as head nurse, penetrated the fingernail with his penknife. Pus and blood spurted out of the opening, and after a while the finger shrank to nearly its normal size. The blade was not sterile, but the gusher probably carried away any infectious bacteria introduced into the wound.[7]

By mid-afternoon the *San Demetrio's* bows were riding lower, and she was responding sluggishly to the rudder. With the delicate, fire-damaged helm a constant threat to break away from its post, steering the ship by its surviving spokes took fingertip handling. Hawkins and Pollard went forward and found that water was entering shell and splinter holes and cascading into the fore hold. The added weight was pressing the stem deeper into the sea. As the water level rose in the hold, the ship grew less responsive and more unstable. Pollard and some of his men tried to solve the problem by repairing steam pipes to the forward ballast pump. They struggled to keep their footing as the seas broke over the settling fo'c'sle. Some of their tools washed overboard, and they gave up just before dark.

It was too rough the next day for men to work on the deck. Though the gale protected the tanker from U-boats and the German bombers that swept the western approaches to Britain, it increased the rate of water flow into the fore hold. The ship was down deeper by the head and responding to commands like a fractious camel. Hawkins and Pollard decided to transfer aviation fuel from the forward No 9 tank to the empty No 6 below the aft part of the bridge. The engineer, together with Jones, who volunteered for the hazardous assignment, went down to the dark pump room with a safety torch. The small chamber was filled with noxious fumes. They quickly found the right set of colour-coded wheels. Using a spanner they had brought with them, they opened the pipeline to the No. 6 tank, opened the outlet valve from No 9, and started the pumping. Then, they escaped from the toxic gas of the pump room as fast as they could. More than a thousand tons of fuel flowed aftward. The shift in weight distribution brought up *the San Demetrio's* head and created a slight, but not bothersome, list to the starboard. From then on, she rode more easily and shipped less water.[8]

Since it was Sunday, Hawkins held a brief, nondenominational service. He used the only book on the ship not scorched, the Yank's

Bible, which had been given to him by his children. The Lord's Prayer came first. Then Hawkins recited what he remembered from 'The Form of Prayer to Be Used at Sea': 'Look down, we beseech Thee, and hear us calling out of the depth of misery, and out of the jaws of this death that is now ready to swallow us up... Oh, send Thy word of command to rebuke the raging winds and the roaring sea.'

All the while, Boyle drifted into a darkening haze. Crew members dropped into his cabin, asking how he felt, trying to comfort him, rearranging the bedclothes over him. The Yank was the last man to speak to him, around midnight. Before morning, the young greaser was dead. He was buried at sea by his shipmates. They could not talk without tears about his courage in doing his share of hard work through his pain while his blood drained away into his abdominal cavity.[9]

The gale gradually reversed its direction to southwesterly, and by Tuesday 12 November it began to moderate. Hawkins calculated that land might be sighted that evening. To everyone's disappointment, their straining eyes saw nothing but wet horizon.

'Don't worry,' the Yank cracked,' by tomorrow, we're bound to make landfall somewhere between Narvik and Gibraltar.'

Early Wednesday afternoon, in a calm sea, Hawkins with binoculars to his eyes suddenly raised his left thumb. The sighting quickly spread through the ship. Men excitedly gathered on the main deck. There it was. Cliffs topped with grass and low stone walls. White cottages scattered throughout the landscape. The surf crashed against some massive black rocks. It looked like Ireland. But it could be Cornwall or Brittany. Hawkins was convinced their navigation was precise enough and that they were near County Mayo. He took the ship along the coast, and by twilight they came to an inlet, which, sure enough, was Blacksod Bay. The young acting captain was tempted to take shelter in the bay. It appeared deep enough, but dropping the anchors meant losing them, for the damaged windlass could not raise them again. He remained in the bay by running the wounded *San Demetrio* in slow circles all night 'like a mouse in a pail.'

At daybreak, to everyone's joy, the tug *Superman* chugged up and, seeing 'SOS' and 'HELP' all over the tanker, her captain offered them a tow. Hawkins proudly but politely refused. In response to the tug's radioed report, the destroyer HMS *Arrow* approached and signalled that she would escort them to the Clyde. Hawkins, however, wanted to patch up his ship before entering a home port. The destroyer commander sent over a boarding party to help cover the holes and do some repairs in the engine room.

The *San Demetrio* started for the Clyde that night, heading around

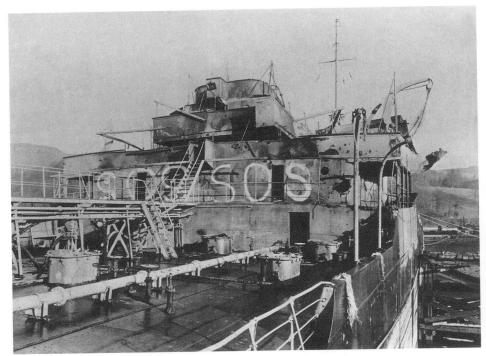

The *San Demetrio,* emblazoned with painted 'SOS' signs, reaches Rothesay Bay after enduring hard shelling by the *Scheer,* abandonment, reboarding, and an arduous trip with a skeleton crew to her destination port, where she unloads 11,000 tons of sorely needed aviation fuel. *(Imperial War Museum)*

Northern Ireland accompanied by the Arrow until they were well down the Northern Channel. The tug stayed with her all the way, in case she needed assistance. By the night of 15 November, ten days after convoy HX 84 was attacked by the *Admiral Scheer,* she lay at the mouth of the River Clyde. At first daylight fifteen elated men sailed her into Rothesay Bay. Halloran and Davies were bundled off to a hospital, and the other ten crewmen were given a day's shore leave to rest and refuel. Hawkins, Pollard, and Fletcher remained on board for the night. On 17 November, with the men back from their liberty, they prepared to unload the cargo. Two days later, the patchwork tanker sidled up to a discharging berth. Valve connections were made, and the San Demetrio's own repaired pumps delivered 11,000 tons of fuel to keep the RAF flying.[10]

On top of the happy ending to this maritime saga, the Eagle Oil & Shipping Company, owner of the *San Demetrio,* gladly participated in a salvage claim hearing. The presiding judge said he never had a more satisfying task to perform. He decreed that the men who brought in the ship be paid £14,700, many times the value of the same amount today. Hawkins and Pollard each received £2,000. The other men's awards averaged £823. The judge was delighted when the rest of the crew unanimously requested that the at first irresponsible, then irrepressible Yank also be given the red ensign that flew from the *San Demetrio's* mast.

When the men in the lifeboat reboarded the burning tanker, their focus was on surviving, saving their ship, and delivering her vital cargo. Thoughts of salvage awards did not occur to them during their ten-day ordeal. The subject was first mentioned by a company representative after they had reached port.

For their courageous 'rescue' of the *San Demetrio* and her load of aviation fuel, Hawkins and Pollard were appointed Officers of the Order of the British Empire (civil); Willey was made a Member of the Order of the British Empire (civil); Preston (the Yank), Davies, and Fletcher, who later was found to have three broken ribs, were awarded the British Empire Medal; and Boyle received a Posthumous Commendation.

Their greatest rejoicing came with the news that all of their shipmates in the other two lifeboats had been picked up and were delivered to Canada.[11]

18 End of the String

DESPITE mistakes, fate, and circumstances that cost him the distinction of sinking virtually the entire HX 84 convoy, Theodor Krancke proved himself an exceptional commander. During the remainder of the *Admiral Scheer*'s cruise, which extended into the Indian Ocean and concluded in early spring 1941, the raider sank or captured ten more cargo ships. Each confrontation was different, and in each the captain employed a different tactic.

In one of them, a mid-December capture in the South Atlantic, *Scheer* commandos boarded the refrigerated, 8,652-ton *Duquesa* and discovered in her holds 3,000 tons of meats, 15 million eggs, vegetables, fruits, whiskeys, wines, liqueurs, and stores of other goodies. Christening her 'The Floating Delicatessen,' the raider's men kept provisioning themselves (and other German raiders and resupply ships) for two months until she ran out of coal and was scuttled. During that time they could well have been the best-fed crew of the war.

The most unusual encounter involved two freighters simultaneously and, due to a freak accident, almost resulted in the *Scheer* sending herself to the bottom. On the morning of 20 January 1941, a cargo ship was sighted on a northerly course. The pocket battleship began tailing her, but at 3:00 pm the temporarily patched-up radar spotted another vessel heading south. Krancke repaired to his darkened cabin and lit up a cigar. As he considered the alternatives, his nose glowed softly with each draw on his black Brazil. Before long he emerged and told his officers they were going to get two for the price of one: 'I think the time has come for us to try a little guile.'

The British refrigerated ship *Duquesa* (left), captured and manned by a boarding crew, provides the *Scheer* and other German ships with meats, eggs, cheeses, and vegetables for several months before she runs out of coal and is scuttled. (*Bordkameradschaft* Admiral Scheer)

He rang for full speed and turned east, away from the freighters. Beyond naked-eye visibility, he came about and waited until they were about to pass each other along the *Scheer's* line of sight. Then he moved at top speed toward the nearer southbound ship. As the other one disappeared behind her, the *Scheer's* course was altered slightly to the south. This kept her hidden from the northbound merchantman while approaching the first target. When the raider's signalman flashed the British recognition code, the freighter showed her stern—the normal reaction on sighting another vessel—and then she blinked a response. The Germans flashed back: 'Have secret orders for you. Put about to facilitate delivery.'

One forward 11-inch gun had been lowered out of sight, masking the defining triple turret characteristic of the pocket battleship. The freighter reversed her course and, with her wireless still silent, approached the supposed British warship. By the time the captain of the 5,200-ton Dutch cargo carrier *Barneveld* recognised the enemy, it was too late to transmit an 'R R R' signal, despite the insistence of a British lieutenant, one of fifty-one Royal Navy passengers. An armed prize crew boarded the *Barneveld* and discovered to their chagrin that they were outnumbered nearly four to one by enemy naval officers and ratings. Since Krancke had already taken after the second freighter, they were in a vulnerable position. They pointed their guns menacingly, quickly disarmed the few men who carried weapons, then herded the passengers and the fifty Dutch crewmen into a confined space and waited for their ship to return.

At twenty-six knots the *Scheer* rapidly overtook the 5,600-ton *Stanpark*. The freighter's captain, not realising the other cargo vessel had been seized, stopped his ship, put on his white uniform, and prepared to greet the expected Royal Navy boarding party. He dropped Jacob's ladders for them. When bearded German commandos with guns and grenades clambered over the railing, an awful moment of hallucination overcame him. He quickly recovered his composure and handled the situation with British aplomb.

Krancke was not interested in the cargo of cotton seed from Bombay, and after transferring the crew to prison compartments, he ordered the *Stanpark* scuttled. Following the explosions, she settled about ten feet and stopped, apparently due to swelling seeds. Fires broke out amidships and spread rapidly. The captain feared the flames and oily smoke would make her visible beyond the horizon, and he ordered a torpedo coup de grace. The weapon was discharged electrically from four hundred yards. It missed. Krancke shook his head in disbelief.

'Try another one, Schulze,' he told the torpedo officer.

'By the way,' he asked the lookout, 'where's the [commando's cutter]?'

'On the port side , sir.'

'Starboard tube, fire.'

The torpedo sprang out of its compressed-air launcher on the quarterdeck. Plunging about twenty feet into the water, its steering gear struck the cutter's gunwale. *How in hell,* the captain wondered, *did the motor launch get from port to starboard so fast?*

Following the projectile's wake, the officers and men on the bridge were horrified as they saw it describe a U-turn and head straight back at the *Scheer*. The ship was not under way, and the captain could do nothing to avoid it. A strange silence descended over everyone who could see the oncoming torpedo.

'It was just unbelievable,' Krancke later wrote. 'No one could really grasp what seemed to be the obvious fact that the *Scheer* was about to be hit fair and square amidships by one of her own torpedoes.'

Twenty yards from the ship the torpedo nose-dived and disappeared.

'You were right, Voichekovski,' Krancke told the signals officer.

'Me, sir?'

'Wasn't it you who said the *Scheer* is a lucky ship.'

The third torpedo blew the *Stanpark* in half, and both sections went down without ceremony.[1]

In the Indian Ocean on 21 February, with her cruise tally grown to sixteen cargo ships and the *Jervis Bay*, a message came to Krancke from Grand Admiral Erich Raeder: 'The Führer has been pleased to award the Knight's Cross [to the Iron Cross] to you.' It was preceded by an order to come home. During the forty days back to Kiel, the *Scheer* ran a Royal Navy gauntlet.

When the ship was spotted by a British reconnaissance plane from the heavy cruiser *Glasgow* at the beginning of the return trip, Krancke immediately changed her heading from southeast to eastnortheast, hoping to deceive the observer. She stayed the course for more than an hour into the deepening twilight and then switched back to her original direction. Just after midnight, the *Glasgow* closely passed the pocket battleship (radar again out of commission) with neither of them spotting the other. The *Scheer* evaded six more cruisers and an aircraft carrier, rounded the Cape of Good Hope at least four hundred miles south of the nearest enemy airbase, and sailed up the Atlantic to a rendezvous on 10 March with the *Nordmark*. She took on fuel, ammunition, and provisions, including meat and eggs saved from the late 'Floating Delicatessen.'

Then Krancke headed toward the Denmark Strait, along the way picking up a replacement radar crystal from a U-boat. On 25 March the ship raced by the lower tip of Greenland and swung northeasterly for the crucial passage. The wind was almost at zero; the air was cold, brittle, and transparent; and visibility stretched to the horizon. Krancke was sure his ship would be sighted. He decided his best opportunity was to get close to the Greenland ice pack, where the sharp temperature difference between ice and the Gulf Stream might produce fog. The *Scheer* quickly reached the ice barrier, where the temperature dropped and, as the captain anticipated, fog enshrouded them. Then, instead of edging along the pack, Krancke took the ship on twelve hours of mysterious manoeuvring—due east, due south, due west, then eastnortheast toward the narrows.

On 27 March the *Scheer* encountered a snow squall and for a while depended entirely on her electronic eyes. At 7:52 am the radar room reported, 'Large objective at 337 degrees, range 20,000 yards.'

'That's probably one of their heavy cruisers on patrol,' Krancke said. 'Naturally she's looking for us where the visibility's poorest, near...the ice pack.'

'She's making for the narrows now,' said Navigation Officer Hubner.

'[I expect] she's not alone. Probably meeting a second cruiser there,' the captain said. 'We'll continue this present course, but we'll go up to twenty-three knots.'

They sighted two other cruisers but remained undetected by the British warships, which apparently had not yet been equipped with radar. Then, the *Scheer's* radar again went out of action.

At about 3:00 am the next day the raider broke out of the narrows and cut through the arctic seas toward Norway as fast as she could go. No more distant masts or shadowy shapes. On 30 March she put into Grimstadfjord off Bergen for an overnight stay. The following afternoon she set out for home escorted by two destroyers and aeroplanes.

It was an auspicious day, 1 April, when the *Admiral Scheer* docked in Kiel after her successful 161-day cruise of 46,419 nautical miles: seventeen enemy ships sunk or captured and the British fleet discombobulated on at least four separate occasions. It was her eighth birthday. She had been launched with the words, 'Serve your Fatherland loyally and may good luck go with you.' It did, except for the less than triumphant action against the *Jervis Bay* and her convoy. The spruced up *Admiral Scheer* and her 1,300 officers and ratings, in their best uniforms, docked and piped Grand Admiral Raeder aboard. After his inspection, Raeder announced that Iron

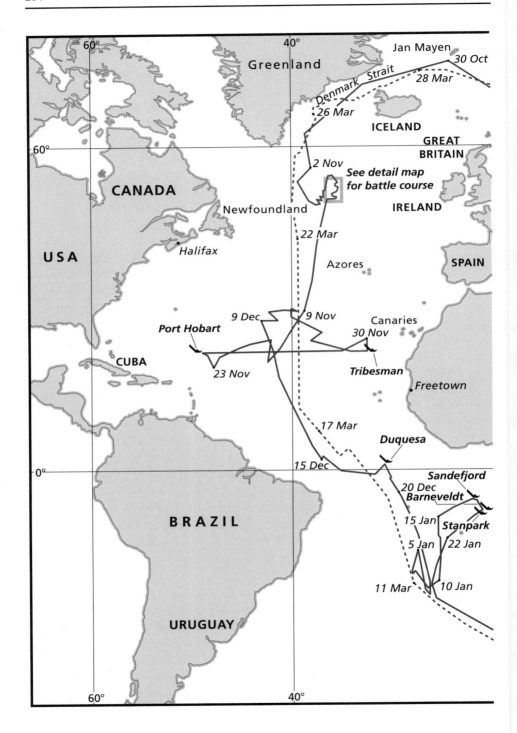

The *Admiral Scheer*'s cruise. *(Chris Robinson)*

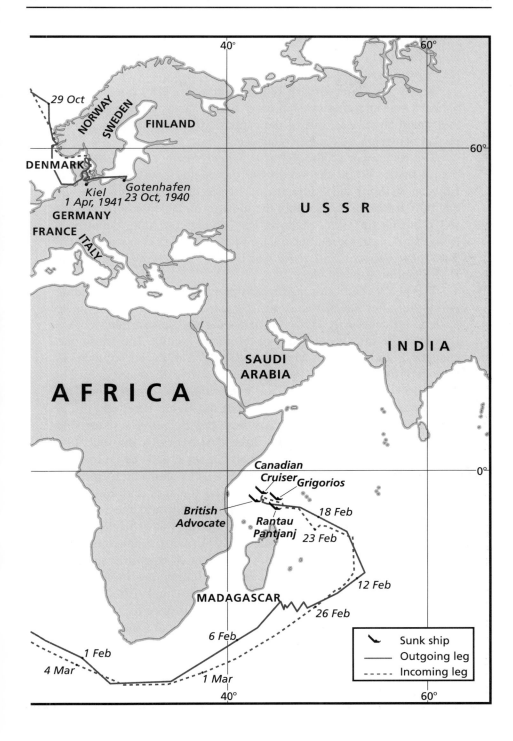

Crosses would go to all members of the crew, one of the few such awards in the history of the German navy. And Krancke was told of his promotion to rear admiral.

Three days later British bombers attacked Kiel harbour. The *Scheer's* anti-aircraft guns shot down two of them. When asked what their main target was, one of the captured flyers said: 'Your bloody pocket battleship, of course. What else?'[2]

The remainder of the *Admiral Scheer's* career was little more than a fizzle. While she was being thoroughly overhauled in Kiel between 15 April and 1 July, the new pride of the Reichsmarine, the 45,000-ton *Bismarck*, probably the most formidable battleship in the world at that time, was sunk on her commerce-raiding debut by a Royal Navy task force after a long running battle. Two weeks later, the *Scheer's* sister ship *Lützow* was hit and severely damaged by an RAF Beaufort torpedo plane.

The pocket battleship had begun preparing for a second raiding cruise, but after the *Bismarck* and *Lützow* calamities, German naval leaders, influenced by Hitler, treated what was left of their surface fleet as if the ships were in a long-term-care facility. The cruise was cancelled, and Wilhelm Meendsen-Bohiken replaced Krancke as captain of the *Scheer*.

Following several Baltic Sea workouts, the former lone-wolf raider was assigned to Group North of the Baltic Fleet and on 23 September sailed toward Norway with the *Bismarck's* sister ship *Tirpitz*, two light cruisers, and three destroyers. A day out, two mishandled depth charges exploded on her deck, and she returned to Hamburg for repairs, with her renown as a lucky ship a bit blemished.

After the war the Germans realised the incident was truly fortunate for the *Scheer*. Through intercepted messages, the US Navy had discovered that the pocket battleship was scheduled to be in the Denmark Strait on 5 November 1941 (the first anniversary of the *Jervis Bay* encounter). Under President Roosevelt's standing order to 'shoot on sight' any German or Italian warship entering America's defence waters, the navy sent a task force of two battleships, two heavy cruisers, and three destroyers to waylay her. (Jürgen Rohwer, vice president of the International Commission on Military History, speculated that had she blundered into the trap, Hitler might have been compelled 'to declare war [on the United States] four weeks before Pearl Harbour.')[3]

Not until 23 February did the *Scheer* join the *Prinz Eugen*, five destroyers, and two torpedo boats in heading for Narvik on what promised to be her first offensive action in almost eleven months. Along the way the *Prinz Eugen's* stern was blown off by a torpedo from a British submarine. The *Scheer* retreated to an anchorage near Trondheim and lay idle for two and a half months. She moved north to Bogen Bay on 10 May with two destroyers and was joined two weeks later by the rehabilitated *Lützow* and three more destroyers. They all sailed to Kaafjord in early June and consolidated with the vessels of No 1 Battle Group: the *Tirpitz*, the *Admiral Hipper*, two destroyers, and two torpedo boats.

This force was assembled to attack Archangel-bound Allied convoy PQ 17 carrying military supplies in thirty-six freighters (twenty-two of them American) and one tanker to the Soviet Union (by then at war with its former friend Germany). The convoy was escorted by eight destroyers, four corvettes, two anti-aircraft ships, and two submarines.

What was a tactically sound plan for the Battle Group ended up as a tragi-comedy of errors that the British also contributed to. It started when the *Lützow*, as jinxed a ship as the *Scheer* was lucky, ran aground on 2 July. The following day three destroyers ploughed into the sands of an uncharted shoal. And the departure of the *Tirpitz*, *Scheer*, and *Hipper* was delayed until 5 July by Hitler, who wanted to be sure the convoy escort did not include an aircraft carrier.

In fear of the *Tirpitz*, Sir Dudley Pound, now the first sea lord, chose to scatter the cargo ships and sent the escorts home. This horrendous operational switch presented a tailing U-boat pack and the Luftwaffe with a golden opportunity. As soon as the escorts left the scene, the slaughter began. They sank twenty-four ships carrying 210 aircraft, 430 tanks, 3,350 vehicles, and 100,000 tons of stores. It was the greatest German naval victory of the war.

But not for No.1 Battle Group (including the *Scheer*), which never got close enough to the convoy to fire a shot. For them it was a huge frustration.[4]

After idling for another month and a half, the *Admiral Scheer* was sent on a curious operation into the Kara Sea off northern Siberia. Her mission was to attack shipping and destroy some coastal facilities. But no traffic was known to be in the area, intelligence was scanty, charts were unreliable, and two earlier forays had accomplished nothing. She spent several days picking her way through increasingly thick ice fields and swarms of icebergs. Trapped once, she managed to jam through the drifts into open water. On the eighth day of the sortie she encountered a small icebreaker, the *Alexander Sibiriakoff*. She fired one across the bow, her first serious shot since the Indian Ocean action a year and a half earlier. The Soviet crew returned fire, and their ship was quickly sunk. Twenty-two of them were taken prisoner.

The *Scheer's* next target was the Port Dikson communications station overlooking the Gulf of Yenisey. The morning of 27 August, she shelled the harbour with 456 medium and smaller rounds, damaging radio installations, port facilities, a patrol boat, and a small (433-ton) steamer.

All told, the strenuous sortie resulted in little of note, but it boosted crew spirits. When the *Scheer* returned to Norway for a boring two-month vacation, their morale waned again. Worse yet, in late September she docked in Wilhelmshaven for a much needed overhaul of her diesels and armament. During the lay-up, Meendsen-Bohlken was succeeded as commander by Captain Richard Rothe-Roth and half the crew was replaced. The ship was still in dry-dock on 26 February 1943, when about sixty-five RAF and American four-engine planes dropped more than 200 high-explosive bombs on harbour and dock installations. Though the *Scheer* received one hit, her pact with the Devil was still in force: it was a dud. Ten other bombs came down on the two adjacent docks, causing her minor splinter damage and one death.[5]

Following a failed attack on a convoy in the Barents Sea, Hitler petulantly ordered the decommissioning of all heavy surface ships. For the most part, the Führer was ignored. But the *Scheer* was given an ignominious assignment to the new Fleet Training Group. She took aboard companies of about five hundred cadets for several three-month indoctrination cycles until November 1944.

The men recouped some of their pride when she was sent to provide cover for an evacuation of German troops trapped on the narrow Sworbe peninsula in Lithuania by overwhelming Soviet forces. Using her surveillance aircraft for spotting, she fired on enemy positions. The German soldiers escaped during the night of 21 November, but the Arado was shot down. The *Scheer* passed through heavy Soviet bomber and torpedo-plane attacks with one dud hitting her upper deck, and with her charmed life extended. She returned to Gotenhafen for two more months of unemployment. In late January and early February 1945, she was stationed off East Prussia, lending artillery support to the retreating army. In her final action, for a few days the next month she bombarded coastal areas being overrun by Soviet forces. Then, with her guns sorely in need of reboring, the former ocean raider docked in Kiel on 18 March.[6]

The end of the *Scheer's* string of good luck was presaged by an air-raid warning on the night of 9 April. Her crew, except for about ninety officers and men, had been sent ashore. At 10:30 pm, the first of 600 Allied planes began dropping their loads. The *Scheer*, now as defenceless as her raiding victims had been in 1940 and 1941, was hit eight minutes later. This time the bomb exploded. More bombs tore holes in her starboard side and put her command and lighting systems out of commission. She listed 16 degrees away from the dock. By 10:45, further hits and near misses increased the list to 28 degrees.

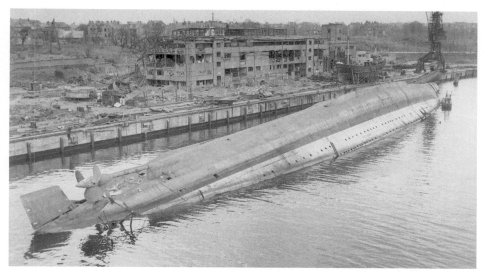

In a 600-bomber Allied attack on Kiel near the end of the war, the undefended *Admiral Scheer* takes multiple hits and capsizes. A shipping raider by design, she was used in that role only once—a mostly successful, 161-day cruise from late 1940 to early spring 1941 through the Atlantic and Indian Oceans, which included the classic *Jervis Bay* engagement. For the remainder of the war she was used ineffectively. *(Imperial War Museum)*

An 'abandon ship' order was given. Men climbed through slanted smoke-and-flame-filled spaces, up strangely tilted companionways, and through portholes. But due to electrical failure many of the skeleton crew did not hear the order. Fifteen of them were killed by explosions, fire, asphyxiation, sliding machinery and other heavy equipment, and drowning. A few minutes later the ship capsized in about 50 feet of water.

After the war, under British supervision, valuable metals, gun housings, and turrets were removed, and the mangled torso was covered over with rubble. In 1950 the remains of the magnificent, innovative *Admiral Scheer* became the foundation for a British-built car park.[7]

Epilogue

KING George VI was at Windsor on 5 November 1940 when news of the attack on the *Jervis Bay* convoy reached him. He followed the reports with the intense interest of a naval officer and made fragmentary entries in his diary:

November 6 & 7 (Wednesday & Thursday)
'On Tuesday evening a report came in that a convoy in the Atlantic was being shelled 'at leisure' by a German pocket battleship the '*Admiral Scheer*.' The War Cabinet decided to send the Fleet in various groups to its rescue in an attempt to catch the '*Scheer*.' No news was heard from the convoy on Wednesday and Thursday.'

November 8 (Friday)
'At last we have heard from one ship of the 'shelled' convoy, which means that there are probably more safe.'

November 9 & 10 (Saturday & Sunday)
'Fourteen ships of the convoy have now reached harbour. There were 38 ships in it [one of them had fallen behind], but as they all disperse in an attack it is difficult for them all to reform again at once.'

November 11 (Monday)
'27 ships have now reported out of the 'shelled' convoy. The AMC '*Jervis Bay*' put up a gallant fight to give the convoy time to disperse.'

The escort's sacrifice stirred the king deeply. At his request the Admiralty on 15 November presented His Majesty a recommendation for award of the Victoria Cross (VC), Britain's highest recognition of wartime valour, to Captain Edward Stephen Fogarty Fegen. The king was gratified at the speed of the response to his wish and was greatly pleased to put his signature on the document two days later.

He entered in his diary: 'I have awarded Captain Fegen the Victoria Cross posthumously. When he attacked the '*Admiral Scheer*' he knew he was going to certain death.' In a note to Queen Mary, the king wrote: 'The story of the *Jervis Bay* is an epic & the award of the Victoria Cross was my idea & I am glad it has come out at once.' (It was the war's only VC for convoy defence.)[1]

In his book *Convoy,* John Winton said, 'Fegen...became the first and greatest convoy hero of the war.'[2]

Prime Minister Churchill also had his say to the House of Commons on 13 November: 'The spirit of the Royal Navy... is... exemplified in the forlorn and heroic action... fought by the captain, officers and ship's company of the *Jervis Bay* in giving battle against overwhelming odds in order to protect the merchant convoy which they were escorting, and thus securing the escape of by far the greater part of that convoy.'[3]

The king personally presented the VC to the captain's sister, M C Fegen, at Buckingham Palace on 12 June 1941. He received her in private with the captain's elder brother, Commander Frederick Wilfrid Fegen (who had been King George's classmate at Dartmouth and Osborne), and told them he had met

Captain Fegen's Victoria Cross.
(picture courtesy Mike Chappell)

several members of the *Jervis Bay's* crew and was moved by their stories of Captain Fegen's heroism.[4]

Rear Admiral H G Thursfield later explained Fegen's action in this way: 'For a convoy escort, the ideal is that it should be strong enough to destroy any enemy liable to attack the ships under its charge. If that standard cannot be reached, it should be...capable of providing a large measure of safety for them; and that is what Captain Fegen succeeded in doing, though only at the sacrifice of his ship and himself. Rarely can a VC have been better earned.'[5]

Fifty years after the medal was awarded, it was entrusted on a long-term loan to the Royal Naval Museum in Portsmouth by Barbara Fegen, wife of the captain's late nephew Anthony, and the captain's niece, Gillian Cooper. Mrs. Fegen said, 'It was a shame to leave the medal locked in a bank vault, where nobody could see it.'[6]

Other awards were documented in the Admiralty's Board of Inquiry report, issued 13 November 1940, by Rear Admiral Stuart S Bonham-Carter:

'I know from my experience of the last war how difficult it is to select men for special recognition... when all must have

Presentation of Captain Fegen's Victoria Cross to the Royal Naval Museum, 19 September 1991. Left to right, Barbara Fegen, Admiral Sir Anthony Morton, Sam Patience, and Gillian (Fegen) Cooper. *(Barbara Fegen. Photo by J A Hewe)*

upheld the highest traditions of the Navy. I therefore ordered the Board of Inquiry to endeavour to discover any outstanding acts [and they provided the following]:

'*James Harold Wood, Leading Seaman, C/JX.134126* [Conspicuous Gallantry Medal] showed outstanding leadership and initiative on the raft after the ship was abandoned. He gave everyone confidence and encouragement and concealed the fact that he was wounded in both thighs.

'*Mr. Ronald Alfred Gardyne Butler, RNR* [Distinguished Service Cross] was one of the last to join the raft having been in the water for some time. He immediately took charge and showed outstanding leadership and initiative.

'*Mr. Hugh Williamson, Senior Radio Officer* showed initiative and devotion to duty in passing enemy reports on Home Station frequencies direct to the Admiralty although on the America and West Indies Station. He was killed in the wireless office whilst transmitting the report on a third frequency. [His award was gazetted as 'Mention in Dispatches (Posthumous)' and was exemplified as representing the many among the survivors and those who went down with the ship who, if the truth were known, deserved decoration.]

'*Donald 'Danny' Bain, Seaman, TRN.R X.9978* [Distinguished Service Medal] was extensively burnt endeavouring to save one of the same gun's crew who was on fire. He had previously been slightly wounded on the scalp.

'*Lieutenant Norman Edgar Wood, RNR (T 124)* [Distinguished Service Order] is the senior surviving officer. I was impressed by his modesty and by the manner in which he took charge of the survivors in the *Stureholm* and since arrival at Halifax.

'*Charles Castle, Petty Officer, C/J.101048* [Distinguished Service Medal] displayed marked courage and leadership both during the action and later on after the ship had been abandoned. His example under most trying circumstances was a great help.

'*John Christopher Egglestone, Able Seaman, RFR, B20971* [Distinguished Service Medal]...was No. 1 of P.2 gun. He was wounded but remained at his post and by his example kept the surviving members of the gun's crew together.

'*Dennis Drury, Stoker, T124* [Distinguished Service Medal]... took a prominent part in organising the launching of the rafts. The ship was being heavily shelled and Drury's coolness and determination were an example to everyone.

'*William Barnett, Assistant Steward, T124* [Distinguished Service Medal]...was stationed in the foremost shell room, when things went wrong and the lights went out. Barnett stuck to his post endeavouring to get the emergency lighting to work. He would not leave his post until [receiving] orders to do so although he could serve no useful purpose by remaining below.

'*William James Albert Cooper, Able Seaman, RNVR C/LDX.3515* [Distinguished Service Medal]...was sightsetter at P1 gun. Orders had been given to abandon the forecastle and all the surviving men had left except Cooper. He had received no orders through his telepad and remained at his post alone. He stayed there quietly awaiting orders until he realised that the fore part of the ship had been abandoned. Then only did he leave.

'*G Beaman, Stoker, RCNVR A2445* [Distinguished Service Medal]...did excellent work in getting the rafts out and later on dived into the water several times in attempts to rescue...men.'[7]

If it is legitimate to anthropomorphise a thin-skinned, vulnerable old cargo liner, then HMS *Jervis Bay* was a heroic ship. She stands memorialised at six places around the British Commonwealth:

A twelve-foot granite shaft with a bronze plaque originally set on the grounds of the Saint John Tuberculosis Hospital (Saint John, New Brunswick) opposite the site of the *Jervis Bay*'s final refit, and now relocated at the Jervis Bay–Ross Memorial Park.

A small riverside park named for the *Jervis Bay* in Owen Sound, Ontario.

A bronze plaque in the Church of Saint George at the Royal Naval Barracks, Chatham.

The RNVR Memorial on the Liverpool pier.

A large granite sundial in Hamilton, Bermuda.

A copper wreath and gold laurel leaves with an inscription at the Seamen's Institute in Wellington, New Zealand.

The dining room of the New Merchant Navy Hotel in London, though not precisely a memorial, is known as the Jervis Bay Room.[8]

Several ships have been named or renamed in honour of the armed merchant cruiser:

> The first commemorative *Jervis Bay* was a British container ship run by Shaw Savill & Albion. The 26,876-ton vessel began her maritime life in 1970 and sailed until the mid-1980s.
>
> The 5,431-ton HMAS *Jervis Bay* GT 203, like the original, was converted from a merchant vessel, the *Australian Trader,* commissioned by the Royal Australian Navy in 1977, and used as a training ship (decommissioned in 1994).

This twelve-foot granite shaft, with its commemorative plaque, at Jervis Bay-Ross Memorial Park, Saint John, NB, Canada, is one of six memorials to the *Jervis Bay*. The others are located in Chatham and Liverpool; Owen Sound, Ontario, Canada; Wellington, New Zealand; and Bermuda. *(Courtesy of #53 Jervis Bay Branch, Royal Canadian Legion, Saint John, New Brunswick)*

Another container ship, the 50,350-ton *Jervis Bay*, was put into operation by P&O Nedlloyd in 1992. Her chief engineer Bernie Jones is the son of Charles Edward Jones who went down with Captain Fegen's ship in 1940.

The Royal Australian Navy's 1,250-ton sea-lift catamaran *Jervis Bay* was commissioned in June 1999. Three months later she transported 500 fully equipped troops and their land vehicles at more than 40 knots to Dili in East Timor as part of the United Nations–sanctioned 'operation Stabilise.' All told the 282-foot vessel made twenty round trips between Darwin and Dili carrying more than 2,800 troops and passengers, 217 vehicles, and hundreds of cargo pallets.[9]

Among the four vessels named *Jervis Bay* in honor of the armed merchant cruiser are (above) the 50,350-ton P&O Nedlloyd container ship and (below) the 282-foot Royal Australian Navy catamaran that carried troops and vehicles to East Timor for the United Nations during 'operation Stabilise.' *(above: P & O Nedlloyd, below: Incat Australia)*

Tom Davison was featured in a widely published, three-panel cartoon advertisement with a headline, 'Hero *of 'Jervis Bay'* sea battle tells his story.' In it, he recounts how his soaked flashlight attracted the Swedish freighter *Stureholm* which picked up the survivors from his raft. 'Without those dependable 'Eveready' fresh dated batteries,' he says in the ad, 'we would have died miserably.'[10]

The *Gloucester City* left Britain in outward-bound convoy OBM 234 a day or two after HX 84 departed Halifax. Capable of only nine knots, she fell behind the other ships and soon lost touch with them. With U-boats and long-range German bombers on the hunt in the North Atlantic, it was a scary time to be alone, especially knowing that independently sailing cargo ships were sunk far more frequently than those in convoys.

Early in the evening of 5 November, the radio operator picked up an 'SOS' from the *Rangitiki* reporting that her convoy was being shelled by an enemy raider at a position about 290 miles to the

Eveready Battery ad featuring a survivor of the *Jervis Bay* engagement.
(Eveready Battery Company)

southwest. *Gloucester City*'s master S G Smith felt there might be survivors in the water. He chose, like the *Stureholm*'s captain, to ignore the Admiralty's stay-away-from-sinking-ships stricture. He immediately altered course toward the attack position. The 3,071-ton freighter, with no cargo to stabilise her, ran into a force-10 gale that nearly swamped her on the night of 6 November. The storm tailed off by morning, and thirty-seven hours after receiving the distress call, at about 6:00 AM, she reached the scene of the encounter, where seas again were heavy.

Smith charted a back-and-forth search pattern over a 15-mile radius. It accounted for surface currents and prevailing winds expected to move lifeboats away from the battle site. The possibility that the German raider was in the vicinity was ignored as he started the traverse. An hour into the search the lookout sighted a *San Demetrio* boat with nineteen survivors. They were taken aboard and given hot food and dry clothes.

About 9:00 AM, the *San Demetrio's* Captain Waite with three other men in the second lifeboat hoisted sail and headed eastward. Thirty minutes later, they saw a freighter flying the red ensign. They came alongside, climbed the Jacob's ladder dropped down to them, and had a rousing reunion with their rescued shipmates. No one had a clue to the location or fate of the tanker's third boat. Nor could they imagine that Hawkins, Pollard, and the others were off on an extraordinary adventure.

Captain L Daneil, in the No. 1 lifeboat with three of his *Trewellard* crew, saw a ship to the north and then a small sail just west of themselves. It was about 10:00 AM Their own boat's sail had been torn in the shelling and was useless. The other craft, which turned out to be the *Trewellard*'s No. 2 lifeboat with nine more of her men in it, came alongside. After accepting a tank of drinking water and two oars, Daneil instructed the others to sail to the unidentified ship and bring help. About one o'clock they climbed aboard the *Gloucester City* and were astonished to come face to face with twelve men from their ship's No. 3 boat.

Captain Smith and his men persisted another nine hours in their hunt for survivors. They picked up twenty-four from the *Fresno City* and twenty from the *Kenbane Head*. On 13 November, they landed at St. John's, Newfoundland.[11]

Captain Lawson in the *Fresno City*'s starboard lifeboat figured his freighter had been shelled eighty miles from where the German raider had opened her attack on the convoy. He thought there was a good chance that a rescue vessel would search around that position.

His men hoisted a lug sail, and at about noon on 7 November they arrived where the *Jervis Bay* had mounted her last-ditch defence. If any Royal Navy ships were in the area, their paths did not cross.

Two of the nine survivors were wounded able seamen Mackie and Finnis. The captain had them wrapped in blankets and made them as comfortable and protected as possible athwart the bottom.

The only choice left for them in the middle of the North Atlantic was to head for home, a full thousand miles to the east. By then the southwesterly gale was pounding. A heavy gust from the starboard side could blow the big lug sail down and capsize the boat. Lawson replaced it with a light jib. They made good time running mostly before the wind. The craft rode the high, bucking seas with remarkable stability. On the morning of the ninth, after they had sailed nearly two hundred miles, they sighted smoke. Lawson altered course to the southeast across the unknown vessel's track.

A lookout on the 3,286-ton Greek freighter *Mount Taygetus,* sailing with outward-bound convoy OB 238, spotted the rising and falling jib a few miles northwest. Captain Samathrakis (first name missing) thought the boat most likely came from the convoy that had been attacked four days back. He swung his ship out of formation and picked up the nine men. Macke and Finnis were immediately put to bed in the sickbay and looked after by the chief officer, who had some medical expertise. Other men were treated for minor wounds and exposure.

'No more thoughtful care and attention could have been given us by our own families,' Lawson said.

The survivors were delivered to St. John's on 18 November, where they were reunited with the twenty-four shipmates rescued by the *Gloucester City.*

All told, the two freighters saved 101 merchant seamen from the wild, freezing North Atlantic. One hundred sixty-eight cargo ship sailors lost their lives in the attack.[12]

In recognition of his bold initiative in rescuing ninety-two convoy survivors, the Admiralty, with King George's approval, appointed *Gloucester City* captain S G Smith an Officer of the Order of the British Empire (Civil).

An excerpt from a Halifax newspaper covering the survival of *Jervis Bay* crewman Warren Stevens came to light shortly before publication of this book and is partly corroborated by the *Stureholm's* ship's log which mentions taking survivors from 'three remaining rafts'. Possibly it described Steven's hatch cover as a raft:

Mr Stevens said he jumped over the side not knowing what he was going to find to keep him afloat.

When he first struck the cold water it was all he could do to keep breathing. He remembers making his way over to the cable which had lowered the lifeboat (more likely the jolly boat) and holding on for a few minutes to collect his thoughts...

After a few minutes he found a small hatch cover, crawled upon it and drifted away from the burning wreckage. 'All I had on was my navy sweater, pants and sneakers. As I drifted I happened to see a navy duffel coat floating in the water and I pulled it around me.'

...Shortly before midnight he saw flashlights and knew the men in the lifeboat had been rescued.

'It was the Swedish ship that had waited for us. It went to the liferaft and picked up the survivors. They came very close to me but they couldn't see me and I didn't have a light to signal them. I yelled as loud as I could and I took down my hood so they could see my face,' he said.

It was 10 minutes to five in the morning when he was finally plucked from his small wooden hatch cover.

Oddly, no official notice was extended to the captain and crew of the Swedish ship *Stureholm,* who rescued the sixty-five *Jervis Bay* sailors. Another of the men they picked out of the sea spoke for the rest of his mates, as reported in *The War Illustrated* (which failed to identify him): 'He [Captain Sven Olander] is a great man. He didn't have to risk himself and his ship to help us, but here he was right on the spot when we needed help badly. All the fellows are...well, we just can't put it into words. But we have the highest admiration for the Swedish captain and his men.'

At an annual gathering of the Royal Naval Association in 1959, two years after his death, the British finally managed to scratch out a semi-official appreciation of the Swedish captain's selfless action. The meeting program carried the following words: 'We pay tribute...to Captain Sven Olander and the crew of the...*Stureholm,* without whose gallantry, in rescuing survivors, it is unlikely that any member of the crew of the *Jervis Bay* would have lived.'[13]

The 5,299-ton *Trefusis* rode through a set of misadventures after the *Scheer* attack. Twenty-two years old and slow, she was overloaded with steel and timber in her holds and a deck cargo of eight-foot stacks of timber. She averaged 6.4 knots, plodding and swaying like

an old plough horse in the increasing storm. The captain opened his
emergency routing instructions, which told him to rendezvous with
other surviving ships at a position off the coast of Northern Ireland.
He felt the ship was too slow to follow that directive, and he stayed
the course for four more days. Because of sea conditions and reports
of U-boat activity, the captain headed into the Minches, the two
channels between Lewis and Harris Island and the Island of Skye. It
was a passage the Admiralty prohibited to independently sailing
vessels. The consequences were to be tragic.

Third Mate H C Fellingham was at the bridge just after 8:00 PM on
11 November. The wind was strong, laced with frequent squally
showers, and it was dark. He made out a large black shape. At first, he
'thought it was land [because] it looked so big.' Then he realised it
was a closing ship. The *Trefusis* was running without navigation lights
because her degaussing coils had been energised with all available
electric power for protection against magnetic mines. The approaching
vessel switched on her lights. Fellingham shouted 'Starboard!' (a rule
of the road) to the wheel and delivered a short blast on the whistle. He
was horrified to hear two short blasts from the other ship, indicating a
port turn. The *Trefusis* rammed the *Duchess,* a 1,200-ton coastal
steamer, amidships. The third mate took out a lifeboat with six
volunteers. They heard cries for help, but because of the wind and the
heavy seas, they could not maintain a proper heading. The voices
weakened until they faded out. As Fellingham and his rowers then
approached the sinking *Duchess,* a man jumped into their boat. He
told them the rest of the crew, eleven of them, had launched a dory
that had capsized. He was the only survivor.

As the *Trefusis* finally sailed up the Clyde with a pilot aboard,
she was struck dead centre by an off-course Swedish freighter. She
managed to stay afloat and reached her berth in Rothesay Bay.[14]

Three days after the attack, the 2,734-ton *Vingaland,* carrying steel
and general cargo from New York to Glasgow, approached the
rendezvous position for the scattered ships about 250 miles off the
Irish coast. According to Captain W H Lawrence of the convoy ship
Briarwood: 'I saw the Swedish ship *Vingaland* attacked by a German
plane, which I believe was a Dornier [a nearby destroyer captain
thought it was a Focke-Wulf]. This plane dropped a bomb that struck
the vessel. She immediately caught on fire amidships. Nineteen
survivors…were brought in by the *Danae 2* [another HX 84 ship].'[15]

Following her return to Halifax with the sixty-five *Jervis Bay*
survivors, the *Stureholm* lost most of her crew. Captain Olander gave

up his command because of bleeding ulcers. Hilding Tiderman, a deck hand on the Swedish freighter, said: 'Around 25 men [including myself] left the MS *Stureholm*. The reason: The attack on the HX 84 convoy was very traumatic. I think that most of them were tired of war. The *Stureholm* had made previous convoys to England under submarine and air attacks.'

Four men stayed with the ship: a steward, a cook, an able seaman, and Second Mate Berner, who served as captain in the next convoy. He mustered a new crew, mainly an assortment of Britons and Canadians, including several *San Demetrio* survivors, one of them the tanker's first mate. They sailed with convoy HX 92. At 1:56 AM on 12 December the *Stureholm* was one of four convoy ships torpedoed by U-96. The crew had no chance to abandon her as she plunged to the bottom with her dense load of steel.

Fourteen days later, the compiler of the Admiralty's War Diary, apparently not aware of the ship's rescue action and later fate, printed an advisory: '*Stureholm* was in HX 84 and in vicinity of sinking of *Jervis Bay*. Galveston previously reported crew and officers pro-German. If ship is located, suggest she be carefully watched in future.'[16]

The 6,078-ton *Jumna* had left her convoy and was sailing independently to India on Christmas day. The commodore, Rear Admiral H B Maltby, who had survived the *Jervis Bay* attack seven weeks earlier, was in command. The ship was stumbled upon out of a haze by the German heavy cruiser *Admiral Hipper,* running from pursuing British cruisers. The raider's guns destroyed the radio room and the bridge. Then, anxious to keep moving, she fired two torpedoes and left the scene. Both struck the empty freighter, and she sank with all hands.[17]

Captain J A P Blackburn—Captain Fegen's able executive officer who was given his own AMC command just before the *Jervis Bay*'s final voyage—had escorted Halifax convoys all through the winter. Now, he was taking his 13,301-ton *Voltaire* to her newly assigned home port at Freetown, Sierra Leone. About seven hundred miles westsouthwest of the Cape Verde Islands, on the morning of 4 April 1941, he sighted what looked like an ordinary freighter. But through his binoculars he saw what appeared to be an after deckhouse vanish and reveal two guns. Forward sections of her side swung away and more guns appeared.

She was the German auxiliary cruiser *Thor*. Her armaments, unlike those of British AMCs, were modern, efficient, and accurate.

She rapidly opened fire, and her second salvo hit the starboard bridge and silenced the wireless and one of the guns. In quick order, the *Voltaire*'s fire-control system was knocked out, her sickbay destroyed, fire-fighting mains punctured, and her engine was put out of action. Incendiary shells started fires all over the ship. During his ship's continuing destruction, Blackburn's remarkable gunners, firing their antique artillery at extreme range, managed to get a few hits and cause minor damage. The *Voltaire* lost ninety men. One hundred ninety-seven, including Blackburn, were taken prisoner.

This action prompted the Admiralty finally to give up the use of the slow, poorly armed, thin-hulled AMCs as convoy escorts and on naval patrols. Losses of such ships and their crews had become severe. The remaining AMCs were converted into troop carriers, a vital function for which they were admirably suited.[18]

All afternoon on 16 March 1942, Captain C Vidot of the repaired and refitted *San Demetrio* noted that a small fishing boat was following his ship. Though he changed course several times and zigzagged continuously, the boat stuck behind her like a ravenous hyena. The tanker carried 11,700 tons of alcohol and refined petroleum and was en route from Baltimore to Halifax to join a convoy to Britain. About eighty miles off the mouth of Chesapeake Bay, U-404 abruptly surfaced and fired two torpedoes. One of them struck the starboard side aft, putting the engine out of commission and killing most of the black squad. The other blew the No. 2 tank on the same side, transforming its cargo into a fire ball. The *San Demetrio* immediately began listing to the starboard. When last seen she was burning, but this time her bow was up and she was sinking. Twenty-nine of her crew were rescued and twenty-four lost.[19]

Joe Refi was the captain's steward aboard the HX 84 convoy's 4,571-ton Swedish freighter *Delhi*. A distinct Austrian accent was welded onto his English. After the ship delivered her cargo of wood and steel at Immingham on the Humber, he seemed to develop a fetish for keeping his clothes perfectly cleaned and laundered. One of his shipmates said: 'Joe, not to the laundress again! Your shirts don't even have time to get dirty.'

Refi smiled sourly. 'Dere iss no crime in keeping clean.'

Just before the *Delhi* left port, he made a hasty last visit to the laundry woman. The ship landed at Seattle, moved to Tacoma, Washington, and on 19 April 1941 docked at Esquimalt, British Columbia. Tipped that Refi had been acting suspiciously, the Royal Canadian Mounted Police boarded the ship and removed him from his cabin. He tore his arms free for a moment, spat at his captors, raised the stiff-armed Nazi salute, and snapped, 'Heil Hitler.'

The RCMP knew that the laundress in England or someone in her house received messages in his bundles of laundry and passed them on to Germany. Among Refi's things they found a detailed map of Immingham harbour, including its naval defences. He insisted he was Hungarian, but the Canadians knew 'Refi' was an alias. His real name was Gottfried Sohar and his home was Graz, Austria. Sohar was convicted of spying and interned at Fredericton, New Brunswick, for the remainder of the war. It is not known whether his information led to the *Admiral Scheer*'s attack on the *Jervis Bay* convoy.[20]

The highlight of Theodor Krancke's naval career was his cruise as captain of the pocket battleship *Admiral Scheer*. He understood his mission, and he alone devised the tactics. It was a classic naval officer's experience. It meant so much to him that he wrote a book about it, *The Battleship 'Scheer,'* first published in English in Britain in 1956, and then under the title *Pocket Battleship* in the United States in 1958. After his promotion to rear admiral on 1 April 1941, the day he brought the *Scheer* back to Kiel, his career advances came in quick succession: vice admiral after a year and admiral eleven months later.

Upon leaving command of the pocket battleship in June 1941, Krancke moved to naval warfare headquarters as chief of logistics. While he held that position for nearly two years, he represented the navy at Hitler's daily briefings, where his role was to take and follow orders, for a year until March 1943. Along with his rise to full admiral, he was placed in charge of the Naval Group Command, West, and then the Naval High Command, West, where he led the navy's effort to build defences against the coming Allied invasion of France. It was an extremely important responsibility, but Krancke had big problems with the army. As he put it in a message to the naval staff on 10 August 1944:

> I am most doubtful as to the merits of the steadily increasing authority of the Army in the Western Theatre. The more...our defence shifts to the land, the more the Navy becomes subordinate to Army commanders who are given the authority of joint commanders, but who lack the proper appreciation of naval requirements...
>
> Wrong decisions are the natural result, and the Naval Group Command has to try again and again to rectify such errors.

The admiral apparently did the best he could under frustrating conditions. A few weeks before the war ended, he was put in charge of Naval High Command, Norway. Imprisoned after the German surrender, he was released in October 1947. Krancke died in Wentorf, near Hamburg, on 18 June 1973.[21]

When World War II ended, Bernard Edwards wrote in *They Sank the Red Dragon:*

> The final reckoning was 2,426 British merchant ships of 11,331,933 tons sunk and 29,180 merchant seamen lost. For almost three years, the outcome of the [Battle of the Atlantic] had hung in balance, needing only the merest wavering to tip the scales [one way or the other]. Between May 1940 and July 1941, sinkings were averaging 66 ocean-going ships a month, the climax being May 1941, with 20 ships lost for every seven days... It would then have been easy for Britain's merchant seamen, poorly paid and casually employed, to have adopted the attitude of many dockers, miners, and shipyard workers who, conscious of their indispensability, regularly held their country to ransom using the now fashionable weapon of industrial action. If the merchant seamen, who strictly speaking were civilians, had refused to sail the ships—and the temptation to do just that must have been very great at times—then Britain would have gone under, for no nation can fight for long with stomachs empty and arsenals unstocked.[22]

Appendix 1

HMS Jervis Bay Officers and Crew
5th November 1940

Name	Rank	Service	Status
Abbott, JM	Coder	RNVR	lost at sea
Alldridge, H	Petty Officer	RN	lost at sea
Anderson, J	Seaman	RNR	killed
Appleyard, AR	Able Seaman	RFR	survived
Armstrong, JR	Stoker	RCNR	survived
Avery, W	Able Seaman	RN	lost at sea
Bain, D	Seaman	RNR	survived
Bain, J	Seaman	RNR	missing presumed killed
Bain, JM	Seaman	RNR	lost at sea
Baker, L	Able Seaman	RNVR	killed
Baldwin, JT	Able Seaman	RN	lost at sea
Ball, FJ	Able Seaman	RN	lost at sea
Banks, G	Able Seaman	RN	lost at sea
Barham, W	Fireman	NAP(MN)	lost at sea
Barker, J	Able Seaman	RNVR	survived
Barnett, W	Asst Steward	**	survived
Barry, JWP	Lieutenant (E)	RNR	lost at sea
Bartle, AHW	Lieutenant	RNR	lost at sea
Beal, FC	Chief Petty Officer Sick Berth	RN	lost at sea
Beaman, G	Stoker	RCNR	survived
Beland, AW	Able Seaman	RN	lost at sea
Bigg, DJH	Lieutenant (E)	RNR	lost at sea
Billings, FWG	Able Seaman	RFR	survived
Blanchard, JHG	Stoker lst Class	RCNR	missing presumed killed
Blyth, J	Leading Seaman	RFR	missing presumed killed
Bonney, HL	Leading Seaman	RFR	survived
Bowles, HJ	Able Seaman	RN	lost at sea
Boyce, JH	Pantryman	NAP(MN)	lost at sea
Boyland, VD	Able Seaman	RNVR	lost at sea
Bradley, WL	Carpenter	NAP(MN)	lost at sea
Bremner, DR	Seaman	RNR	lost at sea
Bremner, W	Seaman	RNR	lost at sea
Brewis, PW	Able Seaman	RNVR	lost at sea
Bruce, WR	Carpenter's Mate	NAP(MN)	lost at sea
Butler, RAG	Midshipman	RNR	survived
Byam-Corstiaens, GF	Sub.Lieut E	**	survived
Carr, AJ	Assistant Steward	NAP(MN)	lost at sea
Carson, MW	Ordinary Signalman	RCNVR	lost at sea
Castle, C	Petty Officer	RN	survived

**denotes not known

Seaman
James Anderson,
RNR.
(James Anderson)

Able Seaman
Sidney Horace Cheesman,
RFR.
(Sheila Niven)

Carpenters Mate
Arthur William Desborough
NAP(MN).
(via Hilary Cooke)

Able Seaman
Henry Frank Ferguson,
RNVR.
(Josie Norris)

Able Seaman
Jack Hudson,
RN.
(Peter Hudson)

Able Seaman
Michael McNamara,
RN.
(via Denis McNamara)

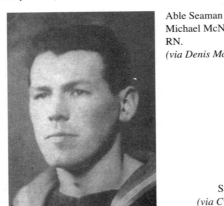

Able Seaman
Sam Miles RFR.
(via Cynthia Bridges)

Name	Rank	Service	Status
Chappell, J H G	T/Commander(E)	RNR	missing presumed killed
Charlton, JG	Signalman	RNVR	lost at sea
Cheesman, SH	Able Seaman	RFR	killed
Christie, D	Asst Steward	**	survived
Clark, LE	Assistant Cook	NAP(MN)	lost at sea
Clark, WJW	Petty Officer	RN	lost at sea
Clarke, P	Petty Officer	RN	lost at sea
Cole, FS	Able Seaman	RN	lost at sea
Collins, RG	Able Seaman	RN	lost at sea
Colloff, JA	Chief Cook	NAP(MN)	lost at sea
Condon, JH	Able Seaman	RNVR	lost at sea
Cooke, JH	Pantryman	NAP(MN)	lost at sea
Cooper, W	Able Seaman	RNVR	survived
Costello, T	Greaser	NAP(MN)	lost at sea
Crane, CWR	Carpenter's Mate	NAP(MN)	lost at sea
Crouch, RA	Assistant Steward	NAP(MN)	lost at sea
Crowson, G	Stoker 1st Class	**	survived
Currie, JH	3rd Sub.Lieut E	**	survived
Curry, R	Ordinary Seaman	RN	lost at sea
Danby, WH	Ordinary Signalman	RCNVR	missing presumed killed
Daniels, JRH	Able Seaman	RNVR	lost at sea
Darnborough, WL	Able Seaman	RCNVR	survived
Davenport, H	Scullion	NAP(MN)	lost at sea
Davey, BW	Captain's Steward	NAP(MN)	lost at sea
Davison, T	Able Seaman	RNR	survived
Day, AG	Fireman	NAP(MN)	lost at sea
Demeza, AFW	Writer	NAP(MN)	lost at sea
Dennis, PI	Able Seaman	RN	lost at sea
Desborough, AW	Carpenter's Mate	NAP(MN)	lost at sea
Doull, G	Seaman	RNR	survived
Dove, C	Asst Steward	**	survived
Draper, B	Able Seaman	RFR	survived
Driscoll, AW	Lieutenant Commander	RNR	killed
Drury, D	Stoker	**	survived
Dunbar, D	Seaman	RNR	survived
Dunbar, S	Baker	NAP(MN)	lost at sea
Durham, C	Leading Sick Berth Attendant	RN	lost at sea
Durrand, JS	Seaman	RNR	survived
Durrant, R	Seaman	RNR	survived
Egglestone, JC	Able Seaman	RFR	survived
Ellender, FE	Chief Engine Room Artificer	RN	lost at sea
Ellmes, SC	Stoker 1st class	**	survived
Esmond, H	Watchkeeping Officer	NAP(MN)	lost at sea
Evans, JR	Writer	**	missing presumed killed
Evans, TG	Lieutenant Commander Surgeon	RNVR	lost at sea

**denotes not known

Name	Rank	Service	Status
Farmer, R	Greaser	NAP(MN)	lost at sea
Farthing, MF	Able Seaman	RNVR	killed
Fegen, ESF	Acting Cpt VC	RN	missing presumed killed
Ferguson, HF	Able Seaman	RNVR	missing presumed killed
Finch, G	Able Seaman	RN	lost at sea
Findlater, TH	Chief Petty Officer	RN	lost at sea
Funge, C	Stoker RCN	survived	
Galloway, FG	Greaser	NAP(MN)	lost at sea
Gibbs, F	Leading Seaman	RFR	survived
Gibson, J	Chief Petty Officer	RNVR	lost at sea
Gospage, DH	Fireman NAP(MN)	lost at sea	
Green, D	ERA	RCNVR	survived
Green, GD	Acting Sub Lieutenant (E)	RNVR	lost at sea
Greenley, W	Seaman	RNR	missing presumed killed
Griss, WG	Assistant Storekeeper	NAP(MN)	lost at sea
Grubb, V	Able Seaman	RNVR	survived
Gulless, AT	Able Seaman	RNVR	lost at sea
Gunn, R	Seaman	RNR	survived
Hall, RL	Sub-Lieutenant (E)	RNR	lost at sea
Handley, A	Able Seaman	RFR	survived
Hanlon, JTW	Leading Seaman	RFR	survived
Hart, R	Fireman	NAP(MN)	lost at sea
Hart, W	Greaser	NAP(MN)	lost at sea
Hawn, DE	Leading Seaman	RCNVR	lost at sea
Heard, H	Seaman	RNR	lost at sea
Hennessy, M	Assistant Cook	NAP(MN)	lost at sea
Hill, W	Lieutenant	RNR	missing presumed killed
Hinstridge, HE	Second Cook	NAP(MN)	lost at sea
Houghton, WO	Able Seaman	RNVR	lost at sea
Howes, EG	Assistant Steward	NAP(MN)	lost at sea
Hudson, J	Able Seaman	RN	lost at sea
Innes, J	Seaman	RNR	died of wounds
Ireland, AS	Junior Engineer	NAP(MN)	lost at sea
Jarvis, WJ	Chief Petty Officer	RN	lost at sea
Jeffcott, JS	Able Seaman	RNVR	lost at sea
Johnson, AM	Stoker	RCNR	missing presumed killed
Jones, CE	Watchkeeping Officer	NAP(MN)	lost at sea
Kelly, C	Assistant Baker	NAP(MN)	lost at sea
Kershaw, JH	Master At Arms	RN	lost at sea
Kilgour, R	2nd Electrician	NAP(MN)	lost at sea
Lane, JD	Fireman	NAP(MN)	lost at sea
Lane, HJ	Able Seaman	HO	survived
Lang, HSG	Carpenter's Mate	NAP(MN)	lost at sea
Latch, CCT	Midshipman	RNR	missing presumed killed
Lattimore, NWG	Able Seaman	RNVR	lost at sea

Name	Rank	Service	Status
Lecomber, TW	Fireman	NAP(MN)	lost at sea
Leddra, MR	Lieutenant Commander (E)	RNR	lost at sea
Lee, WH	Saloon Steward	NAP(MN)	lost at sea
Lethby, GE	Able Seaman	RNVR	lost at sea
Liddle, RG	Able Seaman	RNVR	lost at sea
Lis, FS	Seaman	RNR	survived
Lloyd, J	Donkeyman	NAP(MN)	lost at sea
Lowe, RB	Ordinary Signalman	RNVR	lost at sea
Mabbott, LE	Assistant Steward	NAP(MN)	lost at sea
Macdonald, A	Stoker	RCNVR	lost at sea
Macdonald, W	Jnr Watchkeeping Officer	NAP(MN)	lost at sea
Mackay, WA	Engine Room Artificer	RCNVR	lost at sea
MacQueen, WG	Storekeeper	**	survived
Major, HR	Able Seaman	RN	lost at sea
Mallon, FR	Able Seaman	RNVR	lost at sea
Mardell, WC	Cooper	NAP(MN)	lost at sea
Margetts,WJ	Petty Officer	RN	lost at sea
Marginson, K	ERA4	RCNVR	survived
Martin, HF	Assistant Baker	NAP(MN)	lost at sea
Martin, JW	Plumber	NAP(MN)	lost at sea
Matcham, HT	Petty Officer	RN	lost at sea
Matheson, WJ	3rd Electrician	NAP(MN)	lost at sea
May, TJ	Leading Seaman	RNR	lost at sea
McConnell, J	Stoker 1st class	**	survived
Mcnamara, M	Able Seaman	RN	missing presumed killed
McRae, HS	Engine Room Artificer	RCNVR	missing presumed killed
Miles, SJ	Able Seaman	RFR	killed
Miller, L	Watchkeeping Officer	NAP(MN)	lost at sea
Miller, WB	Seaman	RNR	lost at sea
Milroy, GD	1st Electrician	NAP(MN)	lost at sea
Mitchell, AW	Assistant Steward	NAP(MN)	lost at sea
Moonie, A	Seaman	RNR	survived
Moore, D	Chief Yeoman Signals	RN	lost at sea
Moore, HAJ	Engine Room Artificer	**	lost at sea
Mordaunt, C	Asst Steward	**	survived
Morgan, JA	Able Seaman	RNVR	missing presumed killed
Morrill, TA	Able Seaman	RFR	survived
Morrison, KM	Lieutenant Commander	RNR	missing presumed killed
Morrow, E	Scullion	**	survived
Moss, HO	3rd Sub.Lieut	**	survived
Munro-Cormack, J	Seaman	RNR	lost at sea
Newton, W	Lieutenant (E)	RNR	lost at sea
Nicholls, HJ	Able Seaman	RFR	survived
Oag, W	Seaman	RNR	survived
Ogilvy, D	Watchkeeping Officer	NAP(MN)	lost at sea

**denotes not known

Name	Rank	Service	Status
O'kane, J	Greaser	NAP(MN)	lost at sea
Ormston, SW	Asst Butcher	**	survived
Owen, SG	Ship's Cook	NAP(MN)	lost at sea
Owens, RF	Midshipman	RNR	killed
Parent, JLJP	Fireman	NAP(MN)	lost at sea
Parker, CW	Able Seaman	RNVR	lost at sea
Parker, G	Engine Room Storekeeper	NAP(MN)	lost at sea
Patience, SS	Seaman	RNR	survived
Pattinson, HM	Acting Sub Lieutenant (E)	RNVR	lost at sea
Payne, PC	Asst Steward	**	survived
Peskett, HT	Storekeeper	NAP(MN)	lost at sea
Peters, SA	Chief Butcher	NAP(MN)	lost at sea
Porter, W	Carpenter's Mate	NAP(MN)	lost at sea
Price, AE	Engine Room Artificer	RCNVR	lost at sea
Rainsbury, TF	Able Seaman	RNVR	lost at sea
Randall, RK	Fireman	NAP(MN)	lost at sea
Read, BG	Leading Seaman	RN	lost at sea
Reeve, JF	Writer	NAP(MN)	lost at sea
Reid, J	Boatswain/Bosun	NAP(MN)	lost at sea
Reid, J	Seaman	RNR	survived
Rice, OGA	Able Seaman	RN	lost at sea
Robertson, AJ	3rd Sub.Lieut E	**	survived
Robins, W	Assistant Steward	NAP(MN)	lost at sea
Rockhill, HA	Able Seaman	RNVR	lost at sea
Roe, GL	Lieutenant Commander	RNR	lost at sea
Rooney, J	Fireman	NAP(MN)	lost at sea
Rooney, T	Fireman	NAP(MN)	lost at sea
Ross, PL	Ordinary Signalman	RCNVR	lost at sea
Rushall, FB	Leading Seaman	RFR	survived
Sargeant, JG	Pay Sub. Lieut	RNR	survived
Saville, S	Fireman	NAP(MN)	lost at sea
Searles, JW	Greaser	NAP(MN)	lost at sea
Shackleton, R	2nd Radio Officer	**	survived
Sheppard, GK	Ordinary Seaman	**	killed
Simmons, EH	Chief Steward	NAP(MN)	lost at sea
Sinton, G	Assistant Steward	NAP(MN)	lost at sea
Skinner, AE	Leading Seaman	RN	lost at sea
Smith, DJ	Able Seaman	RNVR	lost at sea
Smith, JT	Stoker	RCNVR	survived
Spencer, SA	Able Seaman	RN	lost at
Spiller, CHJ	Able Seaman	RFR	survived
Squires, GM	Ordinary Seaman	HO	survived
Squires, RA	Seaman	RNR	survived
Stamp, JJ	Ordinary Seaman	RN	lost at sea
Stannard, ER	Gunner	RN	lost at sea

**denotes not known

Name	Rank	Service	Status
Stansbury, C	Ordinary Seaman	RN	lost at sea
Staples, FG	Carpenter's Mate	NAP(MN)	lost at sea
Stevens, WD	Stoker	RCNR	survived
Stevenson, J	Junior Engineer	NAP(MN)	lost at sea
Story, TW	Able Seaman	RN	lost at sea
Stott, AW	Lieutenant (S)	RNR	lost at sea
Sullivan, J	Greaser	RNR	lost at sea
Taylor, AW	Ordinary Seaman	HO	survived
Taylor, HJ	Able Seaman	RCNVR	lost at sea
Thiselton, WE	Midshipman	RNR	lost at sea
Tilley, L	Ordinary Seaman	HO	survived
Tolfree, AE	Able Seaman	RN	lost at sea
Toop, WF	Leading Seaman	RN	lost at sea
Turnbull, FG	Able Seaman	RNVR	lost at sea
Urquhart, RW	2nd Radio Officer	**	survived
Voaden, FC	Able Seaman	RNVR	lost at sea
Waldron, W	Assistant Steward	NAP(MN)	lost at sea
Walker, B	Leading Seaman	RN	lost at sea
Wallis, WR	Petty Officer	RNR	survived
Ward, AC	Petty Officer Regulating	RN	lost at sea
Ward, AHG	Lamp Trimmer	NAP(MN)	lost at sea
Warren, AJ	Boilermaker	NAP(MN)	lost at sea
Waters, W	Assistant Steward	NAP(MN)	lost at sea
Watts, RF	Able Seaman	RN	lost at sea
Webster, A	Seaman	RNR	lost at sea
Weightman, RL	2nd Steward	NAP(MN)	lost at sea
White, EW	Lieutenant Commander (S)	RNR	lost at sea
Whiting, HD	Petty Officer Pensioner	**	survived
Williams, EA	Able Seaman	RNVR	lost at sea
Williamson, H	1st Radio Officer	NAP(MN)	lost at sea
Wood, GEC	Lieutenant Commander	RN	killed
Wood, JH	Leading Seaman	RNR	survived
Wood, NE	Lieutenant	RNR	survived
Wood, RM	Stoker	RCNR	lost at sea
Wooldridge, GW	Able Seaman	RN	lost at sea
Woollett, AE	Third Cook	NAP(MN)	lost at sea
Young, HE	Painter	NAP(MN)	lost at sea

Information courtesy of Harold E. Wright, Heritage Resources, Saint John

**denotes not known

Notes

Introduction A Climate of Desperation

1. *World Almanac*, 14–15, 33–36; Shirer, *Rise and Fall of the Third Reich*, 290, 292, 299, 417, 420, 448, 461–62, 483, 499, 541; Dear, *Oxford Companion*, 954.

2. Dear, *Oxford Companion*,140; *World Almanac*, 37–40; Shirer, *Rise and Fall*, 622, 633–35 (quotes), 645; Barnett, *Engage the Enemy*, 65.

3. Shirer, *Rise and Fall*, 671–72, 717, 719 (quotes), 745; *World Almanac*, 46, 56, 59, 64; Dear, *Oxford Companion*, 408–14, 709 (quote, 408).

4. *World Almanac*, 53; Gilbert, *Finest Hour*, 410, 418–21 (quotes, 418, 419).

5. Dear, *Oxford Companion*, 312–13; *World Almanac*, 61, 64; Gilbert, *Finest Hour*, 463, 468 (quote).

6. Kennedy, *Rise and Fall of British Naval Mastery*, 355 (quote); Shirer, *Rise and Fall*, 740; Dear, *Oxford Companion*, 594; *World Almanac*, 63, 65; Cruikshank, *German Occupation*, xiv, 55, 58, 251.

7. Possony, 'Decision without Battle,' 764–65; Callahan, 'Invasion's Moment Lost,' 46.

8. Possony, 'Decision without Battle,' 765, 767; Callahan, 'Invasion's Moment Lost,' 45; Assman, 'Operation 'Sea Lion,'' 4 (quote).

9. Assman, 'Operation 'Sea Lion,'' 4; Shirer, *End of a Berlin Diary*, 341–42 (quote, 341).

10. Gilbert, *Finest Hour*, 272 (quote).

11. Shirer, *Rise and Fall*, 782 (quote).

12. Gilbert, *Finest Hour*, 672 (quote).

13. Callahan, 'Invasion's Moment Lost,' 46–47; *World Almanac*, 68 (quote).

14. *World Almanac*, 66–69; Dear, *Oxford Companion*, 315.

15. Dear, *Oxford Companion*, 1134; Shirer, *Rise and Fall*, 763; Gilbert, *Finest Hour*, 778; Fleming, 'Operation 'Sea Lion,'' 201, 205.

16. Giles, 'Operation Lucid,' 1–3 (quotes); Roskill, *Churchill and the Admirals*, 120–21; Gilbert, *Finest Hour*, 815; Fleming, 'Operation 'Sea Lion,'' 209 (quote).

17. *World Almanac*, 76–79; Dear, *Oxford Companion*, 955; Shirer, *Rise and Fall*, 814–17 (quotes, 814–15); Collier, 1940: *The Avalanche*, 245–48.

18. Shirer, *Rise and Fall*, 775–77 (quote, 776); *World Almanac*, 70–73; Dear, *Oxford Companion*, 159, 331, 490; Budiansky, 'Britain: Defeating the Luftwaffe,' 68 (quote), 74–76.

19. *World Almanac*, 64; Gilbert, *Finest Hour*, 580–83; Dear, *Oxford Companion*, 331.

20. Shirer, *Rise and Fall*, 777–81 (quotes, 778, 781); *World Almanac*, 72–74, 77; Ruge, *German Navy's Story*, 111.

21. *World Almanac*, 40; Ruge, *German Navy's Story*, 60–61, 33–36, 41; Barnett, *Engage the Enemy*, 79; *New Grolier Multimedia Encyclopedia*, 34.

22. Barnett, *Engage the Enemy*, 70–71; Doenitz, *Ten Years*, 69, 71; Padfield, *War beneath the Sea*, 60–64.

23. *World Almanac*, 37, 42–53, 60.

24. Ibid., 55; Davies, 'Iceland,' 230 (quote).

25. Marder, *From Dardanelles*, 180, 182, 191–94, 211–12, 235, 238–39, 253–55, 262, 283; Churchill, *Their Finest Hour*, 232 (quote).

26. Barnett, *Engage the Enemy*, 195, 255; MacIntyre, *Naval War*, 54; Dear, *Oxford Companion*, 63–65; Doenitz, *Ten Years*, 19–20, 46–47, 61, 102, 104–5, 109, 117 (quote); *World Almanac*, 65–69; Gasaway, *Grey Wolf*, 87; Bekker, *Hitler's Naval War*, 190–91.

27. Bailey and Ryan, *Hitler Versus Roosevelt*, 82–87, 90, 93; Ketchum, *Borrowed Years*, 476–80; Abbazia, *Mr. Roosevelt's Navy*, 93.

28. *World Almanac*, 73, 78–79; Doenitz, *Ten Years*, 106; Collier, 1940: *The Avalanche*, 235–36; van der Vat, *Atlantic Campaign*, 147; Dear, *Oxford Companion*, 63; Churchill, 'On War Problems,' 2 (quote).

1 The *Scheer* Breaks Out

0. The first names of several officers and crew of the *Admiral Scheer* are not known.

1. Krancke and Brennecke, *Pocket Battleship*, 20–22 (quote, 21); 'Operation of the 'Admiral Scheer,'' 3; Brown, *Bodyguard of Lies*, 263; Whitley, *German Capital Ships*, 130.

2. Krancke and Brennecke, *Pocket Battleship*, 22, 26.

3. Ibid., 22–26, 29, 237 (quote); Beaufort Wind Scale, 5; National Geographic Society, telephone by Segman; Tolman, telephone by Segman.

4. Krancke and Brennecke, *Pocket Battleship*, 23, 26 (quote).

5. Ibid., 26, 29; 'Operation of the 'Admiral Scheer,'' 3.

2 A Family Reborn and Death of a Sister

1. Van der Vat, *Grand Scuttle*, 11, 17–18, 20–21, 171–73.

2. Ibid., 11, 102–4, 129–130, 159, 219.

3. Ibid., 107 (quote), 134, 143, 147 (quote), 149.

4. Ibid., 150, 153, 155, 157, 160–62, 164–65, 169, 170 (quote).

5. Ibid., 170–71, 174–76, 183 (quote).

6. Thomas, *German Navy*, 23–27; Barnett, *Engage the Enemy*, 15; Kennedy, *Rise and Fall of British Naval Mastery*, 331.

7. *World Almanac*, 10; Humble, *Hitler's High Seas Fleet*, 25–27; Ireland, *Jane's Battleships*, 40–43; quote from Elliott, 'Treaty Warship,' *New York Tribune*, 1.

8. Ireland, *Jane's Battleships*, 42, 43; quote from Thomas, *German Navy*, 9.

9. Koop and Schmolke, *Pocket Battleships*, 24–25, 31; Ireland, *Jane's Battleships*, 42; Divine, *In the Wake*, 21; Krancke and Brennecke, *Pocket Battleship*, 34; Green, *Warplanes of the Third Reich*, 42.

10. Whitley, *German Capital Ships*, 83–89; Frank, 'Misperceptions and Incidents,' 35–39; Gray, *Hitler's Battleships*, 24.

11. Bekker, *Hitler's Naval War*, 35 (quotes); Terraine, *Time for Courage*, 99; Whitley, *German Capital Ships*, 104–5.

12. Bekker, *Hitler's Naval War*, 46–47, 104; Lippman, 'Showdown on the River Plate,' 50; Whitley, *German Capital Ships*, 96–99, 102; Humble, *Hitler's High Seas Fleet*, 40–41; Koop and Schmolke, *Pocket Battleships*, 171.

3 In Command

1. Bradley, *Germany's Generals and Admirals*, 1–2; Krancke and Brennecke, *Pocket Battleship*, 7.

2. Raeder, *My Life*, 300; Shirer, *Rise and Fall*, 674–76 (quote, 676).

3. *World Almanac*, 46, 47; Raeder, *My Life*, 306, 310; Kersaudy, *Norway 1940*, 43–44 (quotes).

4. Barnett, *Engage the Enemy*, 101–9, 113, 120, 138–39; Shirer, *Rise and Fall*, 679–80; Petrow, *Bitter Years*, 16.

5. Rohwer, letter to Segman; Krancke and Brennecke, *Pocket Battleship*, 7–8, (quote, 13).

6. Raeder, *My Life*, 287 (quote).

7. Krancke and Brennecke, *Pocket Battleship*, 13–17 (quote, 15); Reinicke, 'German Surface Force Strategy,' 182; Whitley, *German Capital Ships*, 129.

8. Krancke and Brennecke, *Pocket Battleship*, 28–32; Ireland, *Jane's Battleships*, description from photo, 45; Pollock, *Jervis Bay*, 86, 90–91; description from Pollock photo, opp. 128.

9. Krancke and Brennecke, *Pocket Battleship*, 32–34 (quotes, 33, 34).

4 The Conscripted 'Cruiser'

1. Poolman, *Armed Merchant Cruisers*, 98 (quotes).

2. Rowbotham, 'Armed Merchant Cruiser,' 85–88; Chatfield, *It Might Happen*, 61; Creswell, *Sea Warfare*, 65; Bowen, *Flag of the Southern Cross*, from photo, opp. 4.

3. Rowbotham, 'Armed Merchant Cruiser,' 90 (quote).

4. Creswell, *Sea Warfare*, 65; Rowbotham, 'Armed Merchant Cruiser,' 88, 90; Pollock, *Jervis Bay*, 20, 27; Isherwood, 'Aberdeen & Commonwealth,' 148–150; Dunn, *Book of Ships*, 128; 'List and Particulars of A.MCs,' 2.

5. Morning Leader, 'No Mutiny on '*Jervis Bay*,'' 1; Pollock, *Jervis Bay*, 24–25; Eldridge, *History of the Royal Naval College*, 1.

6. Pullen, 'Sinking of the *Jervis Bay*,' 10; Hampshire, *Blockaders*, 112–14; Poolman, *Armed Merchant Cruisers*, 96, 102–3; Pollock, *Jervis Bay*, 17; Crosse, letter to Duskin, 1.

7. Eldridge, *History of the Royal Naval College*, 1; Poolman, *Armed Merchant Cruisers*, 102–3; Pullen, 'Sinking of the *Jervis Bay*,' 10.

8. Pollock, *Jervis Bay*, 33–40 (quotes, 40).

9. Pink List October 1939, 2; Pollock, *Jervis Bay*, 40–43, 47; Thorpe, 'Memories of the *Jervis Bay*,' 650–51; Purcell, letter to M J Petch, 1–2 (quotes).

10. Thorpe, 'Memories of the *Jervis Bay*,' 651 (quote); Brennen, Australian Commonwealth Shipping Line, 50; Pollock, *Jervis Bay*, 48.

11. Pollock, *Jervis Bay*, 49.

12.Ibid., 50; Ireland, *Jane's Battleships*, 46–47; Poolman, *Armed Merchant Cruisers*, 109, 121–22 (quotes), description from photo following 86; Whitley, *German Capital Ships*, 105.

13. Pollock, *Jervis Bay*, 54–55; Poolman, *Armed Merchant Cruisers*, 126–29.

14. Pollock, *Jervis Bay*, 56–57 (quotes).

15. Ibid., 58–64; Pink List October 1939, 5–6.

16. Pollock, *Jervis Bay*, 63–67 (quote, 67); Pink List October 1939, 6, 14.

17. Pollock, *Jervis Bay*, 67–69; Pink List October 1939, 15–16; Poolman, *Armed Merchant Cruisers*, 165 (quote).

5 The Captain

1. Winton, *Victoria Cross at Sea*, 192; N Fegen, letter to Duskin containing family genealogies, 2nd chart; Fegen family from naval lists (ADM 51/4069, ADM 11/47, and ADM 196/40); Woodward, 'Despatch,' *London Gazette*; B Fegen, letter to Duskin containing more genealogies.

2. 'Edward Stephen Fogarty Fegen' (ADM 196/54), 1; Cooper, letter to Segman, 1; Bywater, *Cruisers in Battle*, 1, 7–8 (quotes), 14; Carr, *Brass Hats*, 35, 36.

3. ADM 196/54, 1–4 (quotes, 3).

4. Winton, *Victoria Cross at Sea*, 192; Turner, *V C's of the Royal Navy*, 54–55; 'Story of 'Hedwig,'' South China Morning, 1, 2; ADM 196/54, 3 (quote).

5. ADM 196/54, 2; Draper, *Operation Fish*, 33; Agar, *Footprints in the Sea*, 248 (quote).

6. Morgan, taped interview, 3 (transcript).

7. Gillespie, transcript of telephone interview by Duskin, 1; C G (full name unknown), HMS *Emerald* newsletter; Draper, *Operation Fish*, 42; and Agar, 'Personal Tributes,' combined quote.

8. Draper, *Operation Fish*, 42 (quote).

9. ADM 196/54, 2; Agar, *Footprints in the Sea*, 251 (quote).

10. MacDonnell, *Valiant Occasions*, 216; Poolman, *Armed Merchant Cruisers*, description from photo after 86; Giles, 'Operation Lucid,' transcript of audiotape, 4 (quotes).

11. Pollock, *Jervis Bay*, 72 (quotes).

12. Watt, *In All Respects Ready*, 48; Cooper, letter to Segman, 1 (quote).

13. Pollock, *Jervis Bay*, 75 (quote).

14. Pink List October 1939, 19; Pollock, *Jervis Bay*, 71 (quote), 74 (quote).

15. Pink List October 1939, 20, 21; 'HMS *Jervis Bay* Roared,' Royal Gazette, 2; Watt, *In All Respects Ready*, 48; Sheridan memo, 'Steel Drums,' 1; McBrearty, letter to Duskin; Hampshire, *Blockaders*, 113.

16. Crosse, letter to Watt, 1 (quote).

17. Pink List October 1939, 21–22; Thorpe, 'Memories of the *Jervis Bay*,' 79 (quote), 80; Slater, *Red Duster at War*, 66.

18. Pollock, *Jervis Bay*, 72–73 (quote, 73).

6 In All Respects Ready

1. Gretton, *Convoy Escort Commander*, 192–98; Macintyre, *Naval War*, 55; Roskill, *War at Sea*, 10, 11; Marder, *From Dardanelles to Oran*, 1 (quotes), 119–21.

2. Watt, *In All Respects Ready*, 1, 2 (quotes), 23; Tucker, *Naval Service of Canada*, 2:107.

3. Tucker, *Naval Service of Canada*, 2:106–8; Watt, *In All Respects Ready*, 7–9, 11, 19, 22–44, 33, 36–46, 63; Kerr, *Touching the Adventures*, 121.

4. Watt, *In All Respects Ready*, 47–49 (quote, 48).

5. Liberty, 12 (quotes), 13; Watt, *In All Respects Ready*, 49.

6. McAughtry, *Sinking*, 92; Pollock, *Jervis Bay*, 73 (quote).

7. Pollock, *Jervis Bay*, 171–72; Patience, audiotape interview by Bailey, 4; Clayton, *Finest Hour*, 358, 359.

8. Pollock, *Jervis Bay*, 69, 70 (quotes).

9. Ibid., 69–70, 80–84.

7 The Fifth of November

1. Watt, *In All Respects Ready*, 11, 12; Wellings, 'Intelligence Report (Enclosure F),' 2; McAughtry, *Sinking*, 111; Maltby, 'Brief Narrative,' 3.

2. Pollock, *Jervis Bay*, 49, 82–83, 97–98; Kerr, *Touching*, 123 (quote); MacDonnell, *Valiant Occasions*, 216; Admiralty reports on HX 84 ships, ADM 199/725 15661T, Waite report, 1.

8 Out of Nowhere

1. 'Operation of the 'Admiral Scheer,'' 4–5; Krancke and Brennecke, *Pocket Battleship*, 34–35.

2. Fellingham, letter to Duskin (15 March 1988), 1–2 (quote on 1); Fellingham, letter to Duskin (10 July 1988), 1; Fellingham, 'Convoy HX 84,' 4.

3. Fellingham (15 March), 1–2; Fellingham (10 July), 4.

4. Krancke and Brennecke, *Pocket Battleship*, 35–37.

5. Ibid., 33–38; 'Operation of the 'Admiral Scheer,'' 5; Pollock, *Jervis Bay*, 102; Monk, letter to Duskin, 2.

6. Peters, audio-tape interview, 1 (quote), 2; Pollock, *Jervis Bay*, 99; Hughes and Costello, *Battle of the Atlantic*, 116 (quote); List of *Mopan* officers and crew, 1.

7. Parsons, 'Elders and Fyffes,' 6; Peters, audio-tape interview, 3; Peters, 'Could the *Jervis Bay*,' 368; Pollock, *Jervis Bay*, 100 (quote).

8. Riley, interview, 1; Krancke and Brennecke, *Pocket Battleship*, 39; Peters, interview, 2 (quote); Hughes and Costello, *Battle of the Atlantic*, 115 (quotes).

9. 'Operation of the 'Admiral Scheer,'' 5; Krancke and Brennecke, *Pocket Battleship*, 38–40 (quotes).

10. Krancke and Brennecke, *Pocket Battleship*, 40–42 (quotes); 'Operation of the 'Admiral Scheer,'' 5; Hughes and Costello, *Battle of the Atlantic*, 117.

11. Jones, letter to Duskin, 2; Riley, interview, 1.

12. Peters, interview, 3 (quote); Hughes and Costello, *Battle of the Atlantic*, 117 (quote); Peters, 'Could the *Jervis Bay*,' 368; List of *Mopan* officers and crew, 2.

13. Riley, interview, 2 (quote); List of *Mopan* officers and crew, 6.

14. Jones, letter to Duskin, 1 (quote), 5; List of *Mopan* officers and crew, 1.

15. Peters, 'Could the *Jervis Bay*,' 369 (quote).

16. Jones, letter to Duskin, 3; 'Operation of the 'Admiral Scheer,'' 5.

9 Ranging In

1. Barnett, interview, 1; Pollock, *Jervis Bay*, 108, 13.

2. Krancke and Brennecke, *Pocket Battleship*, 43–44 (quote).

3. Pollock, *Jervis Bay*, 13–14, 18, 108, 127, 172–73; Patience, interview by Bailey, 2, 3 (quote); Clayton, *Finest Hour*, 203–4.

4. Pollock, *Jervis Bay*, 172–73, 13–14, 18, 108–9; Patience, interview by Bailey, 3–4, 7–8 (quote); Clayton, *Finest Hour*, 204.

5. Pollock, *Jervis Bay*, 109–12, 17 (quote).

6. Barnett, 1; US Naval Attache, 'Detailed Operations,' 1; Pisani, 'Report of Attack,' 2; Pollock, *Jervis Bay*, 113–14.

7. Pollock, *Jervis Bay*, 18 (quote).

8. Ibid., 104, 110, 114–17 (quote, 117).

9. Morrow, interview, 1 (quote), 2.

10. Pollock, *Jervis Bay*, 108–19 (quote, 115).

11. Ibid., 116–19 (quotes); Clayton, *Finest Hour*, 373 (quote).

12. Pollock, *Jervis Bay*, 120–23 (quotes).

13. Ibid., 123; Maltby, 'Proceedings,' Incidents 8 and 9; Maltby, summary of report, 1; Poolman, *Armed Merchant Cruisers*, 167 (quote).

14. Pollock, *Jervis Bay*, 124 (quote); Wellings, *On His Majesty's Service*, 51 (quote).

15. Krancke and Brennecke, *Pocket Battleship*, 45–46.

16. Pollock, *Jervis Bay*, 125–28 (quotes, 126, 128); Clayton, *Finest Hour*, 374.

17. Pollock, *Jervis Bay*, 128–29; Maltby, 'Proceedings,' Incidents 9, 10 (quote); Krancke and Brennecke, *Pocket Battleship*, 46; Morrow, interview, 2; Clayton, *Finest Hour*, 374; McBrearty, letter to Duskin, 1.

10 Rain of Steel

1. Krancke and Brennecke, *Pocket Battleship*, 46–47; Pollock, *Jervis Bay*, 131.

2. Pollock, *Jervis Bay*, 131–35 (quotes, 131, 135).

3. Fraser, interview, 162; Pisani, 'Report of Attack,' 2; Fraser, battle charts; McBrearty, 'The 'San Demetrio' Convoy,' 505; Fellingham, letter to Duskin, 2; Kerr, *Touching the Adventures*, 125, 126 (quote).

4. Kerr, *Touching the Adventures*, 125 (quote), 126; Fraser, interview, 163 (quote).

5. War Diary, 97 (quote).

6. Gerhard, letter to Segman (1998), 3; Krancke and Brennecke, *Pocket Battleship*, 47–49, 56.

7. Pollock, *Jervis Bay*, 133–37 (quotes, 133, 134).

8. Pollock, *Jervis Bay*, 132 (quote), 133, 137, 146 (quote).

9. Ibid., 147, 151 (quotes); Morrow, interview, 4; Clayton, *Finest Hour*, 374.

10. Pollock, *Jervis Bay*, 152.

11. Ibid., 136; 'Commander Butler,' *London Daily Telegraph*, 1.

12. Pollock, *Jervis Bay*, 135, 136 (quote); Barker, audiotape interview, 3 (quote).

13. Quotes from 'Commander Butler,' 1; Pollock, *Jervis Bay*, 38; 'Loss of HMS *Jervis Bay*,' Enclosure 8, p. 4.

14. Krancke and Brennecke, *Pocket Battleship*, 49.

11 The Lower Depths

1. Pollock, *Jervis Bay*, 138–42 (quotes, 142), 147.

2. Ibid., 110, 147–50 (quotes, 148, 149).

12 Someone Else is Getting Away

1. Krancke and Brennecke, *Pocket Battleship*, 48–50.

2. Pollock, *Jervis Bay*, 143–46.

3. Ibid., 152 (quote), 166; Patience, interview by Bailey, 9.

4. Pollock, *Jervis Bay*, 152–54 (quotes, 153, 154).

5. Pollock, 154 (quotes).

13 Every Ship for Herself

1. Hampden, 'Attack on British Convoy,' 2; 'Details of Ships,' 1; Krancke and Brennecke, *Pocket Battleship*, 49, 51; Pollock, *Jervis Bay*, 190.

2. Winton, Convoy, 162, 163 (quotes); Pisani, 'Report of Attack,' 2; Holman, *In the Wake* of *Endeavour*, 148; Krancke and Brennecke, *Pocket Battleship*, 51, 52; Barnett, interview, 2.

3. Krancke and Brennecke, *Pocket Battleship*, 49–52; 'Details of Ships,' 1; Pollock, *Jervis Bay*, 158.

4. Krancke and Brennecke, *Pocket Battleship*, 52, 53; 'Details of Ships,' 1; Kerr, *Touching the Adventures*, 127.

5. Admiralty reports on HX 84 ships, Daneil report, 1–2; Daneil, interview, 1; Gleadow, 'Loss of HMS *Jervis Bay*,' 1; Krancke and Brennecke, *Pocket Battleship*, 53.

6. Gleadowe, 'MV *San Demetrio*,' 6; Pollock, *Jervis Bay*, 192; Admiralty reports on HX 84 ships, Waite report, 1, 2; Krancke and Brennecke, *Pocket Battleship*, 53–54 (quotes).

7. Gleadowe, 'MV *San Demetrio*,' 6–7 (quotes).

8. Krancke and Brennecke, *Pocket Battleship*, 24, 54, 55 (quotes).

9. Admiralty reports on HX 84 ships, Milner report, 2; McAughtry, *Sinking of the* Kenbane Head, 121–23 (quote, 123); 'Details of Ships,' 1; Krancke and Brennecke, *Pocket Battleship*, 55.

10. Krancke and Brennecke, *Pocket Battleship*, 56–58 (quotes, 57, 58).

11. Pollock, *Jervis Bay*, 194–95; 'Details of Ships,' 1; Krancke and Brennecke, *Pocket Battleship*, 58 (quote).

12. Krancke and Brennecke, *Pocket Battleship*, 57–58 (quote).

13. Ibid., 58–60 (quote, 60).

14. 'Details of Ships,' 1; Lawson, interview, 1–3 (quotes, 1, 2); Lawrence, interview, 2 (quote); Pollock, *Jervis Bay*, 196 (time).

15. Krancke and Brennecke, *Pocket Battleship*, 59, 64.

14 Into the Icy Sea

1. Stevens interview; Pollock, *Jervis Bay*, 166, 155–58 (quotes, 156); Morrow, interview, 1–5 (quotes, 3); Barker, interview, 4.

2. Pollock, *Jervis Bay*, 156 (quotes); Morrow, interview, 4–5; 'North Atlantic Ocean— Northern Sheet,' US Defence Mapping Agency.

3. Pollock, *Jervis Bay*, 158–61 (quote); Barker, interview, 4.

4. Pollock, *Jervis Bay*, 157, 159–60 (quotes, 157, 159); Barker, interview, 3–4.

5. Pollock, *Jervis Bay*, 156–58.

6. Ibid., 166–68 (quotes, 167); Patience, interview (Bailey), 1 (quote), 7, 8; Clayton, *Finest Hour*, 375; Patience, interview (Wood), 1, 8 (quotes).

7. Pollock, *Jervis Bay*, 28, 163–66 (quotes, 163–65).

8. Ibid., 168–70, 177 (quotes, 168, 169).

9. Ibid., 169.

10. Ibid., 188; 'Caithness Archives,' 6.

15 We Go Back

1. Pollock, *Jervis Bay*, 171; Clayton, *Finest Hour*, 375–76 (quote, 375); Patience, letter to Duskin (21 August 1990), 1, 2.

2. Pollock, *Jervis Bay*, 173–74 (quote, 173); Patience, letter (Duskin), 2; Patience, interview (Wood), 1 (quote); Patience, interview (Bailey), 1.

3. Pollock, *Jervis Bay*, 175–76 (quotes); Faulkner, 'Recent War Experience,' 8; 'The *Jervis Bay* and the *Stureholm*,' 34–35 (quote, 34); Olander, interview (Duskin), 1.

4. Pollock, *Jervis Bay*, 184–87 (quotes, 184).

5. Ibid., 160–61, 177–81 (quotes, 161, 179).

6. Ibid., 174–75 (quote), 179 (quote), 181–83 (quotes).

7. Ibid., 187–88; Pullen, 'Sinking of the *Jervis Bay*,' 14.

16 Search and Getaway

1. Wellings, '[HMS] *Eskimo* Operations,' 52–55 (quote, 53); War Diary, 97, 102–3; Wellings, *On His Majesty's Service*, 51–54 (quote, 52); US Naval Attache, 'Detailed Operations' (search), 1–2; 'Report of Proceedings' (search), 1.

2. Krancke and Brennecke, *Pocket Battleship*, 60, 64–65, 235; Read, 'Intelligence Report,' 1; G Jones, *Under Three Flags*, 13.

3. Roskill, *War at Sea*, 289; US Naval Attache, 'Detailed Operations,' 8; War Diary, 97, 125, 135 (quote), 137 (quote), 185.

4. US Naval Attache, 'Detailed Operations,' 9–10; War Diary, 138; Report of Proceedings, 3.

5. Krancke and Brennecke, *Pocket Battleship*, 65.

6. War Diary, 102, 133, 136–37, 151, 164, 170, 189, 250, 269, 281, 317; Roskill, *War at Sea*, 289 (quote); Langmaid, *Sea Raiders*, 25; Milner, *North Atlantic Run*, 158 (quote); Pollock, *Jervis Bay*, 202-203; Monk, letter to Segman,1.

7. War Diary, 132, 204, 261, 289, 461 (quote), 476 (quote); US Naval Attache, 'Detailed Operations,' 11–12; Milner, *North Atlantic Run*, 158.

8. Krancke and Brennecke, *Pocket Battleship*, 56, 59 (quote), 66–75.

9. Ibid., 62; 'Operation of the 'Admiral Scheer,'' 9.

17 The San Demetrio Saga

1. Jesse, *Saga of* San Demetrio, 9–10, 14, 16 (quote), 21 (quote), 22; Admiralty reports on HX 84 ships, Waite report, 1–2; Gleadowe, 'MV *San Demetrio*,' 6; Jones, 'Welsh Apprentice,' 180.

2. Jesse, *Saga of* San Demetrio, 23–26 (quotes, 23, 25); Gleadowe, 'MV *San Demetrio*,' 7; Krancke and Brennecke, *Pocket Battleship*, 54; Jones, 'Welsh Apprentice,' 180–81.

3. Jesse, *Saga of* San Demetrio, 26–29 (quotes, 29); Gleadowe, 'MV *San Demetrio*,' 4; Winton, *War at Sea*, 77–78 (quote, 77).

4. Jesse, *Saga of* San Demetrio, 29–31 (quote, 29); Gleadowe, 'MV *San Demetrio*,' 8; Winton, *War at Sea*, 78.

5. Jesse, *Saga of* San Demetrio, 32, 34 (quote), 36, 38; Winton, *War at Sea*, 78, 81–82; Gleadowe, 'MV San Demetrio,' 6–10.

6. Jesse, *Saga of* San Demetrio, 38–39; Gleadowe, 'MV *San Demetrio*,' 8–9.

7. Jesse, *Saga of* San Demetrio, 40–45 (quotes, 44, 45); Gleadowe, 'MV *San Demetrio*,' 9–10; Jones, 'Welsh Apprentice,' 182.

8. Jesse, *Saga of* San Demetrio, 43, 47–48; Gleadowe, 'MV *San Demetrio*,' 9.

9. Jesse, *Saga of* San Demetrio, 46 (quote), 48; Gleadowe, 'MV *San Demetrio*,' 9.

10. Jesse, *Saga of* San Demetrio, 49–54 (quote, 50), 60; Gleadowe, 'MV *San Demetrio*,' 9, 10; Jones, 'Welsh Apprentice,' 182.

11. Jesse, *Saga of* San Demetrio, 56–57, 61–62; 'Salvage—£14,700,' 1; 'Law Report, Jan. 17,' 8; Shaw, *Merchant Navy at War*, 43–44.

18 End of the String

1. Krancke and Brennecke, *Pocket Battleship*, 122, 192, 170–78 (quotes, 171, 172, 177, 178); 'Operation of the 'Admiral Scheer,'' 13, 30–31; Whitley, *German Capital Ships*, 132–33.

2. Krancke and Brennecke, *Pocket Battleship*, 215, 220–24, 229, 231, 234, 239–41, 246–51 (quotes, 215, 240, 241, 250, 251); 'Operation of the 'Admiral Scheer,'' 41–42, 49, 52; 'Heroic Action,' 31; Barnett, *Engage the Enemy*, 279.

3. Koop and Schmolke, *Pocket Battleships*, 53, 127–28; Whitley, *German Capital Ships*, 161; Howarth, *Battle of the Atlantic*, 412 (quote);

4. Koop and Schmolke, *Pocket Battleships*, 127–28; Barnett, *Engage the Enemy*, 710, 712; Whitley, *German Capital Ships*, 184–85; *World Almanac*, 164.

5. Koop and Schmolke, *Pocket Battleships*, 128–29; Whitley, *German Capital Ships*, 187, 204.

6. Koop and Schmolke, *Pocket Battleships*, 129–30; Whitley, *German Capital Ships*, 193, 208–11.

7. Koop and Schmolke, *Pocket Battleships*, 131; Whitley, *German Capital Ships*, 211.

Epilogue

1. Wheeler-Bennett, *King George VI*, 475–76 (quotes); Recommendation for Victoria Cross, 1; Brice, letter to Duskin, 13.

2. Winton, *Convoy*, 164 (quote).

3. James, *Winston Churchill*, 6310 (quote).

4. Winton, *Victoria Cross at Sea*, 192; 'Investiture at the Palace,' 1; Fegen, letter to Duskin, 2.

5. Thursfield, 'Month at Sea,' 424 (quote).

6. Cragg, 'Naval Hero's VC,' 1 (quote).

7. Bonham-Carter, 'Loss of HMS *Jervis Bay*,' 8–9 (quote); *Jervis Bay* awards announcements, *London Gazette*, 23 January 1941, 464, and 11 March 1941, 1440.

8. '*Jervis Bay* Memorial Unveiled,' *Montreal Standard*; 'Stray Notes,' *Chatham News*, 1; *Royal Gazette* (Bermuda) photo caption; Winton, *Victoria Cross*, 192; Woodward, 'P&O Nedlloyd *Jervis Bay*,' 2.

9. Woodward, 'P&O Nedlloyd *Jervis Bay*,' 2; '*Jervis Bay*,' *Lloyd's Register of Shipping* (1970), 1, and (1993), 1; 'Name of Courage,' *Sunday Telegraph* (Sydney), 15; 'HMAS *Jervis Bay*,' *Royal Australian Navy Historic Naval Events of 1977*, 2; '*Chartering*,' *Naval Institute Proceedings*, 75–77; 'HMAS *Jervis Bay* AKR45,' p. 1 of data and p. 1 of operations; Greenlees, 'Forces Secure Streets of Dili,' *Australian*, 1.

10. 'Hero of 'Jervis Bay,'' *Liberty*, 12 (quote).

11. Admiralty reports on HX 84 ships, Smith report, 2, 9; Waite report, 2; Daneil report, 2.

12. Lawson, interview, 3 (quote).

13. Admiralty reports on HX 84 ships, Smith report, 4; '*Jervis Bay*'s' Forlorn Heroic Action,' *War Illustrated*, 567 (quote); 'The *Jervis Bay* and the *Stureholm*,' 27 (quote).

14. Fellingham, letter to Duskin (15 March 1988), 4–7; Fellingham, interview, 3–7; Fellingham, letter to editor, *Sea Breezes*, 2, 3; Fellingham, letter to Duskin (19 January 1988), 2, 3.

15. Lawrence, interview, 2; HMS *Havelock* commanding officer's report, 6; Hocking, 'Dictionary,' *Lloyd's Register of Shipping* (1969), 742 (quote).

16. War Diary, 526, 809 (quote); Westerberg, *Swedish Seamen*, 2; Tiderman, letter to Duskin, 1 (quote); Hocking, 'Dictionary,' 669; Rohwer, *Axis Submarine Successes*, 39.

17. Monk, letter to John M Young.

18. Pollock, *Jervis Bay*, 203–5; Hocking, 'Dictionary,' 745; Creswell, *Sea Warfare*, 65.

19. Monk, letter to Duskin (1 October 1990), 3; 'Summary of Statements by Survivors, M/V 'San Demetrio,'' 1–2.

20. Ketchum, *His Path*, 11, 29–35 (quotes, 30, 35); Royal Canadian Mounted Police (dispatch), 1–3; 'Out-and-Out Nazi Spy,' *Toronto Globe and Mail*, 1; Royal Canadian Mounted Police, 'Re: Gottfried Sohar @ Joseph Refi,' 2; Gottfried Sohar, statement to RCMP, 1.

21. Bradley, *Germany's Generals and Admirals*, 1; Krause, 'German Navy under Joint Command,' 1038–40; Gerhard, letter to Segman (1 October 98), 2.

22. Quote from Edwards, *They Sank the Red Dragon*, 192.

Bibliography

Books

Abbazia, Patrick. *Mr. Roosevelt's Navy.* Annapolis, Md.: Naval Institute Press, 1975.

Agar, Augustus W S. *Footprints in the Sea.* London: Evans Brothers, 1959.

Bailey, Thomas A, and Paul B Ryan. *Hitler versus Roosevelt: The Undeclared Naval War.* New York: Free Press, 1979.

Barnett, Corelli. *Engage the Enemy More Closely.* New York: W W Norton, 1991.

Bekker, Cajus. *Hitler's Naval War.* Garden City, N Y: Doubleday, 1974.

Bowen, Frank C. *The Flag of the Southern Cross, 1939–1945.* London: Shaw Savill & Albion, 1948.

Bradley, Dermot. *Germany's Generals and Admirals.* Vol. 2. Osnabruck, Germany: Biblio Publishing, 1989.

Brennan, Frank. *Australian Commonwealth Shipping Line.* Canberra: Roebick Society Publication, 1978.

Brown, Anthony Cave. *Bodyguard of Lies.* New York: Bantam Books, 1976.

Bywater, Hector C. *Cruisers in Battle.* London: Constable, 1939.

Callahan, Raymond. 'Invasion's Moment Lost.' Excerpt from *World War II.* Leesburg, Va.: Empire Press, November 1987.

Carr, William Guy. *Brass Hats and Bell-Bottomed Trousers.* London: Hutchinson, 1939.

Chatfield (Lord). *It Might Happen Again.* Vol. 2: *The Navy and Defence.* London: Heinemann, 1947.

Churchill, Winston S. *Their Finest Hour.* Cambridge, Mass.: Riverside Press, 1949.

Collier, Richard. *1940: The Avalanche.* New York: Dial Press/James Wade, 1979.

Creswell, John. *Sea Warfare, 1939–1945.* Berkeley: University of California Press, 1967.

Cruickshank, Charles. *German Occupation of the Channel Islands.* Gloucestershire: Allan Sutton, 1990.

Dear, I C B, and M R D Foot. *The Oxford Companion to World War II.* Oxford: Oxford University Press, 1995.

Divine, A D. *In the Wake of the Raiders.* New York: E PDutton, 1940.

Doenitz, Karl. Memoirs: *Ten Years and Twenty Days.* New York: World Publishing, 1959.

Draper, Alfred. *Operation Fish.* London: Cassell, 1979.

Dunn, Laurence. *The Book of Ships (1920–1935).* New York: Time-Life Books, 1968.

Edwards, Bernard. *They Sank the Red Dragon.* Cardiff: GCP Books, 1987.

Eldridge, F B. *A History of the Royal Naval College.* Np., n.d.

Fleming, Peter. *Operation Sea Lion.* New York: Simon & Schuster, 1957.

Gasaway, E B. *Grey Wolf, Grey Sea.* New York: Ballantine Books, 1970.

Gilbert, Martin. *Finest Hour: Winston S Churchill: 1939–1941.* Vol. 6. London: Heinemann, 1989.

Gray, Edwyn. *Hitler's Battleships.* Annapolis, Md.: Naval Institute Press, 1999.

Green, William. *The Warplanes of the Third Reich.* London: Doubleday, 1970.

Gretton, Vice Admiral Sir Peter. *Convoy Escort Commander.* London: Cassell, 1964.

Hampshire, A Cecil. *The Blockaders.* London: William Kimber, 1980.

Hocking, Charles. *Dictionary of Disasters at Sea during the Age of Steam.* London: Lloyd's Register of Shipping, 1969.

Holman, Gordon. *In the Wake of* Endeavour. London: Charles Knight, 1973.

Howarth, Stephen, and Derek Law, eds. *The Battle of the Atlantic, 1939–1945.* Annapolis, Md.: Naval Institute Press, 1994.

Hughes, Terry, and John Costello. *The Battle of the North Atlantic.* New York: Dial Press/James Wade, 1977.

Humble, Richard. *Hitler's High Seas Fleet.* New York: Ballantine Books, 1971.

Ireland, Bernard. *Jane's Battleships of the 20th Century.* New York: HarperCollins Publishers, 1996.

James, Robert R *Winston Churchill: His Complete Speeches 1897–1963.* Vol. 6: 1935–1942. New York: Chelsea House Publishers in association with R R Bowker, 1974.

Jesse, F Tennyson. *The Saga of* San Demetrio. London: His Majesty's Stationery Office, 1942.

Jones, Geoffrey, *Plunder Three Flags: The Story of the Nordmark and the Armed Supply Ships of the German Navy*. London: William Kimber, 1972.

Kennedy, Paul. *The Rise and Fall of British Naval Mastery*. 3d ed. New York: HarperCollins Publishers, 1991.

Kerr, J Lennox, ed. *Touching the Adventures of Merchantment in the Second World War*. London: George Harrap, 1953.

Kersaudy, François. *Norway 1940*. New York: St. Martin's Press, 1991.

Ketchum, Creston D. *His Path Is in the Waters*. New York: Prentice-Hall, 1955.

Ketchum, Richard M. *The Borrowed Years, 1938–1941: America on the Way to War*. New York: Random House, 1989.

Koop, Gerhard, and Klaus-Peter Schmolke. *Pocket Battleships of the* Deutschland *Class*. London and Annapolis, Md.: Greenhill Books and Naval Institute Press, 2000.

Krancke, Admiral Theodore, and H J Brennecke. *Pocket Battleship*. London: Tandem Publishing, 1975. First English edition, titled *The Battleship* Scheer, published by William Kimber and Co., 1956.

Langmaid, Captain Kenneth. *The Sea Raiders*. London: Jarrolds Publishers, 1963.

Layton, Jim, and Phil Craig. *Finest Hour*. London: Hodder & Stoughton, 1999. (Book from BBC television series.)

MacDonnell, J E. *Valiant Occasions*. London: Constable, 1952.

Macintyre, Donald. *The Naval War against Hitler*. New York: Charles Scribner, 1971.

Marder, Arthur J. *From Dardanelles to Oran*. Oxford: Oxford University Press, 1974.

McAughtry, Sam. *The Sinking of the Kenbane Head*. Belfast, Northern Ireland: Blackstaff Press, 1977.

Milner, Marc. *North Atlantic Run: The Royal Canadian Navy and the Battles for the Convoys*. Annapolis, Md.: Naval Institute Press, 1985.

The New Grolier Multimedia Encyclopedia. Online Computer Systems and Software Toolworks, 1993.

Padfield, Peter. *War beneath the Sea*. New York: John Wiley & Sons, 1995.

Petrow, Richard. *The Bitter Years*. New York: William Morrow, 1974.

Pollock, George. *The* Jervis Bay. London: William Kimber, 1958.

Poolman, Kenneth. *Armed Merchant Cruisers*. London: Lee Cooper in association with Secker & Warburg, 1985.

Raeder, Erich. *My Life*. Annapolis, Md.: Naval Institute Press, 1960.

Roskill, Stephen. *Churchill and the Admirals*. New York: William Morrow, 1978.

Roskill, S W. *War at Sea: 1939–1945*. Vol. 2. London: Her Majesty's Stationery Office, 1961.

Rohwer, Jürgen. *Axis Submarine Successes*. Cambridge: Patrick Stephens, 1983.

Ruge, Vice Admiral Friedrich. *The German Navy's Story, 1939–1945*. Annapolis, Md.: US Naval Institute, 1957.

Shaw, Captain Frank H. *The Merchant Navy at War*. London: Stanley Paul, 1944.

Shirer, William L. *End of a Berlin Diary*. New York: Alfred A Knopf, 1947.

———. *The Rise and Fall of the Third Reich*. New York: Simon & Schuster, 1960.

Slater, John. *The Red Duster at War*. London: William Kimber, 1988.

Terraine, John. *A Time for Courage*. New York: Macmillan, 1985.

Thomas, Charles S. *The German Navy in the Nazi Era*. Annapolis, Md.: Naval Institute Press, 1990.

Tucker, Gilbert Norman. *The Naval Service of Canada*. Vol. 2. Ottawa: By Authority of the Minister of National Defence, King's Press, 1952.

Turner, John Frayn. *VCs of the Royal Navy*. London: George G Harrap, 1956.

Van der Vat, Dan. *The Atlantic Campaign*. New York: Harper & Row, 1988.

———. *The Grand Scuttle*. Annapolis, Md.: Naval Institute Press, 1986.

Watson, Bruce. Untitled manuscript (from Michael Chappell), 2004.

Watt, Commander Frederick C. *In All Respects Ready*. Scarborough, Ontario: Prentice Hall Canada, 1985.

Wellings, Rear Admiral Joseph. *On His Majesty's Service*. Newport, RI: Naval War College Press, 1983.

Westerberg, J. ed. *Swedish Seamen in War and Peace. Vol. 1*. Np., n.d.

Wheeler-Bennett, John W. *King George VI: His Life and Reign*. London: Macmillan, 1958.

Whitley, M J. *German Capital Ships of World War II*. London: Arms & Armour Press, 1989.

Winton, John. *Convoy*. London: Michael Joseph, 1983.

———. *The Victoria Cross at Sea*. London: Michael Joseph, 1978.

The World Almanac Book of World War II. New York: World Almanac Publications, 1981.

Interviews

Barker, Jack. Transcript of audiotape interview. London: Imperial War Museum, n.d.

Daniel, Captain L. Report of an Interview by Shipping Casualties Section, 23 December 1940. (ADM 199/2134 178635.)

Fellingham, H C. Transcript of audiotape interview (# 11509). London: Imperial War Museum, 15 July 1992.

Giles, Rear Admiral Sir Morgan. Transcript of audiotape interview on 'Operation Lucid.' London: Imperial War Museum, 12 July 1992.

Gillespie, Captain Patrick. Notes from telephone interview by Gerald Duskin. Grayshott, Hindhead, England, 14 July 1992.

Morgan, Rear Admiral B J. Transcript of audiotape interview. London: Imperial War Museum, 14 July 1992.

Morrow, Everett. Transcript of audiotape interview by Ralph Segman. Guelph, Ontario, 18 March 1997.

National Geographic Society, Washington, DC Notes on telephone interview by Ralph Segman on width of Denmark Strait, 15 May 2001.

Ohlander, Bengt. Notes from interview with Gerald Duskin. Washington, DC, March 2001.

Patience, Sam. Transcript of audiotape interview by Chris Howard Bailey. Portsmouth, England: Portsmouth Naval Museum, 28 November 1991.

———. Transcript of audiotape interview by Conrad Wood. London: Imperial War Museum, 1991.

Peters, Urban. Transcript of audiotape interview (# 11280). London: Imperial War Museum, n.d.

Stephens, Scott. Telephone interview with Ralph Segman. National Climatic Centre, Ashville, NC: 31 January 2005.

Tolman, Hendrik. Notes on telephone interview with Ralph Segman. National Centres for Environmental Prediction, Camp Springs, Md.: 18 May 2001.

Communications

Brice (given name missing; British naval historian). Letter to Gerald Duskin. Np., n.d.

Cooper, Gillian (Captain Fegen's niece). Letter to Ralph Segman on Captain Fegen's naval education. Ballaugh, Isle of Man, UK, 1 September 2000.

Crosse, John (maritime historian). Letter to Commander F B Watt. Vancouver, Canada, 18 March 1993.

———. Letter to Gerald Duskin. Vancouver, Canada, 7 December 1995.

Fegen, Barbara (Captain Fegen's niece by marriage). Letter to Gerald Duskin containing genealogy and family records. Thames Bitton, Surrey, England, 4 January 1990.

Fegen, Nicholas Fogarty (Captain Fegen's nephew). Letter to Gerald Duskin, including Fegen and Fogarty genealogy. London, 28 February 1988.

Fellingham, H C Letters to Gerald Duskin. Droitwich, England, 19 January, 15 March, and 10 July 1988.

Gerhard, Cornelia. Letters to Ralph Segman. Germany, 1998 (date missing), and Heuchelheim, Germany, 1 October 1998.

Jones, Hedley. Letter to Gerald Duskin. Carmel Valley, Calif., 8 October 1992.

McBrearty, Captain R F Letter to Gerald Duskin. Kent, England, 17 April 1988.

Monk, George (naval historian). Letters to Gerald Duskin. Crowborough, England, 19 August and 1 October 1990.

————. Letter to John M Young (copy to Gerald Duskin). Crowborough, England, 7 September 1997.

————. E-mail to Ralph Segman. Crowborough, England, 19 October 2004.

Patience, Sam. Letter to Gerald Duskin. London, 21 August 1990.

Purcell, Frank (HMS *Sabre* crewman). Letter to M J Petch, Royal Australian Navy. Cleveland, England, 7 December 1987.

Rohwer, Jürgen. Letter to Ralph Segman. Am Sonnenhang, Germany, 27 February 1997.

Tiderman, Hilding. Letter to Gerald Duskin. Stockholm, 23 April 1999.

Official Documents

Admiralty reports on HX 84 ships. London, Public Record Office (ADM 199/725 15661T), 14 November 1940. Enclosures: (1) Daneil, (2) Waite, (4) Milner, and (5) Smith.

Barnett, Captain H. 'Report of an Interview with Captain H Barnett, Master of the SS *'Rangitiki''* to the Shipping Casualties Section, Trade Division. London, Public Record Office (ADM 199/2134 157148), 13 November 1940.

Bonham-Carter, Rear Admiral Stuart. 'Loss of HMS Jervis Bay.' Finding of board of inquiry forwarded to Secretary of the Admiralty (No. 816/E.887/6), London, 20 November 1940.

Caithness Archives. HMS 'Jervis Bay' Armed merchant Cruiser—Casualties, 11/22/2000. http://www.internet-promotions.co.uk/archives/Caithness/jervisbaycasualties.htm

Churchill, Winston. 'On War Problems Facing Britain.' Report delivered in the House of Commons, 5 November 1940. New York, British Library of Information.

'Edward Stephen Fogarty Fegen.' Royal Navy assignments and performance ratings. London, Public Record Office (ADM 196/54).

Faulkner, Captain, RN. 'Recent War Experience.' Report to Office of Naval Intelligence, US Navy, Washington, DC, 7 October 1940.

Fegen Family (from naval lists). London, National Maritime Museum (ADM 11/47, November 1966; ADM 51/4069, September 1788[?]; and ADM 196/40, November 1966).

Fraser, W. Battle charts. London, Public Record Office (ADM 223/148 XC/159092).

————. 'Report of an Interview with Captain W Fraser, Master of the MV 'Erodona'' to the Shipping Casualties Section, Trade Division. London, Public Record Office (ADM 199/2134 157148), 14 November 1940.

George VI. Recommendation of VC to Captain Fegen and approval by the King. London, Public Record Office (ADM 1/10496 110366), 15 November 1940.

Gleadow, R. 'Loss of HMS *Jervis Bay*.' Findings of Board of Inquiry held 13 November 1940. No. 816/E.887/6. London, Public Records Office (ADM/10506 173215).

————. 'MV *San Demetrio* Recommendations for Awards.' Commission and Warrant Branch, 30 November 1940. London, Public Records Office (ADM 1-11657 XC 157340).

Hampden, P. 'Attack on British Convoy by Enemy Pocket Battleship.' Report from DEMS Belfast to Director of the Trade Division, Admiralty. London, Public Record Office (ADM 199/725 157148), 13 November 1940.

Lawrence, Captain W H. 'Report of an Interview with Captain W H Lawrence, Master of the SS 'Briarwood'' to the Shipping Casualties Section, Trade Division. London, Public Record Office (ADM 199/2134 178635), 18 November 1940.

Lawson, Captain R L A. 'Report of an Interview with Captain R L A Lawson, Master of the MV 'Fresno City'' to the Shipping Casualties Section, Trade Division. London, Public Record Office (ADM 199/2134 178635), 17 December 1940.

List of *Mopan* officers and crew. Geneva, International Red Cross.

List of Particulars of AMCs (First 50). ADM 116.4182 XC 157227.

'Loss of HMS *Jervis Bay*.' London, Public Record Office (ADM 1/10506 110366), 26 November 1940.

Maltby, Rear Admiral H B. 'Brief Narrative of the Voyage, Noting Any Important Incidents,' from 'Proceedings by Commodore of Convoy' to the Admiralty. London, Public Record Office, November 1940.

'North Atlantic Ocean: Northern Sheet.' US Defence Mapping Agency.

'Operation of the '*Admiral Scheer*' in the Atlantic and Indian Oceans: 23 October 1940–1 April 1941.' Précis of *Atlantic Kriegfuehrung and War Diaries of* the Admiral Scheer. Washington, DC, Library of the Armed Forces Staff College.

Pink List October 1939. Kew, Public Records Office (ADM 187/2).

Pisani, Lieutenant Commander N L (passenger on *Rangitiki*). 'Report of Attack by German Pocket Battleship on Convoy HX 84, 5 November 1940.' London, Public Record Office (ADM 199/725 157148), 13 November 1940.

Read, O M. (On Great Britain convoy operations). Intelligence Report, No. 907-701, from US Naval Attaché, Ottawa, 2 December 1940.

'Report of Proceedings' on search operations. London, Public Record Office (ADM 199/725 157148), 14 November 1940.

'Report of Proceedings—Reference Convoy HX 84,' from commanding officer, HMS *Havelock*, to flag officer in charge, Liverpool. London, Public Record Office (ADM 199/51 110366), 14 November 1940.

Riley, Gerard. Transcript of interview by OIC London, Public Record Office (ADM 199/2134 178635), 31 August 1941.

Royal Canadian Mounted Police (Headquarters). Dispatch to C G Crea, Undersecretary of State for External Affairs. Ottawa, 4 July 1947.

— — —. 'Re: Gottfried Sohar and Joseph Refi, SS 'Delhi,' Victoria, BC' Victoria, BC, 23 April 1941.

Sheridan, Engineer Rear Admiral H A. 'Steel Drums for HM Ships 'Laconia' and 'Jervis Bay.'' Memo to Naval Secretary. Ottawa, Department of National Defence, 10 July 1940.

Sohar, Gottfried. Statement to Royal Canadian Mounted Police. Victoria, BC, 22 April 1941.

'Summary of Statements by Survivors, '*San Demetrio*.'' Memo for File Office, Chief of Naval Operations, US Navy Department. Washington, DC, 9 April 1942.

US Naval Attache, London. 'Detailed Operations for Search for German Ship *Admiral Scheer*, 5-11-40.' Washington, DC, Office of Chief of Naval Operations (Index Guide No. 907-100, Intelligence Division), 25 November 1940.

War Diary—Situation Report. London, Public Record Office (Admiralty reports), 7–15 November 1940.

Wellings, Commander J H. 'Eskimo Operations, October 20th–November 11th, 1940.' Washington, DC, Report to the Chief of Naval Operations.

— — —. 'Intelligence Report.' Washington, DC, Office of Chief of Naval Operations (Navy Department), 21 September 1940.

Articles

Agar (identified as AWSA). 'Personal Tributes [to] Captain E S F Fegen, VC, RN' *Times*, London, 19 November 1940.

Assman, Vice Admiral Kurt. 'Operation 'Sea Lion.'' *Naval Institute Proceedings* (January 1950).

Beaufort Wind Scale. Lymington, England: Richard Paul Russell, Ltd. http://www.r-p-r.co.uk/beaufort.htm

Budiansky, Stephan. 'Britain: Defeating the Luftwaffe.' *US News & World Report*, 27 August–3 September 1990.

C G. 'HMS *Emerald* Newsletter,' n.d.

'Chartering and HMAS *Jervis Bay*.' *Naval Institute Proceedings* (September 2000).

'Commander R A G 'Rags' Butler.' Obituary. *Daily Telegraph*, 14 November 1996.

Cragg, David. 'Naval Hero's VC Presented to Museum.' Np., n.d.

Davies, Major General H L. 'Iceland: Key to the North Atlantic.' *Journal of the Royal United Service Institution* (November 1956).

Davison, Tom. 'Hero of 'Jervis Bay' Sea Battle Tells His Story.' Eveready Battery panel advertisement. *Liberty*, 25 January 1941.

Elliott, John. 'Treaty Warship, Small and Swift, Is Ready at Kiel.' *New York Tribune*, 14 May 1934.

Fellingham, H C. Letter to the editor. *Sea Breezes* (Liverpool), 7 August 1987.

Frank, William C, Jr. 'Misperceptions and Incidents at Sea: *Deutschland* and Leipzig Crisis, 1937.' *Naval War College Review* 43, no. 2, sequence 330 (Spring 1990).

Freeland, Stephan. 'Shoot on sight.' *Sea Breezes* (Canoga Park, CA), September 2001.

Greenlees, Don. 'Forces Secure Streets of Dili.' *Australian* (Sydney), 21 September 1999.

'Heroic Action Saved Ships in Convoy.' *Shipping—Today and Yesterday* (Liverpool), October 1990.

'HMAS *Jervis Bay* AKR45.' Brochure on ship's operations. http://navy.gov.au/9_sites/akr45/ops.htm

'HMAS *Jervis Bay* in Brief.' *Royal Australian Navy Historical Naval Events of 1977* (1978).

'HMS *Jervis Bay* Roared at the Battleship *Admiral Scheer*.' *Royal Gazette* (Hamilton, Bermuda), 4 November 1987.

'Investiture at the Palace.' *Times* (London), 6 December 1940.

Isherwood, J H. 'Aberdeen & Commonwealth Liner 'Esperance Bay' of 1922.' *Sea Breezes* (Liverpool), March 1970.

'Jervis Bay.' *Lloyd's Register of Shipping*, 1970 and 1993.

'The *Jervis Bay* and the *Stureholm*' (translated by Bertil Jacobsen*). Journal of Seamanship* (Goteborg, Sweden, Royal Society of Naval Sciences) (1960).

'*Jervis Bay* Memorial Unveiled.' *Montreal Standard*, 4 October 1941.

Jervis Bay officer and crew awards announcements. *London Gazette*, 2d suppl., 23 January 1941, and 3d suppl., 11 March 1941.

'*Jervis Bay*'s Forlorn, Heroic Action.' *The War Illustrated* (London), 29 November 1940.

Jones, J Lewis. 'The Welsh Apprentice of the San Demetrio.' *Sea Breezes* (Liverpool), March 1987.

Krause, Captain Roland E. 'The German Navy under Joint Command in World War II.' *Naval Institute Proceedings* (September 1947).

'Law Report, Jan. 17.' *Times* (London), 18 January 1941.

Liberty, 1 March 1941.

Lippman, David H. 'Showdown on the River Plate.' *World War II History* (Herndon, Va.) (January 2004).

McBrearty, RF. 'The 'San Demetrio' Convoy.' *Sea Breezes* (Liverpool), July 1987.

'The Name of Courage Lives in Jervis Bay.' *Sunday Telegraph* (Sydney), Navy suppl., 6 July 1986.

'No Mutiny on 'Jervis Bay.'' *Morning Leader*. London, Public Record Office (ADM 116/2615 PFF 124703), 26 June 1928.

'Out-and-Out Nazi Spy Is Jailed at Vancouver.' *Globe and Mail* (Toronto), 5 June 1941.

Parsons, RM. 'Elders and Fyffes: A Short History of the Company and Its Famous Banana Boats.' *Ships Monthly* (London), April–June 1988.

Peters, Urban. 'Could the *Jervis Bay* Have Been Warned?' *Sea Breezes* (Liverpool), May 1993.

Photo and caption. *Royal Gazette* (Hamilton, Bermuda), 4 November 1987.

Possony, Dr. Stefan T. 'Decision without Battle.' *Naval Institute Proceedings* (June 1946).

Pullen, Michael. 'The Sinking of the Jervis Bay.' *Bulletin of Naval Historical Collectors and Research Association* (London) (Autumn 1991).

Reinicke, Captain H G. 'German Surface Force Strategy in World War II.' *Naval Institute Proceedings* (February 1957).

Rowbotham, Commander W B RN. 'The Armed Merchant Cruiser: Has She a Future?' *Journal of the Royal United Service Institution* (London) 92 (February 1947).

'Salvage to One of the *Jervis Bay* Convoy: 14,700 Awarded the *San Demetrio*.' London *Times*, 18 January 1941.

'Story of 'Hedwig.'' *South China Morning*, n.d.

'Stray Notes.' *Chatham* [England] *News*, 7 August 1950.

Thorpe, Adrian. 'Memories of the *Jervis Bay*.' *Sea Breezes* (Liverpool), October 1968–January 1969.

Thursfield, Admiral H G. 'The Month at Sea.' *The Navy* (London), November 1940.

Woodward, Charles. 'P&O Nedlloyd *Jervis Bay*.' 22 November 2000.

Woodward, Captain Robert. 'A Despatch.' *London Gazette*, 12 August 1887.

Index

Aberdeen & Commonwealth Line 62
Achilles. 49
Admiral Graf Spee 26, 45, 49
Admiral Hipper. 207, 221
Admiral Scheer. 11
   attack on *Andalusian* 141
   attack on Delphinula 139
   attack on Fresno City 150-151
   attack on Jervis Bay 112-115,
              119-123, 125, 128, 133
   attack on Kenbane Head 146-148
   attack on Maidan 141-142
   attack on *Rangitiki* 1401-41
   attack on San Demetrio. 143-146,
              185-187
   attack on Trewellard 142-143
   bombing 13, 48, 208-209
   Britain's fear 34
   continuation of raiding cruise 200-206
   damage done 178, 182, 200-202
   damage. 119, 178
   disruption caused 177-182
   encounter with Mopan 98-103
   en route to North Sea 54-56
   entry into service 45-47
   escape 177-184
   final missions 206-209
   gun crew. 148
   identification 111
   to Kiel. 202-203
   Krancke assigned. 48, 50
   in North Atlantic storm 35-39
   Pietsche's reconnaissance flight . . 58, 95-96
   rendezvous with Nordmark 151, 178,
              182-184, 202
   sinking 208-209
   to Spain. 47-48
   stories about in Halifax 83-87
   structure 37, 44-45, 53
Africa 19, 21
Agar, Augustus 12, 75 76
Ajax. 49
Alexander Sibiriakoff 207
Alexandria 29
Algeria 28
Almería. 47
Altmark 52
Amphion 72-73
Andalusian 141
Antigua. 32
Antonescu, Ion 21
Appleyard, Titch 110, 130-132, 156

Arado 196 monoplanes. 47, 58, 208
Ark Royal 182
armed merchant cruisers (AMCs) 59-60,
              63, 222
asdic device. 29-30, 83
ASPIRIN. 25
Attlee, Clement. 16
Aurania. 65
Australia 59
Australia. 182
Australian Trader. 214
Austria 11
Axis Pact. 21

Baden 43
Bahamas 32
Bain, Danny (Donald) 134, 174, 212-213
Baleares 47
Barker, Jack . . . 64-65, 109, 127, 154-155, 169
Barnett, H 140-141
Barnett, William 213
Battle of Britain. 22-26, 107
Battle of the Atlantic. 26-33
The Battle of the North Atlantic
   (Hughes & Costello) 122
The Battleship 'Scheer' (Krancke)
   See *Pocket Battleship* (Krancke)
Bay of Biscay 177, 178
Bay ships. 60-61
Beaman, G 213
Beaverford 90, 91, 149, 150
Bedford Basin. 84
Belgium. 14-15
Benecke, Paul 41-42
Berlin 25
Bermuda. 32, 79
Berner, Second Mate 221
BHX 41. 79
BHX 86. . . . . 89, 180
Biermann, Captain 72
Billinge, Fred 64, 107, 110-111, 134-135,
             156,174
Bismarck. 206
Blackburn, J A P 68-70, 79, 81,
            88-89, 180, 221-222
Bleichrodt, Heinrich 33
Blitzkrieg. 13
Bonaventure 177
Bonham-Carter, Stuart S 211

Bonney, Tiddly. 126, 155, 171
Boyle, John. 186, 187, 189-190,
191, 195, 197, 199
Breithaupt, Kurt. 37-38
Brennecke, H J 123
Bretagne 28, 29
Briarwood. 150, 220
British Guyana 32
Butler, Ronald A G . . . 126-128, 154, 167-168,
169, 171-172, 212

Canada. 178-179
Canadian Naval Control Service. 84-86
Castle, Charles . . 110, 117, 127, 156, 170, 213
Chamberlain, Neville 11-12, 16, 51
Channel Islands. 17-18
Chappell, J H G. 92-93, 124
Chitral, HMS 68
Churchill, Winston . . . .
   Battle of Britain 26
   convoy system 83
   French forces. 13, 28-29
   German invasion. 17-21
   heroism of *Jervis Bay*. 211
   captain and crew, Pierre Laval. 28
   mining Norwegian waters 51, 52
   neglect of British armed forces 13
   negotiating with Hitler 15-16
   repatriation of British prisoners 52
   request for US destroyers 31-33
   search for *Admiral Scheer* 179
   U-boat attacks. 33
Church of Saint George 214
Ciliax, Otto 47-48
City of Benares. 80
Clark, Nobby. 159-160
Convoys . . . .
   formation and procedures 90-92
   to and from Freetown. 69
   history of 82–83
   masters' conference 86–87
   operations at Halifax 83–85
   restrictions and rerouting 180-182
   rules. 86-87
Cooper, Gillian Fegen 71, 211
Cooper, William James Albert 213
Cormorin, HMS 174
Cornish City 90, 104, 114-115
Cornwall, HMS 73
Cossack. 52
Courageous. 26

Crangle, Gerry 148
Crosse, John 80
Cunningham, Sir Andrew. 29
Czechoslovakia 11-12

Dakar 69
Daladier, Edouard 11-12
Dalton, Hugh 716
Danae II 150, 220
Daneil, L 142-143, 217
Daniel, Frederick 62
Danzig. 12
Darlan, François 28, 29
Davies, H L. 28
Davies, John 186, 189, 191, 195, 198, 199
Davies, P J. 118
Davison, Tom. 64, 68, 107, 109, 159-160,
165-167, 174, 216
Defant, Meteorological Officer 38, 97
Delhi. 90, 222
Delphinula 90, 123, 139
Denmark. 51, 53
Denmark Strait 36-38, 53, 56
Deutschland . . . . 26, 45, 47. See *Lützow*
Dickey, Jimmy 148
Doenitz, Karl 31, 33
Doran, K C 13, 48
Driscoll, A W 111
Drury, Dennis. 213
Duchess. 220
Dunkerque 28, 29
Dunkirk 15-17
Duquesa. . . . 200; 'Floating Delicatessen', 202

Eagle Day attacks . . . . . . See Battle of Britain
Eagle Oil & Shipping Company. 198
Edward III, King. 82
Edward VII, King. 72
Edwards, Bernard 224
Egglestone, John Christopher. 213
Elders & Fyffes. 98
Elliott, John. 45
Emden (cruiser) 42, 43
Emden (light cruiser) 44
Emerald. 75-76
Erodona. 117-118
Eskimo, HMS 177
Esperance Bay 60

Eurofeld 183
Evans, Tyrell George 125-126
Exeter 49

Farthing, Maurice 159
Fegen, Anthony 211
Fegen, Barbara 211
Fegen, Edward Stephen Fogarty ....
   alertness for enemy warships 107-108
   appearance and style of command 76-80,
     86-87
   attack on convoy HX 72 31
   background 71–72
   command of *Jervis Bay* 61, 70-71, 76
   convoys 86-87
   discipline and training of crew 87-93
   early career 72-75
   final attempt to defend HX 84 126-128
   morning of 5 November 95
   gifts from Red Cross 85
   heroism 210-211
   injury 117
   outbursts 80-81
   Sam Patience 106
   possible sighting of *Mopan* attack 104
   'if the gods are good' 79
   relationship with Blackburn 88-89
   response to attack by *Admiral Scheer* ....
     111-113, 121, 125, 126-127, 128-129
   'someone else is getting away' 139
Fegen, Frederick Fogarty 71–72
Fegen, Frederick James 71
Fegen, Frederick Wilfrid 211
Fegen, Mary Catherine (mother) 71
Fegen, M C (sister) 211
Fellingham, H C 95-96, 107, 118, 219
Finland 51
Finnis, N J 151, 218
Firth, Dr 139, 140
Fletcher, bo'sun 188, 198, 199
Flying Kestrel 40, 43
Fogarty, Mary Rose Amelia 71
Fox, C H 72
France ....
   armed forces 13, 28-29
   disposition of German
   High Seas Fleet 41
   German land war 11-20
   pact with Czechoslovakia 11
   in Scandinavian countries 51
Franco, Francisco 12, 21-22
Fraser, W 117, 118

Frederick Fales 80
Freemantle, Sir Sydney 43
Freetown, Sierra Leone 69-70
French, Bill 147
Fresno City 90, 150-151, 217-218
Friedrich der Grosse 40, 42

Gallinat (observer) 58, 95
Gensoul, Marcel-Bruno 29
George VI, King 210-211, 218
German High Seas Fleet 40-44
German Naval Academy 50, 75
German navy 26-27, 44-45
Germany ....
   invasion of Norway and Denmark .. 51-53
   air war 22-26
   land war 12-22
   sea war 26-33
   signing of Axis Treaty 21
   and Spanish Civil War 47-48
Gibbs, Fred 156
Gibraltar 22
Gilbert, Sir Martin 16
Giles, Morgan 20, 77
Glasgow 202
Gleghorn, Mister 151
Gloucester City 184, 216-218
Gniesenau 67
Godfroy, René 29
Göring, Hermann 14, 16, 22-26
Gow, W 142-143
The Grand Scuttle (Van der Vat) 43-44
Great Britain ....
   fear of German attack 34
   and German land war 11-24
   pact with Czechoslovakia 11
   in Scandinavian countries 51-53
Greece 21
Greenland 35, 203
Greenley, Bill 157-158
Greenwood, Arthur 16
Gruber, Ernst 35-36, 38

Hackworth, Green H 32
Halifax 79, 80-81,83-84, 87, 89
Halifax, Lord 16, 19
Halloran, Jack 196, 198
Hamilton, Bermuda 214

Hanlon, Tom 70, 107, 125-126, 135-138,
          152-153, 162, 166, 174
Harland & Wolff. 63
Harris, H G 64, 65, 70
Hartesmere 70
Harwood, H H 49
Hawkins, Arthur G . . . 144, 146, 185, 186-199
Hebburn 66, 68
Hedwig 75
Hellgert, Bo'sun 35
HG 46 182
Hitler, Adolf . . . .
    assistance to Ion Antonescu 21
    Axis Pact. 21
    Winston Churchill on negotiating. . . . 15-16
    construction of German ships. 45
    decommissioning of heavy
        surface ships 208
    delay of attack on PQ 17 207
    expansion of Third Reich 11-12
    invasion of Denmark. 51-53
    invasion of France and 14-15
    Low Countries
        invasion of Norway 27-28, 51-53
    meeting with Franco 21-22
    neglect of German navy 26-27
    'Pact of Steel' with Mussolini 12
    plan to attack Britain. 18-19
Hoffman, Kurt Casar 67
Holland . . . . 14-15. See also Netherlands
Hood, HMS. 177, 180
Hopper, J W 151
HX 41 79
HX 72 . . . . 31, 80-81
HX 78 81
HX 84 34
    attack. 104-105,108, 111, 113-114
    Blackburn's response to attack. 89
    departure from Halifax 90-92
    effect of attack 180-182, 184
    Fegen's final attempt to defend . . 126-128
    Keith Morrison on protection. 137
    Naval Boarding Service
        meeting about 86-87
    plan for attack 96-97, 119, 125
    route 57
    scattering. 112, 114, 117-118
HX 85 . . . . 97, 180
HX 86 . . . . 89, 180
HX 89 182
HX 92 221

Ibiza 47
Iceland 28, 35
Iron Cross(es) 202, 203-206
iron ore (Swedish) 51
isolationism 31-32
Italy. 15, 17, 21, 41, 47

Jamaica. 32
James J Maguire. 118
Jan Mayen Island 35
Japan. 11, 12, 21
Jeffcott, John Stanislaus 162
Jervis Bay (Australia). 61
Jervis Bay, HMS 11
    abandoning 137-138, 152-162
    admiration. 118
    arrival in Halifax. 80
    attack 112-117, 118, 123-128, 133-138
    barrels in holds 80, 133, 137, 168-169
    in Bermuda 79
    black squad 129-130
    commemorative ships 214-215
    conscription and conversion 59, 63-64
    with convoy HX 72. . . . . 31, 80-81
    with convoy HX 84 34
    crew. 64-65, 68-69, 77-79, 87, 92-93
    departure from Halifax 90-94
    early problems. 65-66
    Fegen given command 61, 70, 76
    fire control 110
    in Freetown, Sierra Leone. 69-70
    magazine 131-132
    memorials 213, 14
    and Mopan. 98-99, 104
    observations of from Kenbane Head . . . 147
    responsibilities 92
    sickbay. 125-126
    sinking 161, 163, 168
    stowaways 62-63
    structure 59, 61
Jervis Bay, The (Pollock) 77
Jervis Bay–Ross Memorial Park 214
Jervis, Sir John 61
Jervis, William 110
Jodl, Alfred 14, 51-52
Jones, Bernie. 215
Jones, Charles Edward 215
Jones, Hedley 103
Jones, John Lewis. 188, 190, 193, 196
Jones, RV 24-25
Jumna 221

Kretschmer, Otto 33

Keitel, Wilhelm. 51-52
Kelly, HMS. 66   Lamb Holm. 27
Kenbane Head. . . . . 90, 146-148, 217   Lancaster Castle. 114, 118
Kennedy, Edward Coverley 66-67   Lance, HMS 73
Kennedy, Paul. 17   Langsdorff, Hans 49
Kershaw, James Hardy. 162   Latvia 11, 17
Kiel. . . . . 56, 203, 206, 208   Laval, Pierre. 28
Knickebein 24   Lawrence, Captain (Briarwood). 150
Knox, Frank 32   Lawrence, W H. 150, 220
Königin Louise 72-73   Lawson, R 150-151, 217-218
Krancke, Theodor. . . . .   League of Nations. 45
     assignment to destroy   Ledoux, Paul. 80
          Halifax convoy, ... 55, 56-58   Liddle, Bob. 159
     attack on Beaverford. 149   Lincoln. . . . . See Sherwood, HMS
     attack on Delphinula. 139   Lindbergh, Charles A 32
     attack on Fresno City 150   Lindemann, Frederick. 24
     attack on Kenbane Head. 147   Lithuania. 11, 17, 218
     attack on Maidan. 141-142   Lloyd's 82
     attack on Mopan. 99-100   London 25
     attack on Rangitiki. 139-140   London Naval Treaty of 1930 60
     attack on San Demetrio . 143-146, 186-187   Luftwaffe. 22-26
     attack on Trewellard 142   Lützow . . . . 48, 206, 207. See Deutschland
     battle tactic. 115, 133, 135-137, 147
     career . . . . 50-51, 223-224   Macintosh, James 102
     command of Admiral Scheer. . . . 48, 50-51   Mackie, J J, 151 218
     commemoration of   'Maginot Line' 15
          lost shipmates. 179-180   Maidan 90, 141-142
     ontinuation of raiding cruise 200-206   Mainland. 27
     courage and discipline of   Mallon, Frank R 131
          Jervis Bay captain and crew 128   Maltby, H B . . . 86, 87, 96, 107, 112, 114, 221
     death of 224   Manstein, Erich von 15, 16
     encounter with Barneveld   McBrearty, RL 114, 118
          and Stanpark 200-202   McBride, Bill 148
     encounter with Mopan. 99-100   McNeil, Colum. 189, 190
     evasion of British searchers. 155-157   Meedsen-Bohiken, Wilhelm. 206, 208
     at German Naval Academy. . . . . . . 50, 75   merchant ship sinkings 26, 27-28, 30-31,
     initial attack of Jervis Bay. 116, 146   33, 107, 224
     intentions of attack on HX 84 184   Mers-el-Kebir. 29
     invasion of Norway   Micklethwait, Commander. 177
          and Denmark . . . . 50-52, 53-54   Miller, C L 141
     to Kiel. 203-206   Milner, Thomas F 146-148
     Morse flashes to HX 84. 105   Mont Blanc 84
     in North Atlantic storm 35-39   Moore, Dennis 111-113, 126-127, 128
     physical description of 57   Mopan 98-103, 119
     plan for attack on   Morgan, B J 75
          HX 84. . . . . 98-100, 124, 126   Morrison, Keith M 66, 137-138, 153
     promotion of 206   Morrow, Everett 109, 126, 152-153
     recoils of Admiral Scheer's
          guns 119, 148-149
     rendezvous with
          Nordmark. 151, 182-184
     replacement of. 206

Morska Wola 93
Moss, G B......................... 156
Mountbatten, Lord Louis 66
Mount Taygetus 184, 218
Muir, W R......................... 151
Mussolini, Benito 12, 15, 17, 19, 21

Naiad 177
Naval Boarding Service (NBS) 84–86
Nelson 178-179, 180
Nelson, Horatio...................... 61
Netherlands........... 19, 44. See Holland
Newcastle 67
Newfoundland 32
New Merchant Navy Hotel............. 214
'night of the long knives' 33
Nordmark ... 54, 151, 178, 182, 183-184, 202
Norway 28, 51-53

OBM 234 216
OBM 240 180
O'Fogarty, William 71
Olander, Sven David...... 164-165, 171-174,
                                 219, 220-221
Oland, Richard Hibbert 84, 85, 86
operation Catapult 28
operation Lucid................... 20-21
operation Sea Lion 18, 19, 26
operation Stabilise 215
Oran 29
Oxner, Al 84, 85

P&O Nedlloyd 215
Pacific Enterprise................... 150
Paladin, HMS...................... 73
Palma 47
Patience, Sam 87-88
    abandoning of
        Jervis Bay 138, 157-158, 160
    alertness (Fegen's) for
        enemy warships............. 106-107
    attempt to help patients in sickbay.... 126
    background 105-106
    identification of *Admiral Scheer* 111
    P.1 gun 126, 136
    preparation for battle.......... 113-114
    survival at sea 163-164
Payne, S 150, 151
Pepper, Claude 32

Pershing, John J 32
Petersen, Lieutenant 104-105
Peters, Urban.............. 98, 99, 102-103
Phoebe 177
Pietsche, S................. 58, 95, 96, 178
Pisani, N L 108
Pocket Battleship (Krancke) 105, 143-144, 223
pocket battleships 45-47
Point Green 183-184
Poland 12-13
Pollard, Charles 144, 186, 189-190, 191,
                          193, 195-196, 198, 199
Pollock, George 77
Port Dikson communications station 201
Pound, Sir Dudley 83, 207
PQ 17 207
Preston, Oswald..... 187, 188. See The Yank
Prien, Gunther..................... 27, 31
Prinz Eugen 206
Provence.......................... 28
Purcell, Frank 65

Queen of Bermuda 70

Raeder, Erich 27, 27, 51, 54-55, 182,
                                 203-206
Rangitiki 90, 104, 108, 139-141, 177, 216
Rawalpindi 64, 65, 66-68
Refi, Joe ...... 222-223. See Sofar, Gottfried
Reinberger, Helmut 14
Renown.......................... 182
Repulse 177, 178, 180
Resolution 105-106, 111
Reuter, Ludvig von 42-44
Ridgway, Guy....................... 79
Riley, Gerard................... 102-103
Robertson, A J.......... 129-130, 167, 168
Rodney.................... 178-179, 180
Roe, George L 70, 110, 112, 123-124,
                      124, 130, 137-138, 154
Rohwer, Jürgen..................... 206
Romania 17, 21
Roosevelt, Franklin Delano. 22, 31-33, 34, 206
Roskill, S W 182
Rothe-Roth, Richard................. 208
Rothsay Bay 198, 220
Rowbotham, W B.................... 60
Royal Air Force (RAF) 13-14, 22-26, 34

Royal Australian Navy College 75
Royal Navy 29-30
Royal Navy Association 219
Royal Oak 27
Rushall, Crackers 125, 135, 156

Sabre, HMS 65-66
Saint John, New Brunswick 80
Saint John Tuberculosis Hospital 214
Samathrakis, Captain 218
San Alberto 185
San Demetrio 185-199
    attacks 143-146, 185-187, 222
    damage 190-191
    douse fires and repair 189-193
    find and reboard 186-189
    malfunction 94
    observations of *Kenbane Head* 147, 148
    position in HX 84 90
    rescue of survivors 217
    sail home 193-198
    salvage claim 198-199
Sapsworth, S A 98-103
Scapa Flow 27, 40-44, 65, 177, 178, 179
*Scapa Flow: The Account of the Greatest
    Scuttling of All Time* (Reuter) 43-44
Scharnhorst 66-67
Schleswig-Holstein 50
Schumann, Alfred 140, 146
Sea Breezes 103
Seaman's Institute
    (Wellington, New Zealand) 214
Shackleton, Richard . . 110, 112, 115-116, 117,
                                         160-161, 169-170
Shaw Savill 57, 60, 131-132
Shaw Savill & Albion 62, 214
Sherwood, HMS 88, 108
Shipping Casualties Section
    (London Trade Division) 144
shipping losses 27-28, 30, 33, 224
Shirer, William L 13, 26
Slavol 63
SLF 53 182
Smith, Bob 76
Smith, D R 151
Smith, S G 216-218
Sohar, Gottfried . . . . 223. See Refi, Joe
Sommerville, Sir James 29
sonar . . . . See asdic device
Southampton 178

Sovac 177
Soviet Union 12-13, 19, 19, 47, 51,
                                                207-208
Spain 21-22, 47-48
Stalin, Josef 12, 17
Stannard, Edward R 160-161
Stanpark 201-202
St. John's, Newfoundland 217, 218
St. Lucia 32
Storey, Tom 126
Strasbourg 28
Stromness 40, 43
Stureholm 90, 164-165, 170, 171-173,
                                         174, 220-221
Suffolk 75
Superman 197-198
Sweden 51
Sworbe peninsula 208

Taylor, James 40-41
Their Finest Hour (Churchill) 29
They Sank the Red Dragon (Edwards) 224
Thor 183, 221-222
Thorpe, Adrian 66, 81
Thursfield, H G 211
Tiderman, Hilding 220-221
The Times, London 42
Tirpitz 206-207
Tolman, Hendrik 37
Tovey, Sir John 178-179, 182
Treaty of Versailles 11, 42-45
                                    See Versailles Treaty
Trefusis 90, 95, 107, 118, 219-220
Trewellard 90, 142-143, 217
Trinidad 32
Turley, T 147–148

U-boats . . 27-31,33, 41, 44, 80-81, 82-83, 207
Uruguay 49

Van der Vat, Dan 43-44
Versailles Treaty . . . . 11, 42-45.
                                    See Treaty of Versailles
Vichy government 15
Victoria Cross (Fegen's) 210-211
Victoria Louise 50
Vidot, C 222
Vingaland 90, 220
Voltaire, HMS 89, 180, 221-222

Waite, George 144, 185-186, 217
Wallis, Walter. 108, 110, 112, 116, 124
Walsh, Norman. 148
Watt, Frederick B 84-86
Wehrmacht 13
Wehrmacht High Command (OKW) . . . 18-19
Western Albert Dry Dock. 63
Western Approaches. 97
Wheel Principle 97, 125
White, Ernest V 134, 160
Whitehall. 118-119
Widder 183
Wilhelmshaven. 51, 54, 208
Willey, George 190, 191, 196, 199
Williamson, Hugh 110, 112, 115-116,
                                117, 118, 212
Winton, John. 211
Wood, James (Slinger) 155, 169, 171,
                                172-174, 212
Wood, N E 156, 163, 164, 213

'Yank' . . . . 187, 188, 190, 195-197, 199.
                       See Preston, Oswald

Zenker, Hans. 44-45
'Z Plan' 26-27

About the Authors

Gerald L Duskin (deceased)

Gerald L Duskin was a self-taught naval historian, an economist, and a technology-transfer specialist. As a youth, he was entranced by news reports of the heroic action of the *Jervis Bay* against the *Admiral Scheer*. The battle continued to intrigue him as he matured, and naval history remained his avocation throughout his education and career. Duskin received a BS degree in economics from Temple University and an MA from New York University.

After serving in the economic development office of the US Department of Commerce for thirty years, he branched into two parallel courses. A victim of polio from infancy, he helped organize the new field of assistive-technology transfer—the development and commercialization of aids for the physically handicapped. As a member of the National Organization on Disability, he lobbied for and helped gain passage of the Americans with Disabilities Act of 1990.

Simultaneously, toward fulfilling his unending fascination with the 1940 naval engagement, Duskin began collecting information from multiple sources. After twelve years of research in the United States, Britain, Germany, Australia, Canada, and Sweden, he partnered with a professional writer as coauthor and began working on a book-length manuscript.

Ralph Segman

Co-author Ralph Segman is a retired journalist who covered many of the great mid- and late-century advances in science, technology, and medicine. His US Information Agency articles on the Mercury-Gemini-Apollo manned space program were printed in major newspapers and magazines around the world. He ghosted a widely published postflight piece for Alan Shepard, the first American astronaut. During two years with the overseas branch in Calcutta, he wrote features for Indian publications and lectured throughout the country on American science. A stay in Antarctica resulted in a book-length series of articles on the US research program there. Other positions with the federal government were author of the National Oceanographic Program document for the Office of the President and public information chief of the National Oceanic and Atmospheric Administration's research laboratories.

His private-sector work included posts as managing editor of *Technology Review,* news editor of *Science News,* editor of *Technology Transfer,* and writer with Eli Lilly & Company. He also founded, edited, and published *The Reston* (Virginia) *Times.* In a career change, he became a technology-transfer specialist with the US Forest Service, and then joined the National Technology Transfer Centre as assistant director.